SHEVILLE-BUNCOMBE TECHNICAL INSTITUT

Camp Regulations.

American servicemen participating in the wa[...]
US. administration in Vietnam and caught i[...]
barbarous crims against the vietnamese land and peup[...]
have been duly punished according to their criminal acts ; but the
governement and people of Vietnam, endowed with noble and
humanitarian traditions, have given those captured American
servicemen the opportunity to benefit a lenient and generous
policy by affording them a normal life in the detensions-camp
as practical conditions of Vietnam permit it and conforming to
the situation in which the war is still on.

Detainees are to observe and carry out the following regulations
of the camp.

I. Detainees must strictly obey orders and follow instructions
given them by Vietnames officers and army men on duty in the camp.

II Detainees must be polite toward every Vietnames in the camp.

III Inside the detention-rooms, as well as outside when allowed,
detainees must not make noise or create noise. Quarrel and
fighting between detainees are forbidden. In time of rest
total silence is imposed.

IV Detainees must not bring back to detension rooms any
objekt whatsoever without the camp authority permit it.

V In case of sickness or sign of sickness is felt, detainees
must immediately inform the camp for the medical officer
to check and cure.

VI Detainees must assure hygiene of the camp, take care of
personal items provided by the camp as well as of any other
things for collective use.

VII In case of air alarm, detainees must keep order and silence
and follow the camp regulations on security.

VIII In need of something, detainees should address themselves to
Vietnamese army men standing nearby by announcing two
words "Bao cao" (means:"report") and should wait if no
English-speaking people was available yet.

IX In the detension rooms every detainees are equal with each
other. Anyone does have the right to free thinking, feeling,
praying etc... and no one is permitted to coerce any
other into following his own opinion.

X Violation of the regulations shall be punished.

The camp authorities.

Copied by Monika Schwinn in the Mountain Village

ASHEVILLE-BUNCOMBE TECHNICAL INSTITUTE

NORTH CAROLINA
STATE BOARD OF EDUCATION
DEPT. OF COMMUNITY COLLEGES
LIBRARIES

We Came to Help

DISCARDED

AUG 1 2 2025

Translated from the German by Jan van Heurck

Foreword by Colonel Benjamin H. Purcell

We Came to Help

MONIKA SCHWINN & BERNHARD DIEHL

A HELEN AND KURT WOLFF BOOK

HARCOURT BRACE JOVANOVICH

NEW YORK AND LONDON

Copyright © 1973 by Droemersche Verlagsanstalt
English translation copyright © 1976
by Harcourt Brace Jovanovich, Inc.

All rights reserved. No part of this publication
may be reproduced or transmitted in any form or
by any means, electronic or mechanical, including
photocopy, recording, or any information storage
and retrieval system, without permission in
writing from the publisher.

Printed in the United States of America

The drawings on pages 188 and 246 are based on
sketches provided by Colonel Benjamin H. Purcell.

Library of Congress Cataloging in Publication Data

Schwinn, Monika, 1942–
    We came to help.

    Translation of Eine Handvoll Menschlichkeit.
    "A Helen and Kurt Wolff book."
    1. Vietnamese Conflict, 1961–1975—Prisoners and prisons, North
Vietnamese. 2. Vietnamese Conflict, 1961–1975—Personal narratives,
German. 3. Schwinn, Monika, 1942–   4. Diehl, Bernhard, 1946–
I. Diehl, Bernhard, 1946–   joint author. II. Title.
DS559.5.S3813   1976   959.704'37   76–13882
ISBN 0–15–195595–6

First edition

B C D E

FOR GEORG, MARIE-LUISE, AND RIKA:

THE THREE WHO DIED

Contents

Foreword

The return of the prisoners of war from Vietnam in early 1973 was one of the most dramatic and profoundly moving events of our time. Many of the American prisoners have written accounts of their experiences—the years of loneliness, maltreatment, torture, frustrations, and despair—but much remains to be told. People from other countries were detained as prisoners in North Vietnam as well, and this book tells the story of two such persons.

Bernhard Diehl and Monika Schwinn, citizens of the Federal Republic of Germany, were working as hospital nurses for the Aid Service of Malta.* They had come to Vietnam to offer help and comfort; yet they themselves were to suffer anguish and loss. In April 1969, Bernhard Diehl was twenty-two years old and had been in Vietnam for almost a year. Monika Schwinn was twenty-six and had spent eight months working in the children's ward of a hospital in Da Nang. One Sunday they decided to go for a ride in the countryside with three of their fellow workers,

---

* The Aid Service of Malta is a German branch of the Knights of Malta, or the Knights Hospitalers, a Roman Catholic religious order which now bears little resemblance to the Knights Hospitalers of medieval times. The order engages in charitable hospital work. The Aid Service of which the two authors were members was founded by the German branch of the international charitable organization Caritas. The Service is devoted to the care of accident victims, the education of nurse's aides, and the administering of First Aid training. In other words, Miss Schwinn, Mr. Diehl, and their friends resembled Red Cross workers in the United States, rather than members of a religious order. —TRANS.

Georg Bartsch, Marie-Luise Kerber, and Hindrika Kortmann. The trip suddenly turned into tragedy. Only Bernhard and Monika survived the ordeal—almost four years' detention, under the most primitive conditions, in the jungles of South Vietname and the prisons up north.

Before their capture, both authors kept diaries and wrote letters recording their experiences in Vietnam, but all the notes written by Bernhard during his captivity were lost. Monika succeeded in salvaging a portion of hers. To write this book, the two young people, shortly after their release, reconstructed their experiences from memory and from notes. They forced themselves to relive the painful years of their captivity in order to preserve a record of their own and their companions' sufferings.

Though I had heard about them earlier, it was not until January 1973 that I met Monika and Bernhard face to face. To my knowledge, Monika was the only Caucasian woman held captive by the North Vietnamese authorities, but her courage was as great as any prisoner's. During the months just preceding our release she displayed an attitude of strength and determination that served as a guide to everyone who knew her. Perhaps I can best illustrate this point by relating an incident that occurred in December 1972. I was pressing our detainers to end the practice of solitary confinement by refusing to accept their food, a form of protest I had tried before. Monika covertly shared her meager ration of rice with me. This bit of nourishment enabled me to continue the hunger strike for thirteen days, more than twice as long as I had been able to do on the two previous occasions.

None of the American prisoners with whom I had personal contact during my final months of imprisonment annoyed the Vienamese detainers quite as much as Bernhard did. He was bent on causing the prison cadre as much trouble as possible. His spirit was never broken, and to the very end he "bugged" our detainers so much they must have regretted ever taking him prisoner. They were glad to see him go home, but I missed him greatly, for he had been an inspiration to me.

The many accounts of the treatment we received from our Communist captors are so varied that one might draw the conclusion that prisoners were not treated alike, but the aim was the same in every case. The Communist "re-educators" wanted to coerce the prisoner into breaking with his past and to convert him to their cause. This was as true for our German friends as it was for the rest of us. Their accounts of places and events are factual and faithful to life. All the characters discussed in the book are real, and in only one episode has a name been changed, to spare that person any extra pain.

Just how did Bernhard and Monika deal with such a drastic change in their way of life and the sorrow of losing their three friends? Certainly they had to have great inner strength in order to survive these trying times, but they also had to rely upon each other. Their story is of course a significant addition to the literature on the Vietnamese conflict, but even more a remarkable and affirmative human document.

BENJAMIN H. PURCELL

Colonel Benjamin H. Purcell was the senior U.S. Army officer repatri-ated from Vietnam in the spring of 1973. He had been captured in South Vietnam following a helicopter crash on February 8, 1968, taken to North Vietnam within two months, and released from Hanoi on March 27, 1973. Of the sixty-two months he spent in prison, fifty-eight were in solitary confinement. Only after the Paris Peace Accords were signed on January 27, 1973, was he transferred to the "Hanoi Hilton," where he met the authors of this book, Monika Schwinn and Bernhard Diehl.—ED.

We Came to Help

The Rice Farmer

MONIKA SCHWINN

Ahead of us dark blue mountains rose in the distance; behind us
lay the Khe Le River, its yellow mud still clinging to my feet. We
had traveled some distance upstream, wading barefoot through
the shallow water and carrying our shoes. Although it was not
yet noon, the hot sun had driven us to take shelter in a shady
grove. Even here the dark green curtain of banana leaves seemed
to steam in the sunshine.

From inside the grove I had a view of the rice paddies where
the farmer stood. There were many paddies, separated by narrow dikes and covered with gray water whose dull surface was
broken only by the tips of plants stirring in the gentle breeze. If
it had not been for the twitching of the plants, I would not have
known that there was a breeze at all. People had told me that
Vietnamese Buddhists buried their dead in the rice paddies; and
because there were so many dead, there was often not enough
room left for the rice. While the number of dead kept growing,
the crop continued to shrink; and still more dead went on claiming their rights.

I did not know about such things at first; there were so many
things I did not know. None of us knew much about this country.
Eight months here had taught me very little. My work in the Da
Nang hospital run by the Aid Service of Malta kept me busy
from dawn till dusk. Then I collapsed into bed and, if I was

3

lucky, slept until it was time to get back to work again—back to all those children needing care, all that misery needing comfort. The days were always too short; no matter what we accomplished, it was never enough. That was why I had looked forward to our day's outing. That was why I had brought my camera along, the 8-mm. movie camera purchased in Hong Kong. I wanted to take a couple of pictures home, the kind I could show everyone—not pictures of napalm-burned children and the agony of war. *Pretty* pictures, like the laughing children on the black water buffalo whose image I had captured on the first few feet of film, while I was still wading in the river. Or like this rice farmer looking at us as he stood in the middle of his paddy. Yes, this was the sort of theme I wanted, a picture of the man straightening up, arranging the pointed straw hat on his back, and slowly making his way across the water toward us.

I do not know why I did not film him after all. He was no longer young, but then I always found it hard to assess the age of the Vietnamese. He was wearing a black tunic that hung open at the chest. His trousers, rolled high above his calves, revealed legs stained a grayish yellow by the mud. On his feet he wore a pair of Ho Chi Minh sandals with soles cut from rubber tires. His hair was long and as gray as the dirt on his legs, his face angular and broad. But the important thing was that he smiled at us! Still coming hesitantly toward us, he grinned from ear to ear, as if he had to say everything with that smile, as if he knew just by looking at us that we would not understand anything else. Bernhard, who knew a few words and phrases in Vietnamese, called out, *"Chao ông!"* (Good day!)

The rice farmer said nothing. He just went on smiling, revealing that he had lost all his teeth except for a couple of dark brown stumps. We nodded at him and laughed. "It's really sad," I thought to myself, "that you haven't learned any of their language; you could have said something friendly to him."

Earlier, we had noticed a village in the distance. We were planning to go there so that I could film the bamboo huts and the daily life of the villagers. As we started on our way again, the rice farmer stayed behind. He stood watching us depart,

4

looking suddenly pensive and ill at ease. He was no longer smiling.

We walked along slowly, listening to the loud voices of men chopping wood in a nearby grove. Then, as I trailed a little behind the others, I heard the slapping sound of wet feet in rubber sandals. The rice farmer came charging along in our wake.

He no longer smiled, and he seemed a completely different man. His face twisted with anxiety, and, waving his hands in the air, he started to cry, *"Om! Om! Om!"* Pointing in the opposite direction from the village, he kept repeating the same sound over and over.

This *"om!"* was a word I knew. It was the first Vietnamese word I had learned; it meant "sick." This was the word the parents used when they brought their children to our hospital ward. They could not tell us anything more; but once we had looked at the children, we knew all we had to know. I had heard the word so often that it haunted my dreams. At once I exclaimed to the others, "We'll have to go with him! If someone is sick, we must help. We can't possibly refuse!"

I never doubted for a moment that we had to help the farmer. After all, why else had we come to his country? "We can't possibly refuse," I told the others. For I saw that they had not yet made up their minds.

The rice farmer began running, then paused and came back when he saw that we were not following him. He began to entreat us, gesturing wildly, and crying over and over, *"Om! Om! Om!"*

We began to follow him. He kept turning around to make sure that we were really coming. "Let's hope he isn't going to lead us into Viet Cong territory," Rika said. We trotted along behind him like a flock of sheep, while he circled and leaped around us like a frisky dog. The farther we went, the more we hesitated, for he was leading us away from the road and the village. Finally we came to a halt. The rice farmer ran on a little way until he saw that we were no longer following him. Then he came bounding back, his incessant *"Om! Om!"* growing louder and more insistent. He put his whole soul into the words. His unhappy face told us that the sick person would surely die without our help. And so he drove us onward. We half expected him to push and nudge at us and nip our flanks as a sheepdog does his recalcitrant sheep.

Suddenly we all grew puzzled and suspicious. Talking it over, we decided not to go any farther. But we indicated to the man that if he wanted to bring the ailing person to us, we would wait for them where we were.

The rice farmer began to call out. He called in a high-pitched voice that kept breaking off. Then he raised two fingers to his toothless mouth and gave a whistle. Suddenly a man was standing there with a gun.

I can still picture him rising up out of the tall grass, aiming his gun straight at us. It was a long, heavy, black rifle that seemed to dwarf the man, whose thin form barely reached above the reeds. The man with the gun began to talk with the old rice farmer. He wore a faded light-beige jacket and might easily have been a civilian, or perhaps a guerrilla; in any case, he clearly was not a professional soldier. The rice farmer still seemed overwrought; his squeaky voice kept breaking. Finally the old man ordered us, *"Di, di, di!"* (Forward march!) The younger man waved around his black rifle when he addressed us, as if to say, "Go on, do what he says! This is a gun, a fine Chinese gun, and I know how to use it! Get along now!" Silently he pointed the gun away from the path, and, turning around, I saw that he was not alone. Two other men with black rifles were standing nearby.

We walked along in single file. The old rice farmer led the way, while our guards walked along beside us. One guard brought up the rear. Marie-Luise Kerber, a dental assistant in An Hoa and the youngest of us, was walking just ahead of me. Turning around, she threw me a questioning glance. "Are you afraid?" I shook my head. "We should have run away at once," she said. "How could we have run away?" I replied. "How could we run away when there was a sick person who needed us? You'll see, everything's going to turn out all right."

"You really aren't afraid?"

I repeated that I was not. I thought I was speaking the truth, but perhaps I simply did not want to admit how afraid I was. I could not believe that the farmer had set a trap for us; I did not want to believe it.

We were led to a clearing surrounded by a wall of dense underbrush more than two yards high. It had not rained for a long time, and the little meadow showed hardly a trace of green. I was still hoping that the men planned to bring the sick person to us. But soon I saw that I had been deluding myself. I felt as if the ground were giving way under my feet: some twelve to fifteen armed men had surrounded us. Again I was struck by the sheer size of the guns. One man clutched his rifle with only one hand. His left arm had been amputated at the shoulder and his shirt sleeve neatly cut away. He was holding his gun at hip level, pointed at us; the finger of his right hand rested on the trigger. The gun was fastened to his wrist with a leather strap, as if it were the most valuable thing he owned and he did not dare to lose it. All the men looked thin and ill-clad in their pajama trousers. I had heard the Americans make fun of the Vietnamese guerrillas, calling them "pajama boys" and "Charlies"—terms implying that the guerrillas need not be taken seriously and could easily be defeated. But as I watched them standing there holding their rifles with their fingers on the trigger, I took them very seriously indeed.

Hindrika Kortmann, who worked with me in Da Nang, had recently begun to learn Vietnamese. She and Bernhard tried to explain to the men that we were Germans and took care of sick people. But the guerrillas knew that already, for they had seen our clothing, the official uniforms worn by all hospital personnel in the Aid Service of Malta. They paid no attention to our explanations. Clearly they were waiting for something. The rice farmer had scurried away. He returned accompanied by a man in green pajamas—olive-green trousers topped with a plain linen shirt of the same color. He was short, looked better fed than the others, and was well groomed. He was not armed, but from his shoulder hung a canvas pouch resembling a map case. Later I learned that the pouch contained maps, paper, writing materials, and propaganda leaflets. Such pouches were a sort of special insignia worn only by Vietnamese officials.

Apparently this man knew all about the work of our Aid Service, and we could tell that he wanted to let us go. Speaking in the same imploring tones the old rice farmer had used in addressing us, the official tried to convince the partisans, or guerrillas, that we were Germans from the hospital run by the Aid Service of Malta in An Hoa. A violent argument ensued. The more ardently the official pleaded our cause, the louder and more incensed his companions became. Instead of helping us, our defender was making matters worse. I began to think, "Pretty soon now they're going to run amuck and decide to shoot us on the spot!"

Finally the man with the map case gave in. Throwing me a helpless look, he shrugged his shoulders as if to say, "I've done all I can."

Meanwhile crowds of people had gathered to watch the scene. I could not tell where they all came from. Old men, women, and scores of children stood silently by, taking no part in the discussion. There was neither hatred nor compassion on their faces. They appeared indifferent to our fate.

The debate was over; the official had been outvoted. Then one of the men pointed in the air. Thinking that he was pointing to a nearby tree, I concluded that they were planning to hang us. I prayed to be the one they hanged first.

The man's hand was still pointing in the air when we all heard the whirring of a helicopter. Perhaps the guerrilla had only been calling attention to the approaching plane. . . .

We started walking again, closely guarded by the men with their black rifles. Before leaving, the official had told Bernhard that we were being taken back to An Hoa. Even now I was willing to believe him. The old rice farmer had also taken his leave. But he would reappear in my dreams, luring us into prison with a smile. What had we done to him that he should want such a terrible revenge?

We crossed fields and struggled through tall reeds and irrigated rice paddies, always hugging the thickets and underbrush, where we could hide from enemy scout planes. It was past noon, and the sun was scorching hot. Moreover, my feet hurt, for my flimsy thong sandals were completely unsuited to trekking through marshland. I was very thirsty. Even our guards had grown tired and were walking more slowly. They seemed not to know exactly what to do or where to take us.

For a while, as a precaution, the guards had made us circle around any villages we encountered; but now we walked straight through them. I had formed a romantic image of a Vietnamese village: bamboo huts with smoke rising from the roof, pigs and chickens running around, women carrying their children on their backs. This was the sort of thing I had been planning to film. But the huts I saw now were in ruins; some had burned to the ground. The children had the typical symptoms of malnutrition —the distended bellies, the matchstick arms and legs, the flabby buttocks and thigh muscles.

We paused briefly in each village while the men, women, and children ran up to get a good look at us. Apparently our guards wanted them to have a chance to inspect, to curse, and to marvel at these terrible white creatures which they had managed to capture. Once an old woman ran up to us, beaming with joy and holding a card from the hospital in An Hoa, listing her name, her illness, and her course of treatment. Our guards quickly led us away.

The sun's rays were beating down more fiercely than ever. I broke a dark green banana leaf from a tree we passed and used it to cover my head. Here and there we saw craters dug by the falling bombs. We were walking through a region that must recently have been hit with napalm: everything was scorched, and there was such a terrible stench in the air that we could hardly breathe. We also passed the ruins of an American helicopter, one of the large machines called "bananas," which had been shot down over a nearby field.

Once we met another group of armed men dressed in faded gray-green uniforms. They barred our way, crying, *"Cac maô! Cac maô!"* Their violent gestures told us the meaning of the words: "Why are you bothering with them? Go ahead and cut their throats!" But our guards, feeling the pride of possession, answered something that I interpreted to mean, "Hands off! They're our prisoners! If we decide to kill them, we'll do it ourselves!"

After our encounter with the armed guerrillas, we traveled for another hour or so until we came to a pagoda. The Khe Le River lay far behind us. We had been crossing the valley toward the blue-gray mountains; by now the land was covered with dense jungle. Near the pagoda were more ruined, abandoned huts. We were told to sit down in the pagoda and wait. It was the first time that we had been allowed to rest, and we collapsed on the ground, exhausted.

It must have been five o'clock when a short, thin Vietnamese wearing a plain, olive-drab uniform arrived at the village. Apparently someone had summoned him here to take command.

So far, no one had bothered to search us or ask our names. Now a table was brought in, and one by one we were ordered to display our belongings. On the table we placed our passports, watches, car keys, and money, my movie camera, and Marie-Luise's green pocketbook, which she never let out of her sight. The pocketbook contained powder, eye shadow, a mirror, and a comb. This last article led to an incident that, trivial as it may have been, revealed something about the Vietnamese. While searching the bag, the thin little commanding officer came across Marie-Luise's comb with its long, pointed handle. He had no sooner picked it up than he flung it away in horror, as if he had been bitten by a snake. I bent down to retrieve the comb and started to comb my hair with it, trying to show him how harmless it was. This man, who no doubt was fearless in battle, drew back with a shriek of terror. Clearly he and his comrades believed that I was holding a diabolical instrument of torture used to poke out people's eyes. What must their country have suffered for them to believe themselves threatened with such medieval tortures!

The men stuffed all our belongings into a plain gray linen sack which one of the guards was to carry slung over his shoulder. They made no effort to communicate with us or explain their intentions. The five of us were herded together into an outlying hut containing a bamboo cot full of holes, where we could take turns lying down. For the first time we were left alone, but none of us said a word.

Soon it grew dark. A woman entered the hut, built a fire in a hole in the ground between two stones, and placed a soot-blackened pot over the fire. After cooking our rice, she gave each of us a portion in a small plastic bowl. Then she boiled some water, picked up her things, and disappeared again without saying a word.

I could eat nothing. I simply drank some boiled water. We did not talk much. We all seemed dazed, as if we could not understand what had happened to us. Rika said anxiously, "If we're not back tomorrow morning, Dr. Kröger will have to make a new schedule." There were never enough nurses in Da Nang, and Dr. Kröger hated having to make out the daily schedules.

Once I heard Marie-Luise crying. She said, "I only came here to help. My poor parents. What will they think when they hear that I've been taken prisoner?"

Prisoner. I had grown up in the shadow of that word. It stirred old and frightening memories. I was born in 1942, in the middle of the war, and I was barely three when it ended. But I was never able to forget my father, who had been taken prisoner by the Russians and did not return.

I come from Lebach, a small town on the Saar River. We used to live just opposite the railway station. From our kitchen window we could see the station, the trains arriving and departing, and the people getting in and out. I remember only two things about the war. One is the bomb shelter where we hid when the sirens sounded their alarm, and where I used to go to

11

sleep in a laundry basket. The other is the image of my mother sitting by the kitchen window night after night, mending clothes and watching for my father to appear in the door of the railway station. She wanted to have a clear view of the station, so often she did not cover the window at night. Seeing that she was not observing the blackout, the police kept coming to our house to complain; but my mother ignored them. She was waiting for my father. His body was never found. Thus she went on waiting until her death in 1956.

I never knew my father. All I knew about him, all anyone ever said about him, was that he was a prisoner. When I was a child, the very walls seemed to echo with the word.

I could not picture what a prison camp was like and kept asking my mother, "Why won't they let Papa come home?" My mother always described my father as a good man, but how could a good man be a prisoner? What was a prisoner's life like? As a child I liked to paint pictures. Tearing up the old account books in my father's auto repair shop, I could use the backs of the pages to paint on. I wanted to paint a picture of my father in the prison camp and asked my mother to describe one. She told me, "In prison, you are hungry." "But Mother, why doesn't Father go out and pick potatoes from the field and cook them?" "He would be shot if he went to look for food."

For a long time I wondered how a person could be killed simply for getting food when he was hungry. Then, when my brother started school, we acquired an atlas, and I searched the maps for Russia, where my father was. On the map everything looked very small and not at all far away. "Why can't we go there and get Father? Why doesn't he run away?" My mother shook her head, saying, "My God, child, you don't know anything about being a prisoner."

Now I was a prisoner, too. Now I would learn what captivity was like. Sitting in the jungle hut, I tried to console myself with the thought that perhaps I might learn to understand my father better.

It was pitch-dark. Crickets were chirping outside. Through a small opening we could see stars and parachute flares, which the

Americans used to light up the ground beneath their planes. I wondered if the Americans could be looking for us.

Our guards seemed to have been wondering the same thing. We heard footsteps and saw the glimmer of flashlights. In this light the men's weapons looked blacker than ever. Then voices called out, *"Di di mau! Di di mau!"*

Bernhard whispered, "We're moving on. They're telling us to hurry up." I thought to myself, "So, you're going to learn their language after all. Just think what a fine vocabulary you're going to pick up now. . . ."

Amo, amas, amat

BERNHARD DIEHL

That morning, the five of us had set out from the town of An Hoa. The name "An Hoa" means "Vale of Peace"; but when I arrived there, I found that the "peaceful valley" was a battlefield that living and dead alike could leave only by air.

The first dead I saw in Vietnam were three Americans killed near An Hoa, whose bodies had been flown to Da Nang. I was in Da Nang waiting for a helicopter to fly me to the hospital run by the Aid Service of Malta in An Hoa. When the helicopter arrived, I could not get in until some men had unloaded three plastic bags marked with bright yellow tags. The bags contained the remains of three slain marine infantrymen.

The coastal city of Da Nang lies about five hundred miles north of Saigon and a good one hundred miles south of the seventeenth parallel. An Hoa is only a quarter of an hour away by plane. The three hospitals run by our Aid Service were located in Da Nang, in another coastal town called Hoi An, and in the Duc-Duc district of An Hoa.

For a long time heavy fighting raged in the area between Da Nang and An Hoa. On American maps, Viet Cong territory was shaded red. The balance of power in the region continually shifted, but during the early months of my stay in Vietnam, the Americans had marked the disputed area red. Through this region runs the justly infamous Route 1, leading north along the coast from Saigon to Hué, a hotly contested battleground of the Indochina War. The French, too, had fought for this road and had named it *la rue sans joie,* "the joyless highway."

I arrived at An Hoa just after the major battles of the 1968 Tet offensive, when the area around An Hoa was nominally "at peace." The hospital lay beside an artificial lake beneath the towering mountains. Newcomers were invariably charmed by this magical landscape.

I recall a day about six months before our Sunday excursion, when a new nurse arrived from Germany to join our staff. We "old-timers" always gave a party for new staff members, for we knew that after the first day, they would have little time for diversion. The brilliant colors of a rainbow spanned the afternoon sky above the mountains, as if the scenery had been especially ordered to welcome the new arrival. She was enchanted with the rainbow, the lake, and the mountain landscape.

After supper the doctor, the dentist, the medics, and the new nurse all sat outside on the terrace. The air was mild after the rain, the crickets were chirping, and cans of beer and cola were waiting for us on the table. The new nurse went into romantic rhapsodies about the beautiful night. A train went past—"with lighted windows!" The rest of us did not say a word. "And the shooting stars!" She said that she had never seen such large ones before; usually they fell so fast that one did not even have time to make a wish before they were gone, but these stars mounted slowly and just hung there in the sky! Still we did not reply. Around midnight, she began to go into raptures over the glow-worms whose glimmering lights now filled the horizon. I finally ran out of patience. A small group of Viet Cong had approached within a stone's throw of the American camp, and what the nurse had taken for glowworms were really Chinese and American machine guns exchanging gunfire. Her "shooting stars" were flares attached to parachutes, which the marine infantrymen used to light up the combat zone. And the train "moving so peacefully through the night with lighted windows" was a Chinese machine gun shooting long spurts of fire into the American camp. We explained all this to the nurse, who promptly booked her return flight to Germany and left us two days later.

On another occasion, a doctor left An Hoa after spending only a week with us. He, too, was disillusioned by conditions in Vietnam. Our hospital had no EKG machine; the air conditioner in his room did not work; the drain in his sink was plugged up; and at night, when the Americans and the Viet Cong were exchanging fire, his windowpanes rattled.

In my journal I wrote a few stinging comments about our erstwhile colleagues. But looking back at my earlier entries, I saw that when I first arrived in this country, I had been as naïve as they were.

As a child, I dreamed of having a mission, a divinely appointed task to fulfill. I wanted to be a missionary, a converter of souls. This ambition was a reaction against the home I grew up in, where the most important things in life were discipline and good behavior. I come from the imperial city of Worms. In the West End school I attended, teachers still struck students with a cane. In my home was another cane, used for the same purpose.

My father was an assistant teacher of Latin and Greek in a secondary school. Every afternoon my brothers and I came into his study so that he could check our homework. He used to sit there behind a desk heaped with books and notebooks, rhythmically beating the top of the desk while we recited principal parts or conjugated verbs: *amo, amas, amat.* . . .

He raised us to obey the two guiding principles of his own life. First, he told us, "Goodness is self-evident; but you must constantly be reminded of what is bad so that you will know it when you see it." Second, he taught us, "Ten minutes of exposure to evil can undo the good effects of ten years' teaching."

As a child, I lived in another world of which my family knew nothing. Four elderly ladies, one of them my grandmother, had pledged themselves to aid the foreign missions, and they adopted

16

me into their circle. They collected stamps for the missions, made innumerable book covers and bookmarks, and sewed little pouches for rosaries out of scraps of cloth. These articles were sent to African children resembling the tiny black man beside the collection box in St. Paul's Church, who nodded whenever anyone threw a coin into the box. I listened enthralled to the tales the ladies told about priests preaching to the natives, building churches, schools, and houses, and combating wild beasts. Observing my enthusiasm for everything related to the missions, the ladies one day surprised me by buying me a heathen child!

Could a person really buy a heathen child? It seemed easy enough. One simply paid a certain sum of money, and, in exchange, one of those unhappy foreign beings was baptized. Suddenly the child ceased to be a heathen and became a Christian, received into the communion of the faithful. My cousin Michael already had a heathen child, and now I had one, too. He was baptized with my name, Bernhard. Now there was a little Bernhard in Africa, and periodically we were sent reports on his progress. I was always very excited when the ladies read me the letters from Africa. "My" Bernhard was learning his catechism. "My" Bernhard was learning to read and write. "My" Bernhard had been bitten by a snake. "My" Bernhard needed additional financial aid. Then we received a picture of him. He was jet-black, had scrawny legs, and wore the short trousers my grandmother had sent him, which were far too big for him. I was convinced that one day I would travel to Africa to join the other Bernhard, and live out my days in his country, where help was so sorely needed. At age twelve I thought of my future as a life of labor in the jungle, marked by sacrifices and dangers. I would become one of those priests who wore such beautiful white robes; and, of course, my Bernhard would become a priest, too, so that we could work together at a mission house, one black priest and one white!

Then Father Kasimir arrived with his Chinese friends whose skin was yellow, and I grew faithless to my Bernhard. I was serving as an acolyte in the Dominican cloister when Father

17

Kasimir came to visit, a tall Dominican priest in a white habit and black mantle. He had snow-white hair, and his yellowish face made him resemble a Chinese. After spending almost his entire life in China, he had left during the Revolution and was now head of a mission on Formosa.

Once he showed us some color slides. In the darkened room, I heard his soft voice speaking German with a foreign accent. The slides showed yellow sand and yellow people. And, just as in Africa, there were missions, hospitals, and schools for the children. Father Kasimir, too, spoke of a life of sacrifice; but his God seemed a lot more down-to-earth than my grandmother's. He talked about faith, but he also talked about a carpentry shop, various diseases, and people who needed help.

Something else that happened in my childhood influenced me to come to An Hoa—a bad railway accident at Abenheim, near Worms. In summer, when the grain grows tall, you can hardly see the railway crossing at Abenheim, and there is no traffic signal or barrier to warn vehicles when a train is coming through. The bus driver must not have seen the train coming until it was too late, and many people were killed in the ensuing collision. I did not see the accident itself, but only its aftermath. I was spending the day with one of my four elderly lady friends, the director of the local chapter of the Red Cross. After taking the accident victims to the hospital, all the ambulances parked in front of my friend's house, where they were to be cleaned. The ambulance drivers kept handing me blood-soaked pillows and blankets, which I carried into the house to be washed. I also carried buckets of water and cloths to the men outside, who were washing out the blood in the rear compartments. There was blood everywhere. The blankets, which had been washed and hung on the fence to dry, were still covered with dark stains. I was eleven years old, and this was the first time that I had seen human blood. People told me that I turned as white as chalk; but that evening, my friend said that I had done well and predicted that one day I would become a fine doctor. That day I decided to be a doctor as well as a priest.

After graduating from secondary school, I volunteered for

two years' service in the army, where I received training as a non-commissioned medical orderly. For several months before my discharge, I worked in the clinic at the University of Cologne; it was there that I met a member of the Aid Service of Malta.

He was a man in his forties who volunteered for orderly duty on Sundays and spent the day emptying bedpans, serving meals, and helping the nurses change the beds. Although he himself had never been to Vietnam, his friends had told him about the work of the Aid Service in that distant land. He said that they had set up their own hospitals and were free to run them as they chose. Their life was both exciting and dangerous. I began to feel torn. Should I study medicine or go to Vietnam?

A student demonstration in Cologne helped me make up my mind. One day I saw a group of students heading toward the center of town chanting, "Ho-Ho-Ho-Chi-Minh!" They did not seem at all militant, strolling along nibbling sandwiches and drinking Coca-Cola. Most of the boys had a girl on each arm and kept stealing kisses between chants. "Ho-Ho-Ho-Chi-Minh!"

I had already applied to the university, but now I felt the urge to find out the truth about the situation in Vietnam. I wanted to see for myself what was going on. Leaving the scene of the demonstration, I went directly to the General Secretariat of the Aid Service of Malta in Cologne. After making inquiries and thinking things over for a little while, I signed my contract. I had just turned twenty-one, and I was going to Vietnam.

My family and friends seemed at a loss to understand my decision. One friend remarked casually, "That sounds like a good idea. I hear they pay really well." Another said, "Vietnam? Where's that, and how do you get there?" A girl asked, "How can you hurt your parents so?" When my mother heard that I was leaving, she started to cry and said, "Do you have to go? Aren't you happy at home any more? We've always done everything we could for you." My father was angry: "Oh, so you've made up your mind, have you? Well, we'll just see what your parents have to say about that!" My parents and the other adults

I knew seemed to feel insulted when they heard my plans; their faces grew hard, as if they had just received a blast of icy wind through an open window.

I signed my contract on February 14, 1968. On May 3, I left Cologne in a jet with three other medics in the Aid Service. I still had a very distorted picture of conditions in An Hoa. The few brief orientation sessions I had attended in Cologne had done nothing to clear up my misconceptions. I was told that the Aid Service ran three hospitals in Vietnam, but no one mentioned how little they resembled German hospitals. I was told that we would work in surgical teams, but I pictured the well-organized neurosurgical teams I had observed in Cologne.

Not even the eight-millimeter film the four of us saw on the eve of our departure gave us any inkling of the truth. We watched colored images flitting across the screen in the office of the General Secretariat, but no sound accompanied the pictures. We saw wounded men, but we did not hear their screams of pain; we saw mushroom clouds rising from the jungle, but we did not hear the detonations of the bombs; we saw the clumsy, gyrating black canisters of napalm falling from planes, but we did not hear the shrieking of the jet engines that, later, would cut us to the quick. Only a few things in this silent film seemed real. We were told, "That's Da Nang, that's our hospital there; the Bishop lets us use that house, and in return we generate electricity for him. The man on the right there is Mayer; he can polish off five steaks at one sitting. And don't forget, the medical staff are not allowed to keep dogs in their rooms!"

On the final yards of film, we saw a road. At the edge of the road were some rolled-up fiber mats about the size of human beings. When I asked about them, I was hesitantly told that the mats contained dead Viet Cong guerrillas, whose bodies were left on the road for several days to frighten their comrades before being carted away by the garbage trucks.

This revelation did not sway my decision to go to An Hoa; it simply made me stop and think. I had committed myself to

20

spend nine months in Vietnam. There were no longer or shorter terms of service; it was nine months or nothing.

As I climbed into the jet, I reflected that nine months was exactly how much time it took to make a man. I told myself that I was going to be reborn.

APO San Francisco 96337

BERNHARD DIEHL

The first dead men I saw in Vietnam were the Americans whose bodies had been flown out of An Hoa. They were not the only Americans I encountered. The plane that flew me from Saigon to Da Nang was an Air American DC-3; and after arriving in An Hoa, I spent my first few nights in the nearby American marine infantry camp, for the hospital had not yet been equipped with beds. The American forces maintained a supply depot and a landing field in An Hoa, and the camp commander sent us daily reports on combat conditions in our area. The Americans also warned us beforehand whenever the Viet Cong were expected to launch a night attack on the camp. Sometimes members of the hospital staff had to drive around to our outpatient clinics—the dispensaries in Than My, Nong Son, Khuong Que, and Khuong Thuon. Before leaving, we first waited for an American patrol to clear the road of possible mines. Letters we wrote home were flown by helicopter to Da Nang, then across the ocean to San Francisco, from there to New York, and finally to Germany. Letters from Germany followed the same roundabout path. They were not addressed to An Hoa, but to the "Malteser Aid Service, CORDS-REF-III MAF, Drawer 69, APO San Francisco 96337, U.S.A."

Some time passed before I learned the meaning of the baffling word "CORDS." CORDS was an abbreviation for "Civilian

Organization Revolutionary Development Service." Did this mean that the Americans considered the activities of our hospital a form of "revolutionary development"? After my release from prison, I learned that the meaning of the "R" in CORDS had been changed from "Revolutionary" to "Rural." The new title certainly sounded less insidious!

It was reassuring to know that the Americans to some degree "guaranteed" the safety of our hospital and its staff. But the proximity and patronage of the American forces was not an unmixed blessing. As members of the Aid Service of Malta, we considered ourselves citizens of a neutral nation engaged in running a civilian hospital, who would care for the sick no matter what their political allegiance. But our medical staff occupied a somewhat equivocal position in Vietnam. After our capture, we became aware of just how equivocal it was.

During my stay in An Hoa, the German Red Cross ship *Helgoland* was anchored in Da Nang Harbor. The Communists protested against the arrival of the floating hospital, claiming that the Germans were not interested in offering neutral assistance but were merely demonstrating their support of the American imperialist attack on the Vietnamese people and the people's war of liberation.

To function, our hospital staff had to rely on American support. We treated only civilians and treated them without regard to their political loyalties. Yet despite our good intentions, we sometimes found ourselves being drawn into the surrounding conflict.

Since the beginning of September 1968, we had been treating a Vietnamese suffering from a gunshot wound in the upper thigh. We had received a tip that he was really a Viet Cong guerrilla who might actually have wounded himself in order to infiltrate our hospital and make contact with other patients and the hospital staff. This seemed a fine opportunity to demonstrate our neutrality. While continuing to treat the man, we privately told him that when he was well, he should, so to speak, discharge himself and slip away quietly before he could be captured.

One evening a jeep drove up to the hospital, and shortly thereafter an orderly on night duty heard suspicious noises in the doctor's examining room. Quickly investigating, he surprised a Vietnamese standing by a supply cabinet and cutting off long strips of sterile gauze. Petty thefts were an everyday occurrence, but this time the theft had more serious implications. Seizing the gauze, the thief and a companion barged into the room of the alleged Viet Cong guerrilla, bandaged his eyes, and dragged him outside, where they piled him into the jeep.

At the time these events occurred, I was in my room in a separate part of the hospital compound; but I came running as soon as I heard all the uproar. The hospital and our staff quarters both stood beside Liberty Road, and the jeep had to travel along this road to get away. Running outside, I jumped into our own jeep and tried to intercept the kidnapers, but the Vietnamese driver stepped on the gas and sped away.

Later, the Americans explained what had happened. South Vietnamese special police agents had kidnaped the suspected guerrilla and taken him to a prison in Hoi An. The jeep they had used belonged to the district leader, Major Thriem. We were told that the prisoner was still alive.

We were all deeply shocked by this event. Moreover, we were concerned about the possible consequences to the hospital if news of the kidnaping should leak out. We knew that the North Vietnamese might capitalize on the incident to drum up resistance to our work. We had no choice: somehow we had to regain custody of the kidnaped man.

In the end, we achieved a sort of compromise. The suspected guerrilla was returned to the hospital under guard to undergo a "medical examination to establish his mental and physical well-being." When he had been declared healthy, he was officially "discharged" from the hospital—i.e., returned to prison. The examination and discharge took barely half an hour. Our hospital records were now in order, and we had not violated our neutrality. We never heard a word about the fate of the prisoner.

Our hospital staff never doubted the humanitarian value of

24

our work in Vietnam. Monika Schwinn worked long and exhausting hours in the children's ward of the hospital in Da Nang. During our years of captivity, it may have helped her to remember that she had never done any harm to the people of this country.

When we were captured, I doubted that the guerrillas would acknowledge our political neutrality. Throughout my captivity, I continued to be haunted by the kidnaping of the suspected guerrilla agent. Each time I was summoned for interrogation, I used to think, "Well, the game's up, they've found out about it. They're going to accuse you of having betrayed one of their comrades to the enemy!" From the beginning, I was determined not to tell my captors about the kidnaping, and for four years I lived with the fear that they might learn about it from some other source. I could not forget how the guerrilla had looked when the doctor signed his "discharge." He appeared calm, but there was a mocking expression on his face, as if he were thinking, "So, this is the kind of help you have to offer. . . ."

The Aid Service of Malta had begun their work in An Hoa in November of 1966. At first they had no hospitals. A doctor, two nurses, and a medic traveled around in a jeep, administering outpatient treatment in several dispensaries. They were forced to work under unsanitary conditions and with only the most primitive equipment; yet they managed to accomplish a great deal.

When I first arrived in Vietnam, An Hoa was still considered Viet Cong territory; so I worked in Hoi An instead. When it was safe, I moved to An Hoa. At first, there were seven of us on the staff; at the time of my capture, fifteen. On August 10, 1968, the hospital officially opened its doors. The records state that the hospital contained one hundred and twenty beds, but this was a slight exaggeration. We had managed, with the greatest difficulty, to procure some thirty beds. The rest of the promised shipment was still lying somewhere in Hong Kong. We had an X-ray machine, an essential item in view of the large number of broken bones and fragmentation-bomb wounds we had to treat. But for a time we could not operate the machine, for one of its parts was missing. The hospital had no kitchen; and although it sometimes housed up to one hundred patients, there was only one washing machine for the combined laundry of staff and patients. We had an operating room but no equipment for administering anesthesia. Two surgical teams had to get along with five scalpels, three clamps, and two pairs of scissors. Under the circumstances, I was amazed at how much we were able to accomplish.

We kept careful records of our patients. The records show that during December of 1968, we treated 1,256 people and helped to deliver 21 babies. In January of the following year, we treated 2,478 and delivered 11. In February the count rose to 3,710. The most prevalent ailments were tuberculosis, dysentery, muscular atrophy, broken bones, skin infections, and boils. But by far the largest number of our patients—sometimes as many as fifty percent—required surgical treatment for gunshot wounds and wounds caused by fragmentation bombs. These people were victims of the unending battle between the Americans and the Viet Cong.

There was intermittent fighting near An Hoa. On clear nights, everything was fairly peaceful; but during the rainy season, when the patter of rainfall almost drowned out all other sounds, the Viet Cong resumed their night attacks. Marines and Special Forces troops cleared a path from An Hoa to the coast, and for several weeks American truck convoys traveled freely back and forth. Then the Viet Cong began to reinfiltrate the area, and once again the Americans had to mark it red on their maps. The war went on the same way day after day. As long as it was light, American scout planes scoured the jungle, indiscriminately bombing everything that moved. At night the Viet Cong lay in ambush, launched sudden surprise attacks, and then withdrew. In a war like this, there were no victories.

Somehow we felt untouched by all the turmoil. We saw what was going on, but we were not directly involved. The fighting might keep us awake at night, but that was all. We laughed at German newspaper accounts that described us crawling through the battle lines to rescue wounded men, in danger of being

26

caught in the crossfire or killed by exploding shells. In the eyes of our countrymen, we occupied the lowest circle of Hell.

We knew that our lives were not in danger. Moreover, a sort of tacit agreement existed between our hospital and the Viet Cong. Whenever they could, the guerrillas stole bandages, antiseptic, and powdered antibiotics from the dispensaries, often leaving a receipt for the stolen goods. To the Viet Cong, we represented a source of medical supplies they could not have obtained elsewhere. In exchange for the supplies, they left us in peace and did not attempt to interfere with our work. This state of affairs had continued for so long that we had allowed ourselves to be lulled into a false sense of security. Thus my companions and I were not at all afraid that Sunday morning when we set out on our drive into the country.

These little country outings were the only diversion available to the medical staff in An Hoa, Da Nang, and Hoi An. What bothered us most was not the hard work or the war or even the constant tension, but the circumscribed, sterile ghetto atmosphere in which we lived. Week after week, month after month, we saw the same faces, sat on the same terrace, and told the same stories for the hundredth time. We all developed claustrophobia; we felt that we had to get away and do what we wanted for a while.

April 27, 1969, was a beautiful Sunday for our outing. The An Hoa region had been peaceful for several weeks. The security officer in the American camp reported that there had been no sign of trouble; he saw no reason why we should not take a drive in the country. We had gone on many such outings, and the most exciting thing that had ever happened was a collision between a water buffalo and my Willys jeep. The jeep was dented and the water buffalo went lame. The next day I drove back to the village and paid its owner a compensation of three thousand piasters, about one hundred marks or thirty-five dollars.

This time five of us were going into the country. A few weeks before, Rika Kortmann had laid the cornerstone of the new hospital in Da Nang. Just yesterday, a helicopter had flown Rika and Monika Schwinn from Da Nang to An Hoa to pay us a brief visit. Marie-Luise Kerber and Georg Bartsch were two of my co-workers in An Hoa.

The sun was shining. We lowered the hood and windshield of the jeep and drove off along Liberty Road. Later we turned off onto the road to Nong Son. Leaving the jeep beside the ruined bridge on the Khe Le River, we took off our shoes and began wading upstream. . . .

A Jungle Hotel

MONIKA SCHWINN

For eleven days we trudged through a monotonous jungle landscape. Soon every tree began to look like every other tree, every
hut like every other hut. We seemed to be walking in a circle.
Even our guards appeared unsure of our destination.

There were three guards. Sometimes a fourth man would
join them to act as guide, and twice the guards were relieved
by a new shift. Apparently each group of guards was restricted
to a certain area. They always traveled in groups of three,
which I later learned were called *chibos;* they represented the
smallest combat units among the jungle guerrillas. The leader
could always be recognized by the map case hanging from his
shoulder. A second man acted as porter, carrying the back
pack containing our belongings, the hammocks our guards
slept in, a bag full of canned fish, and sometimes the rice, stored
in two long stockings wrapped around his neck. The third man
always kept his gun trained on us. He also served as messenger,
disappearing into the jungle for half an hour or so and then
reporting back.

As a rule, we traveled only at night. As soon as it grew dark
we started walking and kept going until dawn. Moonlight and
glowworms lighted our path, but we could barely see where we
were going and kept stumbling over roots, stones, and branches
hidden in the dark. In time we learned to feel the path with

our feet before stepping down. Our guards seemed to think that we had unlimited strength. We climbed steep, rocky slopes, then descended the dry bed of a mountain spring, cutting our feet on the sharp pebbles. My thong sandals fell apart the first night, and I might have had to finish the trip barefoot if Rika and Marie-Luise hadn't taken turns lending me their shoes. Sometimes we circled the bomb craters, and sometimes we had to scramble through them. We walked through tall grass with blades as sharp as knives; often it took us several minutes to cut our way through a single yard of underbrush; and sometimes we sank deep in the muddy fields. But for the most part we kept to the jungle, climbing higher and higher into the mountains.

We did not utter a word of protest, but simply went on placing one foot in front of the other. What difference did it make if our feet were sore or we fell down? We had no choice but to go on and no strength left for resistance. Toward morning the *"Di di mau! Di di mau!"* of our guards grew sharper and more insistent.

At two or three in the morning, we stopped for half an hour or so to eat rice and drink boiled water before setting out again. The worst hours of the day lay ahead, the hours before dawn lit up the jungle and the birds began to wake up. Our guards became increasingly anxious and treated us roughly; their voices growing shriller by the minute, they drove us along as fast as they could. They urged us on as if we were going to be late for some appointment. In time I realized that they simply feared the light of day.

The first sign of dawn was not the birds or the glow of sunrise, but the arrival of helicopters and scout planes. American planes began to scour the jungle, and the guerrillas no longer felt safe. Some mornings we heard no birds at all, but the planes were always right on time, and once the crew had spotted a man on the ground, they pursued him relentlessly.

For some reason, one day our guards decided to keep traveling after it grew light. Like rabbits, we hopped along from one bush to the next. Sometimes the bushes were thirty yards apart.

On the day of our capture, the guards had made Georg Bartsch put on a dark green shirt to cover his white one. Despite these precautions, a scout plane caught sight of us. We could hear its motors whirring directly overhead.

We were standing in clear view on a small hill. The only available cover was some underbrush growing in a dry river bed at the foot of the slope. When the guards pointed to the bushes, the others tore off down the hill. Seeing me hesitate, one of the guerrillas grabbed my hand, meaning to drag me to cover. Suddenly everything went black. I must have fallen and rolled all the way down the hill. I came to just as the guard was pulling me into the bushes.

I lay there, gasping for air. The Vietnamese was so close to me that I could hear him breathing. The scout plane continued to circle overhead, sometimes pulling away a short distance and then coming back.

Up to this point, we had all been hoping to be spotted by the American planes. We knew how dangerous it would be if they mistook us for the enemy, but the Americans were the only hope we had left. Now, as I lay huddled in the bushes, I feared the plane overhead almost as much as I feared our guards.

For the first few days, I continued to hope that we might be rescued. At night we had seen a glow in the sky coming from the Special Forces camp in Nong Son, where the Americans were shooting off their flares. Parachute flares lit up the night. Sometimes I even hoped that the guerrillas planned to let us go. "Isn't An Hoa somewhere behind that big mountain?" I thought. Perhaps the guards were going to row us across the lake in the boat tethered there. I believed, or I hoped, that they intended to lead us in a circle, so that later we would be unable to supply information about where we had been and what we had seen. But lying under the bushes, I felt that I had no more hope than a butterfly mounted on a pin.

My uncle used to collect butterflies and mount them in cases. Even in death, their colors were beautiful; but the sight of them always filled me with horror. Pinned down beneath the circling plane, I thought about the past. "Why does everything you do

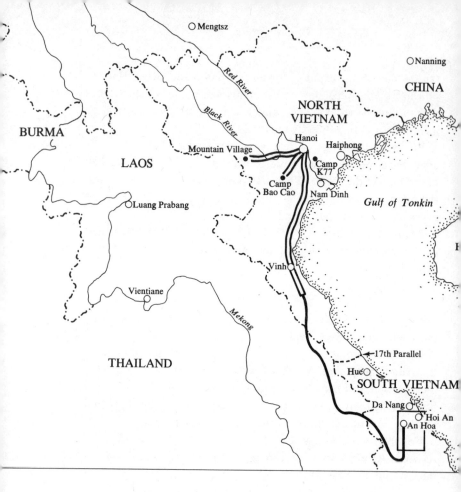

LEGEND

—— Footpath   ═══ Automobile trip

Capture, 4/27/69
Camp I, 5/8/69–5/25/69 (M.S.);
    5/8/69–5/12/69 (B.D.)
American Camp, 5/26/69–9/18/69 (M.S.);
    5/14/69–9/18/69 (B.D.)
Mountain Camp, 9/20/69–3/31/70
    (M.S. and B.D.)
March to the North, 4/1/70–6/3/70

Camp Bao Cao, 6/4/70–6/11/70
Camp K77, 6/11/70–12/11/71
Mountain Village, 12/11/71–1/27/73
Hanoi Hilton, 1/27/73–3/5/73
Release, 3/5/73
Flight from Clark Air Base (Philippines
    3/7/73
Arrival Frankfurt, 3/8/73

go wrong? What are you being punished for, what have you done? Why did you never have a father? Why did your mother die so young? Why can't you form a lasting relationship with a man? Why couldn't you even do the work you had set your heart on?"

As a child, I always loved the theater. At the age of twelve I began to write and perform my own plays, but I knew that I was not beautiful enough to be an actress. I decided to become a make-up artist instead, so that at least I could be near the theater. To transform the faces of others, one did not need to be beautiful oneself. I would learn to understand people's faces, the human emotions that shaped them, and all the expressions they could wear—the joys and sorrows, the passion and awe. As a first step in reaching my goal, I tried to become a beautician, but I could not complete my course of study. I was allergic to the caustic chemicals, fixing agents, fumes, make-up, and creams. When I developed a form of bleeding eczema, doctors advised me to take up another line of work.

I went on thinking about my life until at last the plane gave up and flew away. During that ordeal, each of us was alone with his thoughts, hopes, fears, his hunger and thirst. We all asked ourselves questions. Even during the rest stops, we spoke very little and were lost in our own thoughts. . . .

To avoid the planes, we rested in the daytime. We hid in some ruined jungle hut, nothing more than a roof mounted on six posts. Once we took cover between three boulders covered with a makeshift roof. We slept in small dugouts on the bare ground, while our guards strung their hammocks from the trees.

I envied the others when they managed to sleep. Bernhard could lie down anywhere and fall asleep at once. He often napped sitting down, taking advantage of every spare moment to gather strength for the journey. I rarely got any sleep. I was constantly stung by mosquitoes or was busy driving away the rats and mice. And even during our rest stops, we were never really left alone.

I do not know where all the men, women, and children came from or how they learned where we were. It was as if we left some kind of trail or special scent which they could follow. Suddenly more than a dozen of them would crowd around us, staring at us in amazement. The guards made no effort to drive them away; they behaved like menagerie owners taking their exotic beasts on tour.

Usually one of the women built a fire and cooked rice for us in a soot-blackened pot. We ate rice every day. As long as the supply of canned fish held out, we had a little fish too; and we drank hot boiled water from the empty fish cans. It was as hard for me to eat as it was to sleep. After a mouthful or two, I would put down my rice and begin to gulp the water, which was still so hot that I always burned my mouth.

One day we arrived at a "jungle hotel." We had been traveling for almost eleven days, steadily ascending into the mountains. The higher we climbed, the fewer people we met along the way. Then suddenly, in the middle of the jungle, we came to a neatly swept clearing containing two huts and—O miracle! —clear, bright water flowing from bamboo canes into a hollow tree trunk. Now I remembered the words of a Vietnamese we had met in the jungle. He had told us that in three days we would come to a place he described as *bien confortable*. So this was the comfortable place—a jungle hotel.

The hotel consisted of two huts, one for "guests," the other for the owner. When we entered the clearing, he was sitting in front of his hut with his arms crossed, smoking a fat cigar he had rolled from his own tobacco leaves. A woman with her baby strapped to her back was throwing rice husks to the chickens. The owner sat there and eyed us as he bargained with the guerrillas over the price of our night's lodging.

We ourselves were paying for our food and lodging. When we were captured, the guerrillas had taken seven thousand piasters from Georg Bartsch. I had seen them use it to pay our expenses along the way. They had paid one of our guides, a farmer who gave us rice, the men who supplied our canned fish, and the women who cooked for us. This evening, we were paying for the luxuries of a jungle hotel.

For the first time since our capture, we were allowed to wash. The guards gave us a piece of soap and a towel. There were no holes in our bamboo cots or our mosquito nets. Our guards slept outside in their hammocks under worn, much-mended nets. Besides the usual rice, we were given a salad of finely chopped banana blossoms soaked for a day in onions, salt, and oil and served with a special dressing. There was also dessert—watermelons and peanuts—and anyone who wanted to smoke could gather his own tobacco. Later, when Georg's money was gone, I thought of our meal at the jungle hotel as the last real meal we would ever eat. The next morning we woke up not to the sound of our guards shouting, *"Di di mau! Di di mau!"* but to the noise of monkeys screaming in the trees.

We spent some eighteen hours in the jungle hotel. On the following day, we saw new guests arrive. For the first time I began to understand the system underlying the world of the jungle guerrilla. This almost impassable terrain was really a military stronghold. No wonder the Americans indiscriminately bombed everything that moved. They were fighting an invisible enemy who would never stand and face them, who struck from the jungle and then vanished without a trace.

At first I had believed that our guards had no pre-established plan of action. Now I saw that I had been mistaken. Along the way I had noticed certain facts without knowing what they meant; now everything began to fall into place. I saw that the guerrillas knew exactly where to take us and where to find people sympathetic to their cause. We had seen no sign of radio or communications devices, yet everything went off like clockwork. It was uncanny how the people we met seemed to know all about us and exactly what they were expected to do. Clearly they had never laid eyes on our guards before. Yet whenever we approached a village, peasants armed with rifles swarmed out to meet us, and then scattered to scout the area, as if they were checking to make sure that the village was secure. Men carrying packages magically came to meet us along jungle paths. Once we met a man pushing a chainless and pedalless bicycle loaded down with bundles. Someone had carefully planned our schedule, sent messages ahead, and arranged meetings. All the people we met were obeying orders. But there was no telling where the orders came from. I knew only that everyone turned up at the right place and the right time.

While we were still in the jungle hotel, I suddenly understood an incident that had occurred several days before. Twice during our eleven-day march, we had witnessed a changing of the guard. The guerrillas made quite a ceremony of it. First they emptied out the sack containing our belongings, then carefully examined each object and checked it off on a list before putting it back. During one of these ceremonies, the new guards discovered that Rika's wristwatch was missing. One of the guerrillas had yielded to the temptation to try it on. His wrist was so thin that he had no trouble fastening it. We had all seen him repeatedly glancing down to admire how it looked. But he must have lost it somewhere along the way. Now that the new guards had caught him, he embarked on a long tale of woe, trying to justify his dereliction. The others were not satisfied until they had written a long report and forced him to sign his name. I was struck by the guerrillas' obvious concern to maintain discipline. Red tape had managed to triumph even in the jungle.

Leaving the jungle hotel, we saw at once that our journey must be nearly over. The guards no longer urged us to pick up our pace. Suddenly we seemed to have all the time in the world, and we were even free to travel by daylight.

I could not have gone much farther. By the end of the first day, my feet were badly swollen. Stones and thorns cut them until the toes became infected. I developed chills and felt freezing cold despite the heat of the jungle. Then I broke out in a cold sweat. I was walking more and more slowly. Both my mind and my body were tormenting me.

Finally my feet grew so sore that I could hardly bear to step down on them. They were covered with blood and swollen to twice their normal size. Although they were now thickly callused, the flesh beneath the callus was infected. The big toe on my right foot throbbed with pain; it was bright red and filled with pus. I felt that there was nothing left of me but this throbbing toe and all the aches and pains.

Rika still had a safety pin that the guards had neglected to confiscate. (When we reached the camp, they were severely reprimanded for this oversight, and for having failed to remove the pins in Bernhard's shirt collar.) Rika lanced my toe with the pin. Of course, it was a foolish thing to do, for I had no bandage to cover the wound, which would soon become re-infected. But at least for a moment, as the pus spurted out, the toe did not hurt so much.

Then one of our guards disappeared for half an hour and returned with a man wearing a short, absurd-looking, faded green coat that fluttered as he walked. He was carrying a small wooden suitcase with a metal handle. Putting down the case, he took out a bandage! It was as if an angel had suddenly material-ized from nowhere. When Rika had finished bandaging my feet, the man looked quite proud of his work. Grinning broadly, he pointed first to the case and then to himself, and said in broken English, "*Y si*—medic first class—me!" The *y si* and I were destined to meet again. For now, he packed up his gear and hurried away with his funny coat still flapping against his legs.

Then we traveled on. My bandaged feet felt better for a couple of hours, but then they began to hurt as much as ever. Night was falling, and I longed to reach our destination. I should have known that what lay ahead would be worse than our few days on the trail.

We walked still more slowly, pausing frequently to rest. Later I realized that our guards had purposely slowed our pace so that we would not reach our goal until it was dark. It was as if they wanted to spare us the sight of our prison in broad daylight.

Suddenly lights glowed in the darkness just ahead. Figures

appeared carrying flickering torches and an oil lamp. They were coming closer.

The figures surrounded us, forcing us to line up in a row. Voices bellowed out of the darkness. Now and then a gust of wind made the torches flare, and I saw that we were surrounded by armed soldiers pointing their guns at us.

The ceremonial changing of the guard began. I kept my eyes fixed on the bamboo gate I had just glimpsed in the shadows. We had arrived at the first of a long succession of camps. At that moment, I knew nothing of what was to come. I knew only that we were about to pass through the gate. Then I felt someone take my hand. It must have been one of our three guards, who were standing behind us. I felt him press my hand for a few seconds and then let it go. When I turned around, he had already disappeared.

"That could have meant many things," I thought. "Sympathy, regret, perhaps simply relief because he is free of the responsibility, because he has delivered us safely and is free to return to the jungle world he knows."

The soldiers ahead of us shouted orders and waved their guns, motioning us forward. We walked through the gate. . . .

Give Me, Give Me

MONIKA SCHWINN

This time we awoke to the sound of a whistle at 5:00 A.M. I was glad that it was time to get up. The night before, the soldiers had taken us to a hut and thrown three blankets in after us. Lying on our bamboo cots, we had been freezing all night, for the camp lay high in the mountains.

At least the darkness had kept us from seeing the filth and the slanting walls. The hut had been partitioned to form three separate compartments. We had been assigned the middle compartment. During the night we had heard the sounds of other prisoners behind the bamboo screens.

The whistle was the signal for early-morning exercise. Going outside, we saw the prisoners we had heard the night before. The emaciated figures clad in black pajamas were soldiers of the ARVN, the Army of the Republic of Vietnam, who had fought for the South. The prisoners looked straight through us, indifferent to our presence. They had been in the camps for three or four years, and by now they had lost interest in everything.

Early-morning exercise was a compulsory part of our daily routine. At five o'clock we got up and went outside. At dawn the jungle is a noisy place, resounding with the cries of animals waking up, bird songs, the deafening screams of monkeys. Always audible above the tumult came the sound of the whistle blowing, signaling us to bend our knees. Up, down, up, down,

40

up, down. Running in place. Then it was time for what passed as our breakfast, in the little kitchen that emitted a thin trail of smoke. After breakfast, the South Vietnamese prisoners left the camp to work in the fields. They were considered expendable. No one cared if they were shot down in the fields by American planes.

Watching the Vietnamese prisoners being marched out of camp, I saw the gate that had inspired me with such dread the night before. I could not believe my eyes. Two bamboo posts supported the wooden leaves of a double door. But the gate was standing there all by itself: there was no fence attached to it! The gate solemnly opened and closed behind the departing prisoners, as if it really served some purpose. I felt that at any moment I was going to start laughing hysterically.

Later I saw what I had at first overlooked. Instead of a fence, a barrier of bamboo spikes encircled the camp, beginning at either side of the gate. The spikes were no more than four inches high, but they were hard and sharp as nails and formed a solid carpet almost ten feet across. Our guards knew that, in their weakened condition, none of the prisoners would be able to jump over it. An impenetrable wall of jungle undergrowth began directly on the other side of the spikes.

This was to be the first of many camps. We had names for all the others—the American camp, Camp Bao Cao, Camp K77, the Mountain Village; but our first camp was never anything but "Camp I." Even among ourselves, we used the English word "camp" to refer to our prisons. We were living in a world of foreign sounds and foreign words. Later, when Bernhard said a few words at Rika's grave, he spoke English. As time went on, we spoke German less and less.

We had no reason to give Camp I a name, for none of us spent much time there. Marie-Luise and I stayed for two weeks; Georg, Rika, and Bernhard for only three days. But brief as it was, our stay there left me with bitter memories.

It was not a large camp—only three huts for the prisoners, two for the guards. There was also a kitchen, a shed for the pigs and chickens, and an official lecture hall. No more than twenty

Vietnamese were imprisoned there. The camp was surrounded by jungle. There must have been countless numbers of these jungle camps, all kept small so that they could be abandoned at a moment's notice and the prisoners moved to another location. Prisoners were not closely guarded. The guards took away all our shoes at night. This and the barrier of bamboo spikes were all that prevented our escape.

Early the first morning, the five of us were taken to another hut for interrogation. The guerrillas had already confiscated our belongings, but they had not bothered to find out our names or to ask us any questions. This was the first of many interrogation sessions we would experience in the next four years. Once Bernhard and I were questioned for six days running. But our first interrogation was the briefest and the most bizarre.

The commandant was waiting with three guards. A Vietnamese prisoner named Tat, who claimed to speak fluent English, acted as interpreter, a guard as recording secretary. Tat explained that they wanted to know our names, the names of our parents, our educational background, and so forth. But we never got to tell them any more than our names. Bernhard was the first one they questioned. The moment he mentioned his name, the commandant and his staff looked at each other in amazement and burst into maniacal laughter.

From then on, everything we said was greeted with laughter. "Bernhard Johannes Maria": loud guffaws. "Banhat," one of them mimicked, "Banhat, Banhat, Banhat." "Diehl": they grinned at each other. No one bothered to write down the name. "Monika": giggles. "Schwinn." After a moment of startled silence, the commandant motioned to his secretary to write it down, "Swin, Swin, Swin." "Georg": they held their breaths. "Bartsch": no longer able to sit still, they got up and began to dance around the room, slapping their thighs and holding their sides with laughter. "Marie-Luise . . . Kerber." They were completely out of control. "Hindrika." More imitations: "Dri ka, dri ka, dri ka." "Kortmann." They just sat there, highly amused, and quite content to know nothing about us or why we were here. Then we were allowed to return to our hut. They did not even bother to summon us to the propaganda lectures held almost every evening for the benefit of the South Vietnamese captives.

They had a regular "lecture hall" for propaganda sessions. The best of the huts, it had only three sides and was open at the front. At the head of the room, they had set up a podium, a blackboard, and rows of narrow boards to serve as benches. After a day at hard labor, the Vietnamese prisoners had to sit there enduring two or three hours of indoctrination.

On our trek through the jungle, all five of us had developed the early symptoms of malaria—fever and headache. But sick as we felt, we almost forgot our own misery when we saw the starving, emaciated Vietnamese who had already spent some three or four years in the camps.

In this camp, I learned the real meaning of hunger for the first time. After morning exercise, we ate our "breakfast" in the kitchen with the Vietnamese captives. The kitchen was half buried in the earth, more a windowless dugout than a hut. Inside was a hearth where the food was cooked. On two crooked shelves, the halves of a log, perched two sooty aluminum pots and the small plastic bowls from which we ate our rice. The rice was served with a sauce that sometimes tasted like fish and sometimes like bouillon.

Next to the kitchen was a small dining hall containing three rows of tables so narrow that they could hardly hold our little bowls. Seated on benches, we ate rice three times a day. At my first meal in the camp, I felt eyes boring into my back, and turning around, I saw a Vietnamese prisoner standing just behind me. He had already gulped down his own rice and was staring at my full bowl, his eyes shining with hunger and greed. He said nothing, but his face told me, "Don't eat all that! That's far too much for you!" He did not beg for my food, but I had no choice but to give it to him. The moment I stepped aside, he devoured the rice.

During our four years in the camps, food and the lack of food played a central role in our lives. The word "hunger" conveys nothing of the horror of slowly starving to death. In

43

Camp I, I learned what real hunger was. I saw something that I will never forget.

Our hut contained two partitions separating our compartment from the adjoining compartments. On the other side of one of these partitions lay a Vietnamese so ill that he was unable to work. I never actually saw him, but I could hear him groaning and muttering to himself. Marie-Luise and I were alone in the camp; our three friends had already been transferred. Our food was brought to us in our hut, for Marie-Luise was gravely ill with malaria. As usual, we were served rice. Then one day the guards brought a sweet, gourdlike fruit. After Marie-Luise had eaten a little, I put the rest aside for her to finish later. Suddenly I found that the fruit had disappeared. Another day we were given two bananas. This time I was more cautious and hid them under Marie-Luise's straw hat. They, too, vanished.

One night I saw the man's hand. The Vietnamese in the adjoining compartment had made a hole in the bamboo partition. Sticking his hand through, he began feeling around on the ground. I moved our food to the other side of the compartment. Every time more food arrived, the hand appeared again. We heard his voice begging, "Give me . . . give me . . ."

I was already having trouble getting Marie-Luise to eat. Perhaps the man understood this. Whenever I bent over Marie-Luise, begging her to eat something, the hand reached through the hole and groped around for our bowl of rice. The sight of the hand filled me with horror. Marie-Luise, growing weaker every day, soon lost all interest in food. I myself could hardly eat anything; every bite stuck in my throat. Choking down a mouthful or two, I used to put the rest of my rice into the man's cupped palm. But the more I gave him, the more he seemed to want. The hand was always there, and the voice never stopped pleading.

We were preoccupied with thoughts of food. Bowls of rice helped to break up the monotony of the interminable days. When I was in solitary confinement, the guards who brought

44

my food were the only human beings I ever saw. Three times a day I heard footsteps approaching and waited for the cell door to be opened. We hardly ever talked about anything but food. Humiliating as it was, we cared about nothing else. Only by dreaming of food could we for a few moments break down the prison walls.

In Camp II, the American camp, our hut was partitioned like the hut in Camp I. Bernhard and I often sat for hours back to back on either side of the wobbling wall, making up menus and exchanging recipes. I really entered into the spirit of the thing. "Then we add another egg, to make it good and rich," I would say, actually seeing the golden yolk floating around in the lovely, slightly greenish egg white. I could go on that way for hours until Bernhard exclaimed, "For God's sake, stop it! What kind of idiots are we that we can't talk about anything but food?" We would both keep silent for a while, until Bernhard asked, "What do you do next, after you add the five eggs?"

We all had our specialties. Marie-Luise Kerber always talked about *Wiener Schnitzel,* for her mother was Viennese and a marvelous cook. Georg talked about the snails his father gathered along the banks of the Main River and seasoned with a special herb butter. Rika told us about the cream tarts and tea her mother made. I described my cousin's recipe for squab.

I used to dream about food. The same woman appeared in all my dreams, a war widow friend of my mother's named Frau Gut—"Mrs. Good." The first time I dreamed about her, she was standing in the hut at the foot of my bed, wearing a raincoat, with a kerchief tied around her head, and carrying a brown parcel. I tried to sit up, saying, "Frau Gut, how did you get here?" "Well now," she said, "I wanted to find you, and I did. I've brought you something you need." Then she unwrapped her parcel and took out a large cake. I was not at all surprised to see her. She had always been the sort of woman who could do anything she set her mind to. And how right she was: a cake like that was exactly what we needed!

In another dream, I kept being led away for interrogation.

Each time I was taken to a different room with a different interrogator. But in every room there was a table, and on the table stood a large bowl filled with apricots. People asked me questions and I answered them, but I did not really know what I was saying. I could not take my eyes off that bowl heaped with at least ten pounds of the most beautiful apricots I had ever seen. I kept trying to guess how many there were.

Finally I learned to dream of food while I was wide awake. At mealtimes I would sit there holding my hated bowl of rice cooked in salted water. Bernhard would tell me, "You must eat!" "I can't!" "You must!" I would stare at the rice for a while as if I were casting a spell on it, and then I would begin to murmur, "Well, look at that, the rice is different today! Wherever did they get the sugar and vanilla? They've never given us rice as good as this. Perhaps it's a little too sweet; the cook must have dropped the sugarbowl." While Bernhard stared at me as if I were mad, I would eat a few spoonfuls of the sweetened rice. Then the illusion faded, and I would begin to vomit.

I could not stand to eat the watery boiled rice. There was always rice. Rice with bouillon. Rice with fish sauce. Rice with soybean sauce. More rice.

During our year in the jungle camps, we also ate potatolike roots called manioc, a crop grown in jungle clearings by the Montagnards, or hill tribesmen. Manioc roots have lavender skins and a mealy flesh much whiter than that of potatoes. For weeks on end, I peeled enough for the entire camp. Manioc tasted mealy, like frozen potatoes, and stuck to the roof of one's mouth; we nicknamed it "rubber."

On rare occasions, we were given bananas. In one camp we even had peanuts roasted with salt and pepper. They tasted marvelous. After thirteen months of captivity, we were served a slice of bread. I did no more than look at it, for it was riddled with brown beetles. Then, of course, there were the holidays—Christmas, the Tet festival, and the North Vietnamese Independence Day, celebrated on September 2. Weeks before Independence Day arrived, our guards spread the glad news from cell to cell: "Our holiday is coming; then you'll get something good to eat." On the evening before my first Independence Day, my guard whispered *"tit,"* meaning "meat." The next day I received a beautiful roasted bone. Alas, there was not a scrap of meat left on it.

Two dogs used to run around one of the camps in North Vietnam. One was a yellowish-brown, vicious cur that snarled, barked, and snapped at everyone in sight. The other was a cringing black creature that went around with its tail tucked between its legs. The guards left the vicious dog in peace, but teased, hit, and kicked the timid one whenever they could. They behaved the same way toward people: those who appeared submissive or afraid were cruelly treated. The vicious dog continued to run around the camp; the timid one was fed to the prisoners at Tet.

The last Christmas Eve we spent in captivity, I was allowed to join Bernhard in his cell. Our holiday meal arrived, looking piping hot. We could smell the rabbit and the spices. Grabbing my spoon, I was just about to start eating when I saw the rabbit's eye staring up at me from my plate. Our holiday meals often included unexpected side dishes: a chicken's eye, a beautiful rooster's comb, a set of intestines. Once I collected sugar and candy in a small bag and gave it to Bernhard for Christmas. It was the nicest Christmas we had during our captivity.

Meat bones, rabbit, and candy were holiday fare. The rest of the time we had to be content with manioc, bouillon, and rice. I lost weight and, worst of all, my hair fell out until I was almost bald. When it began to grow back it was no longer dark, but a sort of brown fluff. At our hospital in Da Nang, I had treated children suffering from severe malnutrition. Instead of blue-black, their hair was brown.

In the mountain camp and later in North Vietnam, I stole anything I could lay my hands on. In the mountain camp, I volunteered for kitchen duty. There was not much to steal—

a few peanuts, a couple of fish, a gourd full of water. Sometimes I even stole a little of the rice I hated so much. Bernhard and I secretly roasted it at night on a tin plate, for it was winter and we were allowed to have a fire.

When I swept the courtyard, I always checked the chicken coop to see if the hens had laid any eggs; but the guards always removed them at dawn before I came out. One day I noticed a hen disobeying camp regulations. She was laying her eggs in the husks left after the rice had been threshed. For days I watched the hen, trying to think of some way to get her eggs. I could not manage it during the day, for the commandant's hut stood only a few yards from the nest. I would have to try to steal them at night. Every night there had been a full moon, and I could not decide whether a light jacket or a dark one offered better camouflage. Finally I put on the darker jacket and began to crawl across the courtyard on my stomach. When I passed the chicken coop, all the chickens woke up, grew alarmed at seeing a stranger, and began to cackle and flutter around the coop. I continued to inch forward. Suddenly a door opened, light flooded the yard, and a Vietnamese walked out. But he was simply going to the latrine and soon went back inside. Reaching the nest at last, I thought, "Oh my God, what if she hasn't laid any eggs!" Keeping my eyes closed, I stretched out my hand . . . and touched six eggs! Then I thought, "Perhaps they put the eggs in there to hatch. Or maybe they're trying to trap me." I did not dare to take more than two, one for Bernhard and one for me. We cooked them in our hut and ate them, shell and all. . . .

In North Vietnam, the guards often tried to hand our food through the barred windows so that they would not have to unlock the cell door. But in four years of captivity, I never accepted food offered me through bars. It could have been ambrosia; I would still have turned my back on the guards, thinking, "No, you will never make me eat food you poke through the bars as if you were feeding an animal in a cage!"

Perhaps this sense of pride grew out of what I had witnessed in Camp I. For four years I was half mad with hunger and thirst; many times I would gladly have gone down on my knees and begged for water. Yet I never begged. Whenever my thirst seemed unbearable, all I had to do was remember the prisoner who had stretched his hand through the bamboo partition, imploring, "Give me, give me!" I resolved never to become like him. . . .

The Y Si

MONIKA SCHWINN

A guard wearing an olive-green uniform hung the oil lamp on the wall of the bamboo hut. This was the same lamp the guards had carried when they led us to our hut on our first night in Camp I. The pale, flickering flame gave little light. But the guerrillas clearly treasured the lamp; they always took it away as soon as it was no longer needed. The guard who had brought it to our hut never took his eyes off it.

The small struggling flame was more frightening than reassuring. The light danced along the walls, revealing the dark, soot-blackened bamboo and the grimy floor. It turned our faces brown. Even Marie-Luise now looked like a Vietnamese.

She was lying on the cot suffering from a high fever, chills, and the other symptoms of malaria. The *y si* knelt before her, fumbling in his little suitcase. It was the same man who had miraculously appeared with bandages for my feet, introducing himself as an *y si,* a medic first class. He was wearing the same fluttering, three-quarter-length olive-green coat made of parachute silk. Later I was told that all the *y si*'s wore these green coats when traveling in the jungle, as camouflage to protect them from the American planes. In Vietnamese, *y si* means something like "half a doctor." The *y si*'s were paramedics bearing little resemblance to European paraprofessionals. After two years'

50

training, they received a government diploma. "Our" *y si* later showed me his. One *y si* was assigned to each district. Every village had an *y ta,* a medic with three months' training. A fully trained physician was a *bac si.*

Kneeling beside Marie-Luise's bed, the *y si* seemed at a loss to know what to do. He had opened his case, but the flickering light appeared to disturb him as much as it did me. Inside the case, everything lay in a heap; the tablets and bottles had no labels. The man seemed to be picking up bottles at random. I could not tell what he finally selected to give the sick girl. But at least he was there, at least they had bothered to call him. Even without the lamp, anyone who looked at her could tell that Marie-Luise was gravely ill. . . .

On the morning of our fourth day in Camp I, we were all supposed to leave for another camp, where we had been told conditions were much better. We had put on our hospital uniforms again. The black pajamas we had been wearing belonged to the camp. The night before, we had been told to wash them in the river and give them back to the guards.

As soon as the morning whistle blew, we ate our breakfast of rice, packed our belongings in the rucksack, and stood up, all ready to go. For some time Bernhard, Georg, and Marie-Luise had been running high fevers. Suddenly Marie-Luise, who was standing beside me, said, "I can't stand up any more." I caught her as she started to fall. Her face was very pale. Clearly, she could not walk all the way to the next camp.

We spent the next half hour arguing with the guerrillas. They insisted that the rest of us leave Marie-Luise behind. Finally the commandant gave permission for one of us to stay with her. I was the one who stayed. Holding her up, I led Marie-Luise into the hut, trying to keep her from tripping over the roots in our path. Just before going in, I turned around and saw the others still standing in front of the bamboo gate. The soldiers were binding their hands and arms. I felt uneasy: now that we had separated, we might never see one another again. Would they decide to keep us apart? Would they make sure that none of us ever found out what happened to the others? I was afraid that they might.

It was dark inside the hut. The *y si* had left; the guard had removed the lamp. I did not know what drug the *y si* had given Marie-Luise, when he planned to return, or even *if* he planned to return.

Marie-Luise was sleeping. She was exhausted, and her face was very pale. Seeing her closed eyes, I covered her up. She had placed her shoes at the foot of her bed. They were made of red linen, much nicer than the shoes the rest of us wore. She was still wearing her gray uniform. Her belongings, including her green pocketbook, were in the rucksack the others had taken when they left. No one had remembered to remove them. Apart from her shoes, the only things Marie-Luise had left were her glasses and a Vietnamese straw hat.

For the next few days, her fever continued to rise. Her breathing was labored. Just in front of the kitchen stood a hollow tree trunk filled with water. I used to fetch water and make cold compresses to help bring down her fever. Two or three times a day and at least once during the night, I had to change her sweat-drenched clothing. Fortunately, we had been given back our black pajamas.

Marie-Luise hardly ate anything, but she was terribly thirsty. I spent all my time making compresses and changing and washing her clothes. Accompanied by a guard, I was allowed to go to a nearby river to wash. Here I was in plain view of helicopters and scouting planes and had to be ready to run at a moment's notice. When I had finished washing them, I hung the wet clothes from the trees beside our hut. They did not dry very quickly here, but it was too dangerous to hang them in the sun: the bright patches of clothing might have attracted the attention of American flyers. No one needed to tell me to be careful; fear of the planes had already become second nature.

As time went on, Marie-Luise ate less and less. She kept asking for water. Each morning we were given one bottle of boiled water. Even if we had drunk it all by 10:00 A.M., this was all we were allowed to have. Camp regulations allotted one bottle of water a day to each prisoner; and no one dared to challenge camp regulations.

Even in the daytime, it was very dim inside the hut. The walls were of woven bamboo, and the roofs were very low; thus inside it always looked like twilight. When Marie-Luise was awake, she would ask me to tell her stories. She always wanted to hear funny stories. She was only nineteen, the youngest of our group.

"I used to be a Girl Scout, and we took a lot of trips, even to Italy and Greece."

"Was Greece lots of fun?"

"Not really."

"Haven't you ever had any amusing experiences?"

"Once we had a teacher we didn't like at all. She sent us to her house to get something for her; she gave us the keys and everything. On her desk we saw our notebooks, the ones we had used for our last German compositions. We wrote an 'A' on every composition, using her own red ink!"

She smiled at that, but I did not know many such stories. Then I began to make up my own. It was not easy, but I managed to think up a few tall tales, like one about a man who pulled himself out of a swamp by climbing up his own pigtail. I was trying to pull someone out of a swamp myself, for I saw that Marie-Luise was hanging on every word. She seemed to need to hear cheerful stories in which everyone lived happily ever after. Only once, at the end of one of my tall tales, she said, "You know, people should never talk about happiness out loud." I did not really understand what she meant.

Soon all the days began to seem alike, except for one thing: Marie-Luise was getting weaker. The *y si* paid us a couple of visits. He was always in a great hurry and fumbled aimlessly in his little case. The medicine he gave Marie-Luise did not help. She drifted into a semicoma.

Changing clothes, washing clothes, making up stories. When I was not tending Marie-Luise, I went to sit down outside the hut. My legs were covered with leech and mosquito bites and with running sores from the cuts and scratches I had received. The sores had become infected and were oozing pus. Above all, my toes were badly infected.

One day Marie-Luise's fever rose so high that she became delirious. She kept seeing all sorts of people I did not know. Once I stepped outside the hut for a moment. When I came back, she looked at me with large, feverish eyes and said, "Everything's going to be all right now, the doctor was just here." I looked around. "There wasn't any doctor here." She would not listen. "You must have missed him. He gave me a thorough examination. He promised that I'll be taken to a hospital."

That night, for the first time, I had to carry her to the latrine on my back; she could no longer stand up. Crouching down, I pulled her onto my back. Marie-Luise had been ill for almost two weeks. I had been getting very little sleep, and I, too, was growing weaker. Leaning on a stick for support, I stumbled down the rickety stairs in front of our hut and climbed over a trench. To keep from falling, I had to go very slowly and lean against all the trees we passed. Neither the guards nor the other prisoners paid any attention to me and my burden. Many prisoners were asleep, exhausted by their work in the fields; others were staring into space. Only a few observed without interest the spectacle of one woman trying to carry another across the prison yard without falling down.

The latrine was a hole in the ground covered with a few boards. A space had been left between the boards for the convenience of the prisoners. There were no walls around the latrine, so anyone who wanted to could watch. Afterward I dragged Marie-Luise back to our hut.

At night she continued to hallucinate and talked with people I had never met. Sometimes she herself appeared not to recognize them. Apparently they did not want to enter the hut, for she repeatedly ordered them, "Come on now, come a bit closer!" She called desperately to her father and mother, begging them to help her. Often I could not make out what she was saying, but sometimes she seemed to be reliving our trek through the jungle. She would exclaim, "I can't get up this mountain. You must understand. Can't you see that I'm tired? Do whatever you like, I can't go any farther; I can't get up this mountain." Then she would start crying and fall asleep with the tears still running down her face.

Later in the night she would wake up screaming and sit up abruptly. Then the whole thing would begin all over again. Her attacks continued to grow more violent. One night she began pounding and shaking the walls of the hut, dislodging vermin from the ceiling. It was pitch-dark, but we could feel the insects crawling around in our hair and on our skin. They felt damp and cold and crept into our clothing, seeking warmth. Marie-Luise screamed and banged on the walls until she had used up the little strength she had. Everyone else in the hut seemed to be sleeping. I felt like the only person left alive in the world.

Sometimes Marie-Luise and I used to pray together. Trying to keep up her hopes, I reassured her: "It will take time for anyone in authority to find out that we've been taken prisoner. You have to be patient; in this country everything takes a long time. It will take time for the messengers to get word to their command centers in the jungle. And it will take them just as long to get back here with orders to set us free. Surely by now someone has found out that we only came to this country to help. You know how many people from this area were treated in An Hoa. They'll be questioned, and they'll be witnesses in our defense. But all that will take time."

I described the day when they would set us free. "They'll take us out to a meadow, a big green meadow. They'll send out a radio call—that'll take only a few seconds—and then, before you know it, the helicopter will arrive. It will land right next to us. All you have to do is get through the next few days."

She always felt better when I said that. For the first time, she began to tell me about herself. It was not a long story. She came from a smaller town on the Saar River than I did: they did not even have a Girl Scout troop. When she went to Munich to work as a dental assistant, it seemed like a trip around the world. She had been engaged, but her fiancé, deciding that he loved another girl, had broken the engagement. It was as simple as that. Her fiancé no longer loved her, so Marie-Luise signed up to come to Vietnam, hoping that this gesture would win him back. When he heard the news, he calmly remarked, "The chances are about a hundred to one that you'll never come back alive."

When Marie-Luise had finished telling me her story, I said, "It didn't have a happy ending." She answered, "You'll have to make up one with a happy ending."

As the days passed, I saw that Marie-Luise was feeling more hopeful. But at night, in delirium, she used up the strength she had stored up during the day, screaming and banging on the walls until they shook. But the attacks were brief; it no longer took her very long to wear herself out.

We slept side by side on the same bamboo cot. When she began to twist and turn, I would place my hand on her forehead. Then she would fall asleep for ten minutes or so before growing restless again. Sometimes she would kick me in her sleep like a feverish child. Regaining consciousness, she remembered nothing and assumed that she had been sleeping soundly.

Even when she was delirious, she managed to tell me when she wished to be carried to the latrine. Before picking her up, I would grope my way through the darkness to one of the guards and yell in German, "We're going to the latrine!" The guards did not understand the words, but they understood that we were not trying to escape.

One night there was a torrential downpour. The water came through the thatched roof and soaked the blankets. The floor was flooded. I propped up Marie-Luise's back against one of the corner beams and tucked in her legs. She was sitting on the one dry spot in the hut. Kneeling down, I held her so that she would not fall over and get wet. The water dripped on my head and trickled down my neck and back. We sat in the same position for hours, until it finally stopped raining.

The *y si* came twice a day, morning and evening, to take Marie-Luise's temperature. On good days her temperature registered 102° F. Most of the time it was over 104°. The *y si* continued to give her drugs from his little case.

Marie-Luise's Death

MONIKA SCHWINN

The longer we spent in the prison camps, the harder it became to keep track of time. We developed ingenious methods of counting the days and months. In Camp I, I still knew exactly what day it was. Sundays were no different from other days; yet I know that it was Sunday morning when Marie-Luise woke up, apparently feeling much better. She had slept peacefully all through Saturday night. Mentally I apologized to the *y si* for having doubted his medical skills.

That morning, Marie-Luise wanted to get up and go outside. She said that she could walk by herself and asked me to take her arm and walk with her past all the guards and prisoners to the latrine.

I was amazed that she had the strength to stand up. With the aid of a bamboo cane, she walked out to the latrine. I walked along beside her, supporting her under the shoulder. Then we walked back to the hut, where she lay down on the bamboo cot.

Later she wanted to go outside again, to wash up at the large earthenware jar of water that stood near the hut. For the first time she missed her green pocketbook and began to worry about how she looked without lipstick and eye shadow. I thought it a good sign that she felt well enough to think about make-up. While I held her up, she washed her face and sprinkled water on her neck. That morning she even ate some rice. As usual, the

58

prisoner's hand crept through the partition, and we heard his voice begging, "Give me, give me!"

That day, I paid no attention to the hand. I could not take my eyes off Marie-Luise, who seemed to be getting better by the minute. She had been cooped up for so long that she wanted to go outside and sit in the sunshine.

As she walked unsteadily out the door, I went on lying on the bed. I was worn out from my many sleepless nights. Now that I thought that Marie-Luise could get along without me, I simply collapsed. I could have slept for weeks. I had a terrible headache, and half an hour later I developed chills. Now I had malaria, too.

Marie-Luise sat in front of the hut, resting her head against one of the beams supporting the roof. It was boiling hot inside the hut; but even covered with blankets, I was freezing. Suddenly a tall Vietnamese entered. It was the prisoner who cooked our food in the dugout kitchen. He stood there looking at me, clicking his tongue the way you do to make a horse go faster. He did not move, but I could tell from his face that he felt sorry for me, lying there shivering under my blankets.

Feeling grateful for his sympathy, I thought, "He's a friend, a fellow prisoner; he'll give you water if you ask for it." But as soon as he understood my request, his expression changed. He shook his head firmly, indicating that we had already drunk our ration of water and that camp regulations allowed each prisoner only one bottle of water a day.

When the cook had left, Marie-Luise came in. She told me that she felt strong enough to go to the kitchen by herself. "You'll see, I can manage it; I'll make him give me some water for you!"

"How are you going to do that?" I thought. "How can you deal with people who are sympathetic one minute and won't even give you a swallow of water the next?" She did not return for a long time. When she came back, she told me that the cook had made a fire and was boiling water for me. Later he brought it to the hut.

The *y si* did not come to the camp that day. Marie-Luise's

condition had restored my faith in his little suitcase, and I hoped that he would give me something for my malaria. Perhaps he could even do something for my feet. They were giving me considerable pain, and I could no longer bend my ankles. The toes, which were badly infected, needed to be lanced and drained.

Sunday night, Marie-Luise slept quite peacefully. I had to get up twice to help her outside. By Monday morning, she had grown worse and was too weak to stand up.

Monday evening, the y si arrived. Marie-Luise's temperature was over 104°. For the first time, he gave her an injection. Then she began to rave, screaming, "Help me, please help me!"

All that night, she suffered intermittent attacks of delirium. She would scream for half an hour before sinking back exhausted. After ten minutes' sleep, she would wake up sounding quite lucid. "I don't understand," she said once.

"What don't you understand?"

"That Mrs. Binh; you know her!"

I did not recognize the name. "Whom do you mean?"

"Mrs. Binh in Paris. The woman who represents the NLF at the Paris peace talks.* As a woman, she is sensitive; she must understand what life is like in these camps. She knows all about conditions here. Why doesn't she help us? The men won't help us, but Mrs. Binh is a woman."

Then she began to talk with Mrs. Binh, asking over and over, "Why don't you help us? You are the only woman who can help us. You know what the jungle is like. Have you forgotten everything now that you are in Paris?"

I knew that there had been some dispute over who would be represented at the Paris negotiations. But I did not know that the chief representative of the NLF was a woman. Marie-

---

* On November 4, 1968, Mrs. Nguyen Thi Binh arrived in Paris with her staff to represent the National Liberation Front, the political arm of the Viet Cong, at the expanded Paris peace talks. On June 10, 1969, the NLF announced the formation of the Provisional Revolutionary Government of the Republic of South Vietnam. As Foreign Minister of the PRG, Mrs. Binh was one of the architects of the Paris accords. —TRANS.

Luise seemed to see Mrs. Binh standing before her like a guardian angel and begged her to help us.

All night she clung to the hope that Mrs. Binh was going to save us. In the morning, returning to reality, she said, "If I don't stop seeing things that aren't there, I'd rather be dead." On this, the last day of her life, she was filled with despair. Over and over she said, "I can't go on this way. I would really rather die."

I listened without saying a word. There would not have been any point in interrupting her. Once or twice when she was fully conscious, I tried to reassure her, saying, "You're weak now, Marie-Luise. Just try to get through another day; then everything will look different. I understand how you feel, but you know that people feel wretched when they have a high fever. Just look at all the other prisoners in this hut; they've been as sick and unhappy as you, and they're still alive."

Even as I spoke, I doubted that any of us would live to see home again. I had given up hope. During the night, when Marie-Luise was asleep, I used to get up and go outside the hut so that she would not hear me crying. But I did not want her to lose hope, for people without hope never live very long. I had to think of some way to help her.

Tat, the Vietnamese prisoner who spoke broken English and acted as the official camp interpreter, had told me about the camp where our three friends had gone. In sign language he explained that the other camp had its own resident physician —not an *y ta* or an *y si,* but a real *bac si.* Carried away by his enthusiasm, he described the camp as a paradise where prisoners spent their time drinking beer and whiskey and watching movies! I had already told Marie-Luise what he had said. Now I talked again about the other camp, hoping that she might try to survive long enough to go there. Her eyes lit up as I spoke. "But how will we get there? You don't think I can walk the whole way?"

At noon I cornered Tat. He was supposed to be an interpreter, so let him interpret! With Tat in tow, I went to the commandant and begged him to take Marie-Luise and me to the other camp. Tat did not understand my German and I could barely understand his English; thus it was hard to get my message across. Using signs and gestures, I tried to explain that we needed a simple stretcher and two men to carry Marie-Luise to the other camp. I had been told that it was two days' journey away. I knew that I could not carry Marie-Luise such a long distance on my back. If the guerrillas had allowed it, I would have tried to carry her myself, but I would have collapsed after the first few steps.

I saw that the commandant understood and sympathized with my request. Looking kind, he promised "Swin-Swin" that we would leave for the other camp on the following morning. I was told to begin preparations at once. Above all, I was to wash the black pajamas we had worn, for careful records were kept of camp property, and everything had to be accounted for. I understood that we were to make the trip in our hospital uniforms.

Returning to the hut, I told Marie-Luise the good news. She felt greatly encouraged and said, "Then everything is going to be all right. We'll be saved." Now that she felt better, she began to eat again.

I, too, felt more hopeful. Lying beside Marie-Luise on our last night in the camp, I watched her go peacefully to sleep. Shortly before midnight, she suffered an attack of delirium more violent than any I had yet seen. Calling for help, she screamed so loudly that the neighboring prisoners began to grumble and shout at us. I could hear the guards yelling something outside; but I paid no attention. My only concern was to get Marie-Luise through the night, so that tomorrow at daybreak we could leave this terrible place and join our friends.

Still screaming, Marie-Luise shook the beams supporting the ceiling as if she were trying to bring the whole hut down on our heads. Someone entered the hut holding the oil lamp. He knew a little English and began to shout at Marie-Luise: "Stop . . . shut up! Prisoners must work all day . . . must sleep . . . stop . . . shut up!"

Marie-Luise sat up, staring wide-eyed at the Vietnamese. "But Doctor," she said, "listen to me! The people here are all criminals. They won't help me. Why aren't you helping me?"

The Vietnamese only bellowed, "Stop . . . shut up! Prisoners must sleep!"

I did not know what to do. I tried to pray, but could not. "Our Father": the words were there, but they were meaningless. I knew that Marie-Luise was going to die, and I knew that there was nothing more I could do. She was so young; she had her whole life before her. I felt helpless and sick with misery. Then I had a strange idea.

I had lost everything I owned. I did not even have a pair of glasses or a straw hat like Marie-Luise. I had nothing but my body and the clothes on my back. Or was there something else? Yes, there was my swollen, infected toe, bright red and threatening to burst any minute now. With every beat of my heart, I could feel the pain growing worse.

When we are desperate, we clutch at straws. That night, the only thing that was really mine was the pain in my toe. I had planned to lance the toe before we left. I had no bandages; but I remembered that I had applied leaves to the boils I had lanced on my legs. I planned to incise the toe with a splinter of bamboo, clean the wound, and wrap a green leaf around it. But when I saw that Marie-Luise was getting worse and that there was nothing I could do for her, I tried to use my throbbing toe to strike a bargain with God.

I made him a proposition: "Let her live. Let us get to the next camp, and let her get well again. If you do this, I will leave my toe just as it is, infected, swollen, full of pain. I will suffer as long as you wish. I will endure whatever pains you decree. In return, let her live!"

I had nothing to pawn in exchange for Marie-Luise's life but the sore feet I would have used to walk with her to the other camp. I prayed that God would accept the miserable sacrifice. . . .

Marie-Luise continued to rave until someone sent for the *y si*. Suddenly he appeared in the doorway, then hurried away, and a moment later reappeared with a hypodermic syringe.

After giving Marie-Luise an injection, he made her swallow some pills with a little tea. As usual, he seemed to be in a great hurry and kept darting in and out of the hut.

Marie-Luise quieted down and closed her eyes. The neighboring prisoners seemed to have dropped off to sleep. I sat on Marie-Luise's cot, holding her hands. Her breathing was slow and regular, but very shallow. Her hands gripped mine tightly. Then a shudder passed over her body; her hands loosened their grip. Suddenly she said in a calm, deep voice, "I'm dying." She moaned a little, but her voice sounded relieved. Then she seemed to see something that she could not believe she was seeing and tried to sit up to see it more clearly. Looking surprised but happy, she greeted the visitor who had just entered the hut: "Papa!" The word sounded gentle, as if she were asking him to come closer.

It was then that she died.

Carefully drawing back the covers, I opened her dress and began to massage her heart. Then I laid my ear to her chest. There was no heartbeat. Speaking softly so that I would not wake up the other prisoners, I called to Tat, who slept on the other side of the bamboo partition. I went on calling for half an hour before the other prisoners finally shook him awake.

Tat got up and went to the guards at the gate. It seemed an eternity before the soldiers arrived, carrying bamboo torches. Walking more slowly than usual, they stopped in front of the hut. The *y si* pushed his way through the soldiers and dashed into the hut. Bending down, he touched Marie-Luise's bare feet, which were sticking out from under the blankets. Then he turned to the others and nodded, indicating that she was dead.

For a time the men stood around in front of the hut. It was getting light. It must have been almost five o'clock, for the prisoners behind the partitions were beginning to get up. I did not hear the morning whistle blow.

I was alone with Marie-Luise. She was wearing the nurse's uniform I had dressed her in last night in preparation for our journey. Folding her hands on her chest, I covered her body with the blankets. Then I took the black pajamas and the piece of soap I had been given the evening before and went to the river to wash the pajamas. No one made any move to stop me.

Standing beside the river, I wondered whether I should bother to wash the clothes. "If you run away right now, a scout plane will see you and shoot you down. Marie-Luise is dead. You're going to die, too. They're going to move you deeper into the jungle, and in the end they'll kill you anyhow. They'll make you walk across a meadow and shoot you in the back. Or they'll throw you over a cliff. No one will ever know what happened to you. Why don't you just run away now and be shot from a plane? If you die here, at least everyone will know that you are dead."

Hearing the sound of airplane motors, I began to run toward them. But the soldiers had seen me, and they could run much faster than I could. Catching up with me, they took me back to the camp. Tat and the commandant both began shouting at me. I was a prisoner; what was I thinking of? They themselves would decide if I was to die. They told me that I was going to be taken to the other camp. If I continued to resist, they would tie my hands and feet.

No longer caring what they did with me, I let them lead me back to the hut, where I sat down beside Marie-Luise's body and wept. This time I was asking *her* for help.

The soldiers brought me a small bowl of rice to give me strength for the journey. I never understood the psychological make-up of the Vietnamese. They expected me to eat while I was sitting beside my dead friend! When I did not touch the rice, three or four guards began to shout that I was a prisoner and had to eat. Marie-Luise's death seemed to have upset them all.

Standing up, I followed the guards outside. On the ground I glimpsed a small object shining in the sunlight. It was a nail. Picking it up, I lanced my toe. The throbbing pain I had offered in exchange for my friend's life ebbed away. Clearly I had not offered enough.

Meditations in a Hammock

MONIKA SCHWINN

They had tied my hands behind my back. As soon as we were out of sight of the camp, the guards loosened the knots so that my arms hung down at my sides; only my elbows were still tied together. This way my arms were free to push branches out of the way, clearing a path for my "generous" guards.

Contrary to custom, the guards forced me to precede them along the path. Soon I realized why. It had rained the night before, and the bushes and trees were dripping wet. As I walked through the jungle, branches struck me in the face and bushes brushed against my legs. All the excess water was shaken off onto me as I plowed a path through the underbrush. In a short time I was soaked to the skin. My nurse's uniform clung to my body, my hair hung in damp strands around my face. Behind me, the guards thought that all this was highly amusing and began to laugh. After all, I was only a woman. A woman was nothing; a woman was even less than a prisoner.

During my four weeks of captivity, I had already learned that in Vietnam women held the lowest position of all in the social order. Mrs. Binh, who was representing the NLF at the Paris peace talks, was an exception to the rule. On our eleven-day march to Camp I, the guards had always seemed surprised when Bernhard and Georg talked with Rika, Marie-Luise, and me or took our hands. They appeared to be thinking, "What

66

can a man talk about with a woman? He can make her work, tell her what to do, and beget her children; but what do they really have in common?"

The Vietnamese attitude toward women profoundly affected my life for the next four years. A woman, and a prisoner to boot, possessed no rights whatever. Female prisoners were assigned the worst clothing and lodging, and their needs were always ignored. In one camp in North Vietnam, I was given prison clothing that would have fit an American man about seven feet tall. When the Americans bombed the region around Hanoi, all the male prisoners were removed from their cells and taken to the dugouts. The guards never bothered to take me along, for, after all, I was only a woman; it would make no difference if I was killed. Once, during a typhoon, the water level began to rise in the cells. All the male prisoners were evacuated, but I was left behind. If the water had not subsided, I believe that I would simply have been allowed to drown.

In the prison camps, a woman had only two advantages. Women were considered nonentities; therefore, female prisoners were assigned the most thick-witted interrogators, who could easily be gulled into believing anything. As a woman, I was so insignificant that the Vietnamese did not even bother to search me thoroughly when I was released. Thus I was able to smuggle out the notes I had made during my captivity, whereas all of Bernhard's notes were confiscated. The second advantage lay in the fact that the Vietnamese would never lay hands on a woman prisoner. They used to shout at me or throw a broom at my feet when they wanted me to sweep the courtyard, and once one of them held a pistol to my head when I failed to carry out an order. But in four years, no one physically molested me. To have touched a female prisoner, a creature without rights or honor, would have been an unpardonable crime. . . .

I continued to clear a pathway through the jungle for my guards. For a short time I walked very fast. Some inexplicable force was driving me away from the camp. But I could not keep up this frenzied pace. As the hours wore on, I moved slower and slower. I saw that I could not outrun the thought I had been

67

trying to avoid: Marie-Luise was dead. Would the others still be alive? Was there any reason for me to hurry onward? Perhaps what lay ahead of me would be worse than what I had left behind.

Marie-Luise's linen shoes gave me the strength to go on. I wore the shoes on my journey, and strange as it may seem, they made me hope again. It was sheer luck that I still had them. When the soldiers brought me back from the river after Marie-Luise's death, I arrived just in time to see the interpreter Tat making off with the red shoes. I had laid out Marie-Luise's things the night before—the shoes, the glasses, and the straw hat. Now Tat was wearing her shoes. Suddenly they seemed like a talisman: the shoes were my salvation, and unless I got them back, I would never reach the other camp alive. Furious, I demanded that Tat give them to me.

At first he did not want to take them off. The shoes were already on his feet; *ergo,* they now belonged to him. It occurred to me that I should try to be pleasant to him, for someone would have to bury Marie-Luise. Finally, Tat agreed to give me the shoes in exchange for the four bananas the guards had given me to eat on the trip and the soap I had used to wash the pajamas. There was no time left to bargain. The soldiers had arrived to tie my arms behind my back.

I never learned who buried Marie-Luise. No one knows where her grave is; no one will ever know. They probably dug it in the jungle, or near the river where the ground was softer and there were fewer roots. I would never be able to find the camp again. It probably vanished long ago, swallowed up by jungle growth.

The *y si* left the camp with me and the two guards. At our first rest stop, he came to say good-by. Squatting down before me, he fumbled around in his case. For the last time I glimpsed its hopeless disarray. Then he pulled out a diploma. I could not read the words, but I recognized the official seals. Holding out the paper, he looked at me as if to say, "I did everything I could." He seemed to be waiting for me to absolve him. But I did not absolve him. I thought, "You did not exactly murder her, all of you, but you did not help her to live; and I will never forgive you for that, not ever."

Standing up, he looked back at me once more. Then, seeing that it was hopeless to expect anything more of me, he ran off into the jungle in his fluttering green coat. I never saw him again.

After a brief rest, we continued our journey. The sun had dried out the jungle. We were no longer alone. I saw men carrying heavy burdens on their shoulders. Groups of women walked up and stared at me in amazement. Seeing that I was tied, they touched my arms and face. They seemed both frightened and fascinated. No doubt it was the first time that they had met a white woman in the jungle—a woman, moreover, who was being treated as a slave.

Leaving the well-beaten paths, we moved into wilder country. Once again we were alone. The terrain resembled that of our previous journey. We climbed through dry river beds and over slippery, moss-covered stones; we struggled up and down steep inclines. The guards did not urge me to hurry. They seemed quite friendly. Once, when we crossed a torrential mountain spring, one guard held my hand so that I would not be swept away by the current. Their behavior made me uneasy. Perhaps they had a reason for being so kind. Did they secretly intend that I never complete my journey?

We traveled all day. At twilight, my guards looked at the sky. It looked as if we were in for another downpour. Finally we caught sight of some huts.

The guards began to bargain with an old man who was standing in front of his hut. The man kept shaking his head. Walking over to me with a look of hatred, he spat on the ground at my feet. I believe that he would have killed me rather than have me sleep inside his hut. What must he have suffered to have learned to hate white people so?

Spitting once more, the old man suddenly grabbed a rifle from one of the guards. *"Di, di, di!"* he said, and shoved the gun into my back, showing the guards how to make me move forward.

The old man would not allow us to spend the night in his hut; nor would any of the others. We had no choice but to keep walking. But now, at least, I no longer suspected that my guards planned to murder me.

As night fell, both the guards and I felt uneasy and stayed close together. All three of us experienced the primitive fear of darkness that afflicts anyone who has found no shelter for the night. I was glad of their company, and they of mine. It was as if all our other fears had been forgotten in the deeper fear of being alone.

We heard the rumbling of distant thunder. The guards appeared to have concluded that we were not going to find an available hut. At last we paused at the fork of a stream. One guard gathered brushwood and built a fire. The other suspended a canopy between four trees and strung up three hammocks beneath it. I was given rice and some water from the bottle. The two guards talked in loud voices, as if they were afraid of the silence all around us. When it began to rain, we lay down in the hammocks. I was exhausted.

The storm was circling overhead; the rain beat down on the canopy. Our three hammocks had been strung very close together, but the canopy was too small to cover us all. I had been assigned the least sheltered hammock; half of my body was exposed to the rain. Moreover, the water collected in the canopy above, and periodically it spilled over the edge, directly onto me. In effect I had been given a spot right under the drainspout. It was cold out, and I was freezing. But something besides the cold was keeping me awake.

I kept staring at the shoes on my feet; my hands clutched Marie-Luise's straw hat. "You let her die," I thought. Remembering the old man who had spat at my feet, I longed to be able to hate as purely as he did. But I did not feel hatred. I simply felt empty, like one of those innumerable snail shells we had passed on today's march.

Dead tired, I was shivering with cold. I no longer heard the rain, for someone or something had stopped up my ears. I drifted away. Then I found myself running. I ran until I came

70

to a hut where a truck was standing. Men were unloading crates from the truck. My heart skipped with joy. They were just like the crates sent to us in Da Nang, stamped with the German flag of black, red, and gold, and labeled "DRUGS—AID TO VIET-NAM." The men carried crate after crate into the hut.

At last, Marie-Luise was saved! I entered the hut. The crates were piled up to the ceiling. There was hardly room for them all. A nurse was standing there. "Hurry, hurry," I said. As she turned around, I saw that she was Vietnamese. The nurse shook her head. She spoke in Vietnamese, but I found that I could understand what she was saying: "You've come too early. I have to get everything ready first. The crates have to be unpacked, and then I have to get everything in order. Come back tomorrow."

I returned the next day and the next, but each day she told me, "I'm sorry, but I'm not finished yet. Regulations say that everything must be shipshape before we give out any drugs."

I grew angry, protested, shouted. . . .

"Why are you shouting like that?" someone asked me.

I stared in amazement at the two men who had suddenly arrived at our clearing beside the fork of the river. Both men were dressed very formally in dark suits and ties; both carried black briefcases. One man—the one who had asked me why I was shouting—had a narrow face and wavy blond hair. I thought, "Imagine that! Here he is in the middle of the jungle wearing a formal suit and a fine pair of dress shoes!"

"Calm down now," he said. "And first of all, how do you do! I am so pleased to have found you at last." He spoke in a rather formal, official tone. Then he added, "I wanted to see how you were and whether you were being well treated. Who let the campfire go out?"

"Please just arrange to let me have the drugs," I said. "It's unforgivable that they're taking so long to unpack it. I think they're doing it on purpose!"

"Oh, come now," he said in a soothing voice. "Please, let's not make any wild accusations. We don't want to make a lot of fuss, now do we? Well, that's just fine, I see that there is something that I can do for you after all." He set down his black briefcase. "Now get down out of that hammock. I'm sure you still have strength enough to walk to the car." He laughed. "That surprises you, does it? Of course, it's only a VW, just a Beetle, but I think I can get all five of you inside. If necessary, one of you will have to ride in the trunk. . . ."

"But what if they shoot us?"

"There you go again, making wild accusations! You just go along now." He pointed back the way he had come. "I couldn't drive up all the way, not even with the Beetle; but if you go a step or two, you'll see it just around the bend. Go ahead now, I have a bit of red tape to get through here. After all, we want you to be formally released. Just around the bend . . ."

I ran and ran. Where was the road? Where was the bend? I did not believe what the formal blond gentleman had said about getting me released; but perhaps he merely planned to distract the guards while I escaped. I kept running, but I saw no road and no VW. It was raining. I was running deeper into the jungle, and the rain poured down on me. . . .

The water in the canopy had just splashed down on me again. Startled, I sat up in my hammock. I was not only soaked with water, I was also bathed in sweat.

Beside me I heard the slow and regular breathing of the guards. Glancing at the thin figures, I saw that they were sound asleep, still clutching their black rifles. The fire was smoldering nearby. I heard distant thunder. The storm had passed.

I was suffering from chills and fever. But exhausted as I was, I was afraid to sleep, for I feared my own dreams. I could not bear to be tormented with false hopes. Refusing to close my eyes, I thought about the last few days and about tomorrow.

They had told me that the other camp was only two days' march away. What had happened to my friends? At this moment, were they lying sick in some hut, thinking about me?

I was afraid for us all.

Camp Regulations

BERNHARD DIEHL

His name was John Young. We called him Little John, for he was a scrawny little blond fellow twenty-two years old. During his two years of captivity, he had certainly not grown any bigger. Private First Class John Young had served as a guerrilla fighter in a Special Forces unit. The SF recruited South Vietnamese partisans and trained them as guerrillas to combat the Viet Cong. In retaliation, the Viet Cong repeatedly launched savage attacks on Special Forces training camps. Little John had been captured on one of these raids.

Two years earlier he had lost his uniform and his green beret, and his guerrilla training was no use to him now. But Little John was the most contented prisoner in the camp, for he had something to occupy his time; he had mastered a skill that was in great demand. The tools of his trade were the rearview mirror of a jeep, a comb, and a pair of scissors.

This morning, Little John was sitting in front of my hut, cutting my hair and beard. We were seated on a bench beside a sawed-off tree trunk that served as a table. Draping a piece of gray canvas around my shoulders, the American handed me the rearview mirror so that I could admire his handiwork. He took his time, snipping off a little bit here and there, and finally laid his hand on my shoulder. "Now just take a look at yourself, and don't tell me anybody ever gave you a nicer haircut." He had, in

73

fact, done a fine job, except that he hadn't cut my hair quite as short as I wanted it. Little John always saved a little hair for the next time, for his greatest fear was that he might run out of hair and beards to trim. Picking up his precious mirror and comb and his even more precious scissors, he departed looking quite pleased with his work.

John Young was one of the American prisoners in our second camp. The camp contained about fifteen huts which housed the prisoners, the guards, the commandant and his interpreter, and the resident *y si*. The largest hut was used for propaganda sessions and interrogation. Besides the huts, there were the usual sheds for pigs and chickens, a storeroom, and a latrine. This camp was considerably larger and more spacious than Camp I; yet it was virtually invisible until we were standing almost in the middle of it. All the jungle camps were so well camouflaged that one could approach within ten yards without catching a glimpse of them.

There was no fence around the camp, not even a band of bamboo spikes. But a wall of dense underbrush surrounded the Americans' huts, which formed a sort of camp within a camp. Sixteen Americans were imprisoned there; and even before we saw them, we knew all their names. On the evening of our arrival, when Rika Kortmann was walking to the latrine, something flew over the fence and landed at her feet. It was a piece of paper listing the names of all the Americans in the camp, along with the names of those who had died there. Then Rika received a second note requesting us, after our release, to turn over the list to the nearest American military headquarters. The Americans mistakenly believed that we would be released before they were.

We already knew the names. Soon we learned to know the faces: Willis, the black who always walked around holding a Bible and a machete; Dr. Kushner, who explained mathematical formulas as if they were all that stood between him and madness; Frank, the bomber pilot shot down in a burning plane over the jungle, whose screams we heard at night when he was dreaming; Gus, who liked to amuse us by saying German words with

74

his strong American accent—*Lederhosen, Wiener Schnitzel, Hofbräuhaus*—and, of course, John Young, the barber.

I do not know what would have become of my friends and me if the Americans had not helped us. Later, when we were ill and growing weaker every day, they brought us food and washed our clothes for us.

The American prisoners had all spent two or three years in other camps where conditions were worse than here. We did not learn about their past for some time. After four months together, we were separated and did not see one another for almost four years. . . .

When we first caught sight of the Americans, the guards were leading them into the jungle to cut bamboo for our hut. During our first few days in the camp, we did not have a hut of our own but were quartered with two imprisoned officers of the ARVN. There was room for only five people in the hut. We wondered whether this meant that the guerrillas did not intend to bring Marie-Luise Kerber and Monika Schwinn to join us later. Then we saw the Americans carrying wood from the jungle. The guards set to work erecting a new hut beside the fence surrounding the American compound.

In a few days the hut was completed, and one evening we moved in. The guards had not yet added the finishing touches, but it was a fine, large hut. And, best of all, there were sleeping accommodations for five people. As usual, the bed was very hard. It consisted of a single long bamboo platform raised high above the floor. A thin partition bisected the platform, creating two separate sleeping areas—one for the women and one for the men. There was room for three people in one compartment, for two in the other. Moreover, five "blankets" lay on the floor of the hut. Someone had ripped open empty rice sacks and sewed them together at the sides. We could still read the letters on the sacks—"U.S. AID, Rice for the People"—and see the symbol of American economic aid, two hands clasped in a friendly handshake.

We had heard nothing about our two friends in Camp I. The separation had occurred so abruptly. Before we knew it, our hands were tied and we were led out of the camp. For weeks now we had been wondering how Monika and Marie-Luise were and whether they would soon be joining us.

Once we saw that our hut had been designed for five people, we felt greatly relieved. Obviously the guerrillas intended to bring the others to join us. Rika, Georg, and I were also concerned about our personal safety: we believed that we would not be released until all five of us were together. Once the others had joined us, we felt certain that the guerrillas would let us all go. . . .

By talking with the Americans and observing the planes that continually flew overhead, I tried to guess the location of the camp. Years later, I wanted to find it again, for we had left two graves nearby. Had we been able to find the graves, the bodies of our friends might have been exhumed. I had a vague idea that the camp lay in the mountains southwest of An Hoa, near the Laotian border. The Americans were convinced that we were not far from An Hoa—no more than thirty or forty miles as the crow flies. But there was no way of pinpointing our location.

I took comfort in the thought that we had not yet left the An Hoa area, for this meant that there was still some hope of our being released. The Americans had told me another encouraging fact. After undergoing a period of intensive political indoctrination, a few prisoners had already been released from the camp. In fact, the avowed purpose of this camp was the "re-education," or brainwashing, of prisoners. Soon my friends and I got a taste of re-education.

The evening of the day we arrived, the commandant came to see us, accompanied by his interpreter, Huong. Huong translated the commandant's greeting into English: "We hope that you are well. We hope that you like it here. We hope that you are prepared to learn something here."

I do not know whether Huong translated the commandant's speech accurately. I often suspected him of inventing much of what he told us. Huong could not ask the simplest questions without making a person feel insulted and humiliated. He was the only Vietnamese who ever struck me: he punched me in the face merely because I had dared to ask to speak with the commandant. He used to hit the other prisoners as well. Once he made an American stand for an hour in the hot sun for having failed to use the proper greeting when addressing him. Huong delighted in punishing the *my*'s, the Americans; and when he used the word "punish," his eyes gleamed with hatred. He was feared throughout the camp. I believe that even his own men were afraid of him. Huong, not the commandant, really ran the camp.

A man in his late twenties, Huong had a pudgy face, pendulous cheeks, and a twisted mouth. He kept his hair cropped very short for two inches above the ears; above this point, the hair stuck straight out in a bushy fringe. Although he wore the black linen uniform of the guerrilla fighter, lined with large pockets, I do not believe that he had ever seen real combat. One day we celebrated North Vietnamese Independence Day. Ho Chi Minh had proclaimed Vietnam an independent republic on September 2, 1945. But in the camp, we celebrated the holiday several days early, on August 28. That day, Huong came to me and said, "Do you know why we are celebrating our holiday several days early? Of course, you do not know. I will tell you. Because the actual celebration is of little importance. The real way to celebrate is to fight. On September 2, we will be busy fighting the U.S. aggressors!" But when September 2 arrived, Huong was in the camp as usual, taking a nap in his hut.

On our second day in the camp, the guards conducted me to the hut where interrogation and indoctrination took place. Georg and Rika were too weak to move, so I went alone. At the head of the room, behind the desk, hung the blue and red flag of the NLF emblazoned with its golden star. Handmade posters were mounted on the walls. The commandant spoke and Huong translated, wearing his arrogant smile. "As I do not speak English myself, my young friend here will act as my deputy. He will ask you questions. He will explain everything you need to know. He will inform you about the war and the struggle of the Vietnamese people to become a free and independent nation. You should listen carefully, for what my young colleague tells you will be very important to you."

At this point the commandant departed, leaving Huong free to do as he chose. Our later interviews followed the same pattern: after an introductory phrase or two, the commandant would leave the hut. I always thought that he looked quite relieved to be free of the responsibility. Then Huong would light a cigarette, holding it between his tobacco-stained index and middle fingers. Leaning back in his chair, he would begin.

At my first indoctrination session, Huong told me about the camp regulations, which all prisoners were expected to obey. In the hut that Rika, Georg, and I shared with the Vietnamese officers, I had noticed a small bamboo mat that served as a bulletin board. Fastened to the board was a sheet of paper listing the camp regulations. Huong proceeded to repeat all five:

> Do not attempt to escape!
> Take care to get sufficient exercise!
> Eat as much as possible!
> Sleep as much as possible!
> Do not think about home!

Huong elaborated somewhat on the final point. "If you think about home, it simply weakens your mind. Instead, think about the things I tell you here. This will improve your mind."

He said all this in a completely serious tone of voice, and obviously camp regulations were supposed to be taken seriously. Of course, none of the prisoners could possibly obey them, for we were never given enough to eat, and we were far too weak to do our daily quota of gymnastics. But what did reality matter, when we had regulations?

Then Huong added something that was soon to become an all-too-familiar phrase: "The camp regulations express the lenient and generous policy of the Vietnamese people." In Huong's case, the remark must have been purely sarcastic, for he was an intelligent man who, as he proudly informed me, had studied in Saigon.

78

So ended my first indoctrination session. On the following day, I was taken to the same hut. Clapping Huong on the shoulder, the commandant began his speech, "My young colleague . . . " and disappeared. Huong lit his first cigarette and settled into position. Then he treated me to the first of many lectures, which he claimed were "so very good" for the mind. He always said the same thing. Soon he managed to etch the speech into my brain. Even now I can repeat it word for word.

"We are the Vietnamese people. We are fighting for the freedom of our nation. The National Liberation Front is the only true representative of the peace-loving Vietnamese people. Our brothers and sisters in North Vietnam support our war of liberation. President Ho Chi Minh is the great leader of our people. Uncle Ho is a clear-sighted leader. The Saigon government is a puppet regime. In Saigon, they are all the puppets of Washington. They were appointed by the U.S.A. to serve as lackeys of American imperialism. You, too, are a lackey of American capitalism. The Federal Republic of Germany sold you, a free man, to the United States; it sold you in exchange for a few paltry dollars. The Federal Republic of Germany supports the politics of imperialism; it supports American aggression against the Vietnamese people. The Americans are war criminals. You are a war criminal, too. You have not yet understood these things. You will now return to your hut. You will think about the things I have said to you. This afternoon we will discuss them." At our "discussion," he simply repeated everything he had already said.

Huong also conducted interrogations. He was not nearly as pleasant to deal with as our amused interrogators in Camp I. Huong was a man who knew how to inspire fear, and I feared him.

He began by gathering personal data. His questions were detailed and precise. He seemed to be interested in everything about me. "Did you graduate from secondary school? What subjects were you good at? What were your poor subjects? Where did you usually spend your holidays? When did you sign up to come to Vietnam? Where did you sign up? What did you do in Vietnam?"

"I worked in the Maltese hospital in An Hoa. We took care of sick and wounded people."

"Your hospital served as cover for an espionage ring."

"No, that's not true. Only Germans work at the hospital."

"Do you expect us to believe that? Are you saying that you do not know that the interpreter employed at the hospital in An Hoa is a member of the South Vietnamese Secret Service? You do not know that? You do not know that this interpreter interrogates all the patients? You do not know that he reports to the Secret Service the names of all suspected members of the Viet Cong?"

I did not know this, but suddenly I found myself believing that it might be true. "I know nothing about all that," I said. "We treated civilian patients on both sides. Someone had to take care of them. In one month we treated three thousand patients."

He banged on the desk and shouted, "You tell me that in one month you treated three thousand patients. I tell you that in one month the Americans kill thirty thousand people with their bombs, rockets, and artillery. I tell you that they spray poison gas on the rice paddies. And you support the Americans."

He went on bombarding me with questions. At the end of each session, he always threatened me: "You have not told us everything you know. We will squeeze the truth out of you. We have you in our power. I will ask some of my questions again. Next time, no doubt, you will remember something you have not told us. We have ways of finding out everything about you. If you lie to us, we will know it. You may go now. Do not disobey regulations!"

Two weeks elapsed. My two friends and I were suffering from exhaustion and the aftereffects of the fever we had contracted while marching through the jungle. Once Georg tried to help me dig a trench around our hut to drain off the water that collected when it rained. He had barely started digging when he had to stop and rest. We were so weak that we felt grateful when we were able to perform the smallest task.

During our first week in the camp, I spent several days working on our hut. My first effort was to build a small staircase leading up to the door. Then I made a bench, placing it beside the tree stump that stood in front of our hut. My final creation was a table. After that, I had nothing to do. The days were all alike. We woke up hoping for our release, but by evening we were still in the camp and nothing had changed. We tried to get used to the thought that we were going to be there for a long time.

In the past I had always been a clock watcher. Now I no longer had a clock to watch. During our first weeks of captivity, it was hard for me to keep track of time. I was not even certain what day it was. The position of the sun told me little, for it was May, midsummer, and the sun almost always stood directly overhead.

On our eleven-day march, we knew roughly what time it was, for we still got hungry at regular hours. Moreover, we knew that we had begun the march on a Sunday; thus at first we managed to keep track of the days of the week. But after three or four days in the jungle, we were no longer certain what day it was. The longer we spent in the camps, the more important it seemed to know exactly how much time had gone by. Slowly the months stretched into years. We did not dare to lose track of a single day, for fear that we might lose ourselves.

In our second camp, which we called simply "the American camp," the American prisoners kept a calendar. Thus we always knew what day it was. We also had various means of telling the time of day. Every morning, Huong brought a portable radio into the American compound, and punctually at 7:00 A.M., he turned the radio on full blast. First we heard the time and the date, and then came "The Voice of Vietnam," a propaganda broadcast in English. Huong left the radio there, blaring at the Americans.

The prisoners got up and had breakfast at 5:00 A.M., two hours before the radio broadcast. We knew that it was 11:00 A.M. when the guard gave the signal for lunch by striking his bamboo pipe, which had had a piece of bamboo cut from the middle so that it vibrated when struck. At 1:15 P.M., the same gong signaled the end of our noon rest hour. During this time, no one was permitted to leave his hut. At 4:30 P.M., the gong sounded for the last time, calling us to supper. After supper, we were left alone to face the long evening and the even longer night.

Sometimes the birds helped us to tell time at night. For example, I learned that a healthy rooster begins crowing not in the morning, but around midnight. Certain birds sang only at particular hours. The most remarkable bird of all was one I heard in the Mountain Village in North Vietnam. I never actually saw the bird, for the window of my cell was too high for me to look out. But every evening at six o'clock, I heard it singing in the tree outside. Four times it repeated its call, a long-drawn-out wail: "i—ey, i—ey, i—ey, i—ey." Slowly the sound died away. The bird repeated the same call at seven o'clock and again at eight. If a light was still burning in my cell, it sang once more at nine. Ornithologists may claim that no such bird exists; I know what I know.

Still we had no news of Marie-Luise Kerber and Monika Schwinn. Then one day Bob came over and said, "Don't worry. Marie-Luise is feeling better. They'll both be coming here in a couple of days." We believed him; for if anyone knew what was going on in the camp, it was Bob.

The Deserter

BERNHARD DIEHL

Bob was American. He was a deserter. Perhaps his fellow countrymen will find harsher names to call him, but I cannot condemn him. Whenever I think back to our days in the jungle camps, I cannot help thinking of Bob.

We first saw Bob on our way from Camp I to the American camp. On our second day out, we had to wait in front of some huts belonging to Montagnards, or hill tribesmen. We were waiting for our new guards to arrive and take us the rest of the way to the camp. A gray canvas had already been spread on the ground and covered with our confiscated belongings. The new shift of guards were taking their time about getting there.

Finally they arrived. There were two of them. I could not take my eyes off the taller one, who seemed a giant by Vietnamese standards. He was nearly six feet tall and looked very strong. The man had black hair, dark eyes beneath bristling brows, and a very deep tan. He stood aloof throughout the ceremonial changing of the guard, so that I had time to observe him.

He was wearing the green uniform of the Viet Cong and the broad North Vietnamese belt with its square buckle surmounted by a star. His trousers were rolled up almost to his knees in the style affected by all the "liberation fighters." His feet were clad in Ho Chi Minh sandals, their rubber soles cut from old automobile tires, tied on with four interlacing thongs. On his head perched one of those linen caps the Viet Cong called "water lilies" because their multilayered brims resembled the tiers of petals in the water flowers. His whole outfit bespoke the liberation fighter. He carried a .45, one of the most cherished of all American weapons; his uniform was covered with the flaps and hooks used for mounting camouflage; and, as I saw later, his bulging pockets were filled with everything from drugs to plastic explosives.

Noticing my puzzled expression, he came over and sat down in front of me. He squatted with his weight on both heels in the posture typical of the Vietnamese and quite alien to Americans, who, whenever they kneel, automatically tuck one leg a little behind the other. Then he suddenly addressed me in the purest American: "Why are you staring at me that way? Who do you think I am?" He was smiling at me.

I had taken him for a Vietnamese with a touch of European blood. He looked so authentic, crouching there like that. Clearly he was not dressed that way for the fun of it. He was the very image of a jungle guerrilla fighter.

I continued to study him. His face wore the telltale marks of a jungle existence; his legs were tanned a deep brown; his rough, worn hands were those of a man who hunts and cooks his own food. I asked him in English, "Who are you?"

But suddenly he lost interest in me and began to study Rika. Even now she was still very pretty, and he seemed quite aware of that. "Is she your sweetheart?" he asked me, using the old-fashioned word.

"No," I answered.

"Haven't you got a sweetheart? Not even in Germany?"

"Oh, yes."

"Does she write you often?"

"What, you mean way out here?"

"Would you write her if you could?"

"Would they really let me?"

"We'll see; it may be all right. Lots of things can happen," he said mysteriously. Suddenly he grew serious. "I had a sweetheart back in the States. But I suppose she's married someone else by now. After all, what's a girl supposed to do when a guy like me spends four years running around the jungle and never even lets her know if he's alive?"

That was my first conversation with Bob. It seemed to me absurd to be sitting and talking that way in the middle of the jungle. This was almost the only time that Bob mentioned his past; it was as if he had never existed before the war. That first day I did not really believe his claim that he had been living in the jungle for four years. I could not imagine any white man surviving four years of such conditions and still looking as healthy as he did, flashing his strong, shining teeth and moving with that light and springy step.

We resumed our march silently. I listened to the two guards chatting away in Vietnamese. This "liberation fighter," whoever he was, spoke the foreign tongue with ease. Once, as he was walking along beside me, I asked him the question that concerned me most: "In your camp, who interrogates the prisoners?"

He answered curtly, "An interpreter."

"Is that you?"

"No. A guy named Huong." Then he added, "He's a rat. I hate rats."

That was all he said, and I was still unable to make heads or tails of the man. Just before we entered the camp, he disappeared, leaving us alone with the other guard. From the first I was inclined to trust him. Perhaps I was simply surprised to find a man like him in such a place and desperately hoped that this expert in jungle lore, who dared to be so outspoken about a Vietnamese, might be willing to help us escape.

We saw him again that evening when he entered the hut assigned to imprisoned Vietnamese officers, where we were being quartered. He chatted with the officers in a Vietnamese that seemed quite free of any American accent, and later I learned that he had even mastered some of the Montagnard dialects. With him he brought the camp y si, who reluctantly examined us and then shook his head—meaning, I took it, that he considered us perfectly healthy, and that in any case it would be a mistake to waste good medicine on us. But then the tall liberation fighter reached into one of his bottomless pockets and took out five quinine tablets for each of us, handing them over without a word. I did not even know his name, but one thing I did know: in this jungle, fifteen quinine tablets were a precious gift indeed. . . .

After that, the American often came to visit us, and soon we learned that his name was Bob. Usually he arrived in the evenings after supper. I noticed that after he left us, he always went directly to the commandant's hut; moreover, he slept there at night. The American prisoners had warned us to be careful what we said in his presence, for Bob was a deserter, a traitor.

Bob continued to visit us. Once he brought us a stack of propaganda literature in English, commenting only, "Huong would like you to read these." He also brought us toothpaste and tobacco; and after we had moved into our new hut, he helped us make it more comfortable. A master of jungle crafts, he was as skillful as any Vietnamese. He showed me all the things a man could make with a knife and a piece of bamboo, and demonstrated how to cook a meal with a small amount of plastic explosive. Bob had a passion for an American card game called "casino" and carried around a deck of cards wherever he went. During my first two weeks in the camp, he and I often played cards outside, next to the tree stump.

One day when we were playing casino, I asked him, "How do you come to be working with the Viet Cong? And how did you get into the jungle in the first place? You're an American, aren't you?"

At first he hesitated and looked as if he were about to get up and leave. Then he said, "I don't think the Americans have suffered any great loss because I chose to fight on the other side. In any case, so many Americans are fighting with the South Vietnamese; why shouldn't there be a few fighting with the North?"

I had noticed the large wristwatch he was wearing. Clearly

it was neither American nor Japanese. When I asked him about it, he relaxed for the first time and became talkative. He told me that the watch had been made in the Soviet Union and was a Christmas gift from the guerrillas. He seemed quite proud of it. Bob had, so to speak, a "snug berth" with the liberation fighters. He was paid a stipend from which he deducted "traveling expenses"; and whenever he left the camp, he carried a back pack stuffed full of fine canned goods.

I asked him, "What's the war really all about?"

He laughed and said, "Why do you want to talk about the war? Let's talk about girls."

I knew that he was referring to Rika. He had taken quite a shine to her and often followed her around. One day when she left the camp to gather wood, Bob followed her, sat down beside her, and put his arm around her. Rika ran back to us. Later she felt concerned that by rejecting him she might get all of us in trouble. Remembering how upset she had been, I answered Bob rather sharply, "From now on, you'd better leave Rika alone."

"There are other girls," he said.

"Here in the jungle?"

"Of course in the jungle. You wouldn't believe how many pretty girls there are in the Montagnard villages."

"Well, that's not the story I heard. To hear Huong tell it, Viet Cong soldiers are above that sort of thing."

He laughed again. "Oh, it's the Americans. They're corrupting everybody in this country!"

Again I asked, "But what is this war really all about?"

No longer laughing, he put away his cards. "I don't know. It's all a great big mistake."

"What's your role in it?"

"I'm just a small fish, one of the many small fish who don't need much water to swim in. Do you know what Mao says? Mao says, 'The people are an ocean. The guerrilla swims through this ocean like a fish, but the enemy drowns in it.' The people are on the side of the guerrillas. That's why the Americans will never win this war. Not even with nuclear weapons. The many little fish are stronger than the Americans. They have only a little water to swim in, but a little is all they need."

It sounded like propaganda, but a different kind of propaganda from the phrases Huong spewed out.

Gradually I learned a little about Bob's past. At the age of twenty-one, just a few days before he was due to return to the States, he had been captured by the Viet Cong. He was traveling alone in a jeep, carrying dispatches along the road from Hoi An to Da Nang, which was then nominally under American control. Intercepting the jeep, a troop of guerrillas took him prisoner and blew up the vehicle. Bob walked for two weeks before reaching his first camp and spent the next two years in five different camps. At first he was harshly treated and underwent frequent interrogation. But from the outset he made an effort to learn the language of his captors so that he could communicate with them.

After two years' captivity, he was finally due to be released. But he voluntarily decided to remain in the jungle and fight on the side of the Viet Cong. He never told me how he arrived at this decision. For two years now he had been living in the jungle as a liberation fighter.

"Are you allowed to write home?" I asked him one evening.

"No. But I don't know whom I'd write to anyhow. The jungle is my home."

Then I asked what he planned to do when the war was over.

"The war won't be over for a long time yet."

The American prisoners claimed that Bob belonged to one of the propaganda units which entered the combat zone and encouraged American soldiers to desert. They said that he used to shout into a megaphone, "I am an American. I am a deserter. I recognized the injustice of American intervention in Vietnam. Now I am fighting with the Liberation Front. Come and join us. You will be well treated. The Liberation Front guarantees that any man who voluntarily lays down his arms will be returned to his own country as soon as possible, or given a passport to travel to any country he chooses."

88

The Americans claimed to have received this information about Bob from prisoners they had known in other camps. I do not know how much of what they said was true.

One day Bob left the camp and did not return. The last time I saw him, he was wearing his Ho Chi Minh sandals and his water-lily hat. The sleeves of his green shirt were rolled up to his elbows, his trousers rolled up to his knees. Carrying a small back pack and armed with his .45, he disappeared into the jungle he knew so well.

For a long time I thought that I had heard the last of him. Then, almost four years later, in February of 1973, I met some prisoners who had news of Bob. At that time I was in the Hanoi Hilton, the North Vietnamese camp where we were finally released.

In the Hanoi Hilton was a group of eight Americans who were ostracized by the other prisoners. They called themselves P.C.'s, which stood for "Peace Committee." The other Americans considered them traitors who had sold out their buddies and their country in exchange for a few special privileges. These eight men had requested that they not be released with the other American prisoners, but they were refused political asylum and sent home.

I knew one of these eight men, who had worked in the kitchen in the American camp when I was there and thus knew Bob. Suddenly, after almost four years' separation, I ran into the man in the prison yard of the Hanoi Hilton. At first I did not recognize him. In the past he had looked quite emaciated, but now he had filled out. I asked him whether he had heard any news of Bob.

Looking at me in horror, he replied, "I have nothing to do with Bob. He's a deserter!"

Bob seemed to have no friends on either side.

Later I found out that he was still alive. The prisoners in the Hanoi Hilton told me that he had been made a lieutenant and had gone to North Vietnam. Supposedly, he was now serving in the English-language division of the radio station that broadcast "The Voice of Vietnam."

The rumor that Bob was in North Vietnam may well have been true. He was not among the Americans released from the camps, and he did not return to the United States. His name did not appear on any list. Bob once told me that he might go to Sweden when the war was over. In any case, I could not picture him shut up in some stuffy little office in a tall building bristling with radio antennas. I could imagine him at the front, yelling into a megaphone and trying to persuade American soldiers to desert, but not sitting behind a microphone spouting insincere phrases.

When I think of Bob, I always picture him the way he looked the first and last times I saw him, dressed as a liberation fighter in a water-lily hat and rolled-up trousers. I have always wondered what he was fighting for. Money? Glory? A Soviet watch? His own survival? I'll never know.

Willis's Book

BERNHARD DIEHL

When we learned that Monika and Marie-Luise were coming to our camp, we could hardly wait to see them. Bob assured us that they would definitely arrive "some time today, or maybe tomorrow."

We waited all that day and most of the next. The evening gong had sounded, so that we had to go inside our hut; but we still had a good view of the camp through the open door.

We wrapped the rice-sack blankets around our shoulders, for the evenings were cool. Through the door we could see the yard in front of the hut. A short distance away, the ground sloped gently downward to the stream where we used to wash. Suddenly we saw a pointed straw hat ascending the slope, and a moment later, Monika appeared.

We could tell that her feet were very painful. She could hardly walk. Moving stiffly, she stumbled over a root, then swayed toward our hut looking as if she were in a trance.

We had assumed that Marie-Luise was too ill to walk and might have to be carried in a hammock. Thus we were not surprised that Monika had arrived first. Our friend looked ill and had deep circles under her eyes. She stared at us, unable to speak, and we stared back in silence. I noticed that she was wearing Marie-Luise's red linen shoes, but I was not concerned.

91

Ever since Monika's sandals had been ruined, Rika and Marie-Luise had taken turns lending her their shoes.

Monika stumbled as she tried to climb the low staircase. Laughing, I said, "Come on, Monika! It's not as bad as that. Anyhow, it's all over now. We're all together again."

We pressed her hands. None of us had asked about Marie-Luise. Then, for the first time, Monika spoke: "Don't you know what's happened?"

We glanced at one another, puzzled. In a hollow tone, Georg asked, "What's wrong? What have they done with her?"

"Marie-Luise is dead."

"But that's impossible!" We felt stunned. Then Rika and I both began to talk at once. I noticed that Georg said nothing, but just stood there looking pale. Why was he so affected? He had barely known Marie-Luise on the day of our outing. Then I realized that during our eleven-day trek through the jungle, the two of them had always walked hand in hand. And before we left Camp I, Georg had begged the commandant to let *him* be the one to stay behind with the sick girl.

On the morning we drove into the country, the five of us hardly knew one another. We were just five people climbing into a jeep to take a little trip. We had worked together, but we all had different reasons for being in Vietnam, and we knew very little about one another. Rika was the only one with whom I used the familiar form of address. For the first few days after we were captured, we continued to use the formal address. After that, it seemed quite natural to treat one another as friends, for we were all in the same boat, and we had to help one another. I began to hold Rika's hand to help her over the rough jungle terrain, and Georg helped Marie-Luise. Yet despite the long days of enforced intimacy, in some ways the five of us were almost strangers.

Seeing Georg's pale face, I thought, "He had begun to feel something for Marie-Luise, and you never noticed it. She never knew how he felt, and perhaps Georg himself did not know until this moment."

We could not understand how something so terrible could have happened. Now we all realized how vulnerable we really were. We had thought that, at worst, the five of us might be separated. It was inconceivable that one of our circle was actually dead. It was as if one link in the chain binding us together had been broken.

Suddenly we all stopped talking. Monika began to cry, and Georg helped her onto the bed. Unable to stay in the hut, I went outside, but I could still hear Monika crying. The sky was full of stars. "Dead," I thought. And then, "There must be something left of all those years of religious training. A scrap of faith that everything that happens in the world has some meaning—faith in an absolute, transcendent Being whom you could not know but might nevertheless be able to love—faith in something other than your impotent self." But I could not find the scrap of faith.

I could still hear Monika sobbing inside the hut. Then I heard someone calling my name in a loud whisper. The voice came from behind the fence surrounding the American compound. The guards were not looking in my direction. Approaching the fence, I saw three fires burning in the compound. It was a cold night. In the flickering firelight I saw the shaved head and emaciated frame of Dr. Kushner. He was wearing his olive-drab jacket and the spectacles fastened to his head with a rubber band. These spectacles had once belonged to another prisoner, now dead. Dr. Kushner's own glasses had been confiscated in the first camp in which he had been imprisoned.

"What happened?" he asked.

I told him about Marie-Luise. Then I added, "If only I had a Bible."

Looking slightly surprised, he said, "You really want one?"

"Yes, do you have one?"

"I don't, but Willis has. He has a machete and a Bible. He wouldn't part with the machete, but I think he might give you the Bible."

I watched Dr. Kushner disappear into one of the huts. In a

few minutes he returned with the Bible and handed it over the fence. "Willis says you can keep it for a while."

Taking the Bible back to our hut, I said to the others, "Let's pray for Marie-Luise." Trying to translate the English text into German, I began to read aloud. But Monika was not listening.

The moment she entered our hut and collapsed on the bamboo bed, something strange began happening to Monika. She stopped eating and getting out of bed. She did nothing but sleep.

During her first week with us, we still managed to make her get up for a few hours a day. But each day she spent more time asleep. The rest of us were deeply concerned. We did not know how to help her. At first we sometimes succeeded in getting her outside to sit for half an hour in the sunshine. But once outside, she simply sat on the bench in front of the hut, silent and unresponsive. Then she crept back into bed like an animal. At mealtimes we tried to wake her up, telling her, "You must eat!"

"No, leave me alone!"

A few times we got her to choke down a mouthful of rice, but a moment later she would vomit it up. The camp *y si* came to see her and delivered long, incomprehensible lectures. He did nothing to help her. Monika continued to grow weaker.

Then she became delirious. She no longer knew where she was or what she was saying, and she seemed unaware of what was happening around her. Once, when Rika was washing her, Monika opened her eyes and looked at her friend in terror. Rika had beriberi and was suffering from severe edema. Her face and throat were badly swollen, her eyes looked small and were sunk deep in her flesh. Seeing Rika's face, Monika sat up, saying, "What is that Vietnamese woman doing here? Get her away from me! Make her hurry up and unpack her medicine. It's terrible that she hasn't finished unpacking it yet."

Shaking her shoulders gently, I said, "But Moni, that woman is Rika."

Looking up at me, she suddenly appeared quite rational. "Yes, she must get to a hospital right away, a real hospital.

What are you waiting for?" Then she began to hallucinate again. "Take her to the bend in the road. They're waiting there with the VW. Hurry now. Otherwise she'll die here." Again she retreated into her own world.

As the weeks passed, Monika continued to be almost completely oblivious to her surroundings. For all she saw of us, we might just as well have been phantoms in her delirious dreams.

One day Rika and I lifted Monika from the bed. Gripping her under the shoulders, we dragged her to the latrine, which fortunately was not too far away. Afterward we brought her back and laid her down on the bed again. Throughout this process, she seemed unaware of what was happening. Her eyes were rolled far back in her head, and she muttered inarticulate sounds. Her lips looked very thin and blue. Then, twisting away from us, she turned her face to the wall. Rika and I looked at each other. We did not say a word, but each of us was thinking, "She will be the next one to die."

From time to time, the camp *y si* made his ceremonious entrance, delivered long speeches of which no one understood a word, and proceeded to listen to Monika's heart. He was inordinately proud of his stethoscope. Sometimes he gave Monika vitamin shots, which produced severe abscesses surrounding the area of the injections on her upper arms. She vomited up the medicines he gave her. She vomited everything she swallowed.

Finally the rest of us concluded that nothing could save Monika now. We did not realize how fortunate she was, for nature had devised a way to shield her. She remained unaware of the painful events taking place around her in the weeks that followed. . . .

Now that I had Willis's Bible, I spent most of the day reading, sitting on the tree stump in front of the hut. One day when I was reading, Bob walked over. As always, he had brought his deck of cards along. Sitting down, he began to shuffle, then dealt the cards. "Come on," he said impatiently, "you have your cards; pick them up. It's your lead."

I wanted to go on reading my Bible. Throwing him an angry look, I said, "Can't you see that I'm reading?"

"Come on, you can read your book any time."

"Your book," he had called it, although he must have seen what book it was.

"It's a Bible," I said.

"Well, that's a book, isn't it?" he asked, smiling.

I was angry that he spoke of the Bible as if it were just like any other book. Recalling the propaganda literature he had brought me from Huong, I said, "At least in this book there's no propaganda!"

"Are you quite sure?" Arranging his cards, he smiled and waited.

We ended up playing casino after all.

Rice for the People

BERNHARD DIEHL

Georg Bartsch was a big, strapping man a good head taller than I and more than ten pounds heavier. While we were working together at An Hoa, he never seemed to get tired; he even volunteered for Sunday duty. Physically, he seemed to be the strongest of our group. When we were captured, I consoled myself with the thought, "If things get really bad and you think you've had it, you can always count on Georg to help you out."

Georg and I had hardly talked at all when we were together in An Hoa. I did not even know where he was from. He had arrived at the hospital on April 6; thus, he had only been working with us for twenty days before we embarked on our Sunday outing. When we were captured, I felt safer knowing that Georg was there. He proved to be a loyal friend, always willing to help and to show me how to do things. He even taught me to roll cigarettes, wrapping the coarse Vietnamese tobacco in scraps of paper. Yet to my surprise, it was not I, but big, strong, capable Georg who buckled under the strain.

When we left Camp I, Rika, Georg, and I were all running high fevers and suffering from other symptoms of malaria. The journey cost Georg every ounce of his strength. Every few minutes he had to stop and rest; his pulse was fluttering and rapid—120 beats per minute—and he kept seeing benches and houses that were not there. He talked to us about the lovely, brightly painted green bench he saw above the path, where he was finally going to sit down and rest. Twice he collapsed. His face was pale and drawn, his nose looked pinched. He was running a high fever.

The quinine tablets Bob gave us when we arrived at camp made us all feel slightly better. Georg helped me finish the work on our hut. Then the American physician, Dr. Kushner, took me aside and warned me that it would be dangerous for Georg to go on working. He said that Georg should not participate in our morning exercises, but should simply lie down and rest. I told the doctor about Georg's earlier symptoms. Suspecting that the malaria attack might have damaged my friend's heart, Dr. Kushner attempted to borrow the *y si*'s stethoscope. The *y si* angrily refused.

Monika joined us on May 26, four weeks after our capture. None of us had recovered from our initial attack of malaria. We were also suffering from exhaustion and malnutrition, and Rika had developed severe edema. The unsanitary medical techniques of the camp *y si* made us wince. He used to boil the needles and syringes in a small aluminum pot. Then he took the pot from the fire and, not bothering to remove the sterile instruments, used the same pot to warm ampules of vitamin B₁ and glucose. Having recontaminated the needles, he proceeded to give us our shots. It was these injections that produced the abscesses on Monika's arms.

At least the guards did not prevent the American prisoners' taking care of us. The Americans brought us our food and washed our dishes. We had been given special prison clothing, white pajamas for the women and black for the men. The Americans washed our clothes down at the stream about thirty yards outside the camp.

After Monika brought word of Marie-Luise's death, Georg took a marked turn for the worse. Like Monika, he no longer wanted to eat or get out of bed. One day he was lying down, and I was sitting beside him trying to feed him. Holding out a spoonful of rice, I asked him to sit up to eat it. He answered, "Why should I sit up? You can even eat standing on your head. Try it and see. Even when you're upside down, the food always winds up in your stomach. Why wouldn't it do the same when you're lying down?" He was joking, but the joke was not very funny.

Georg's legs were covered with running sores that refused to heal. The *y si* crushed penicillin tablets and sprinkled the powder on the wounds, but they continued to bleed and ooze pus.

After Monika arrived, we were given tobacco and cigarette paper. No doubt the gifts were intended to cheer us up. Georg had stopped smoking, but he taught me to roll my own cigarettes. He was never quite satisfied with my efforts and sometimes rolled them for me. The guards had also brought us two towels and two pieces of soap. One day the Americans carried Georg to one of their huts, heated a kettle of water, and gave him a good bath. When they brought him back, he was deeply moved and weeping with joy. "They were so good to me," he said. He told us that they had washed him all over and that he would never forget what they had done. He went on crying for half an hour before he grew still.

Our situation was desperate. I was so weak and dizzy that I almost passed out whenever I stood up; Monika was unconscious; and Rika had taken to her bed suffering from a severe case of beriberi. Every other day the *y si* came to see us. Boiling his syringe in front of our hut, he injected each of us with ten cc. of glucose and vitamin B_1. Ten cc. of glucose could do nothing for people in our condition.

When Rika was working in Da Nang, she suffered from insomnia, and the doctor had prescribed sleeping pills. In the camp, the *y si* refused to give her pills, although he had some on hand. Since the day of our capture, Rika had hardly slept at all. She spent most of her time lying down and staring into space.

On the evening of July 7, Georg took my hand and said, "Just feel how cold I am. It feels as if I were already dead." The two of us had to share one mosquito net. Both of us were freezing. I moved closer to him so that we could keep each other warm. "Don't say things like that," I whispered.

Then he said, "Did you know that once I met Death face to face?"

I knew almost nothing about Georg's past. He rarely talked about himself. I did know that he was now twenty-five and that, as he put it, he had had "a devil of a time" getting through school. "Greek, oh my God, I can't bear to think of it; and Latin grammar, oh, it was awful." After serving in the army, he had become a medic and worked in various clinics in Würzburg and Aschaffenburg before applying to come to Vietnam.

"Didn't you hear what I said?"

"Please," I begged, "don't talk so loud, or the others will hear you."

"But it's true, I did meet Death. It happened in Würzburg a couple of days before I flew to Vietnam." And he described in great detail the hospital where he had been working that Sunday.

"It happened in the intensive-care unit on the second floor," he whispered. "We had a patient there in a private room. We all knew that he was terminal, that he could not live for more than a few days. I was taking care of him that Sunday. I'd bathed him, and he was feeling quite well. We both laughed at the stories I told him. Then I walked out into the corridor, closing the door behind me. It was Sunday morning. Visiting hours had not begun yet, and the corridors were all empty. I opened the opaque glass door leading onto the stairwell. A man dressed in a black suit and coat was coming up the stairs; a black hat partially concealed his face. I called out to him, 'Visiting hours haven't begun yet. Where do you think you're going?' But the man simply shoved me aside and kept walking. I watched him open the glass door and saw it shut behind him. Just looking at him made me feel cold all over. Do you need me to tell you what happened next?" he asked in a soft, clear voice.

I wanted to laugh it off and say, "I'm in no mood for ghost stories." But I could not laugh or say a word. He continued his story: "Hurrying after the man, I saw him go into the room of the dying patient. I got there just a minute after he did, but when I opened the door, the man dressed in black wasn't there. The room had only one door, yet the man had disappeared. The patient was lying dead in his bed. Just the moment before we had been chatting away, and now he was dead, and I had to fetch the doctor. . . ."

I said nothing. Feeling colder than ever, I crept closer to Georg so that we could keep each other warm. . . .

By next morning, the weather had changed. It was foggy and drizzling. Georg seemed slightly better. I said, "Come on, get up, it'll do you good to move around a little." He shook his head. I went over to Rika. She shook her head, too. Monika was lying as she always did, with her face to the wall. She did not even hear me.

I went outside and did my morning exercises alone. I ate my rice by myself. "Things have reached a pretty pass," I thought. "We can't even talk to each other any more." Only a few things seemed important enough to talk about. "Eat something." "Don't you want to wash up?" "Don't you want to go outside?" "Oh, what I would give for a piece of meat!" "What I would give for a warm blanket!" That was the sum of our conversation. Nothing else existed. God did not exist. The Bible was just a book. Almost nothing was real to us any more. One day Rika said, "Just once I would like to wash my hair in warm water, with real shampoo. Washing it with this awful soap just makes it dull."

We had lost interest in everything but what concerned the most primitive human needs. I stopped reading Willis's Bible. I do not know whether the others prayed. If they did, they prayed alone.

The day after Georg had told me his story about Death, he did not get out of bed at all. After dark, he allowed me to help him up so that he could go to the latrine. Georg was very modest. As a rule, he would go to the latrine only at night, when he thought that he was unobserved. That evening he put his arm around my shoulders, and we staggered to the doorway. He wanted to walk the rest of the way alone. I let him go, for the latrine was only a few yards away, and in the past he had always managed to get there by himself. This time he collapsed after taking a single step. He lay on the ground, not making a sound.

The night was pitch-black. There was no moon, and not a single star shone overhead. I felt almost as weak as Georg. My knees were shaking and threatened to cave in under me. I said, "Come on, Georg, get up!" With my help, he tried to stand, but fell back exhausted. I tried to lift him, but I was too weak. He said, "Oh, just leave me where I am."

"You can't go on lying here all night."

"Why not? I'll just stay here until it gets light, until they sound the bamboo gong. Then we'll see whether they bother to pick me up; we'll see whether they have any hearts at all."

Somehow I managed to get him on his feet. So this was the man who was going to help me if I started to go under! We had now been prisoners for around ten weeks, and Georg had lost a good deal of weight; but he was still heavy to lift. After dragging him into the hut, I climbed onto the bed and pulled him after me. Then I took off his shoes and lay down close beside him.

It was very quiet. Suddenly Georg said, "Say, can you help me out?"

"Sure, what is it?"

"It's really dumb of me, but I can't remember the Lord's Prayer. I can't get past the first line. 'Our Father, who art in Heaven . . .' That's all I remember."

"It's easy," I said. " 'Our Father, who art in Heaven . . .' " Then I stopped. "Just wait a minute and I'll get it." If I thought about home, surely the words would come back to me. All I had to do was think about dinnertime. First my father comes up the stairs, then my mother says, "Hurry now, the soup's getting cold." Everyone is standing around the table, for we always pray standing up, our eyes fixed on the crucifix hanging over the door. My father has draped his jacket over the chair and unfastened the top button of his shirt. "The eyes of all people await your coming, O Lord. . . ." Now comes the Lord's Prayer. "Just a minute, Georg, and I'll think of it." But the image fades, I cannot hold on to it long enough. I'll think about Christmas instead. The door to the living room is closed. Behind the door, our parents are setting up the crèche and trimming the tree, very simply with nothing but white candles, silver balls, and tinsel. The door opens, but we're not allowed to open our gifts yet. First we must say the Lord's Prayer in front of the crèche. My father leads us in prayer. I can see his lips moving, but I can't hear anything. Perhaps I can read his lips. . . .

"Our Father, who art in Heaven . . ." I had been saying the prayer all my life; I had said it thousands of times. Now I had to say it for Georg, but I could not remember.

"I'm sorry, Georg, but I've forgotten it. I'm just like you, I can't get past the first line."

He seemed shocked. "If even *you* have forgotten it! oh my God, if you've forgotten it, do you know what that means?"

"But Georg, what can it possibly mean? It just means that I'm losing my memory. Starvation and malnutrition make you lose your memory."

"No!" he said fiercely. "Oh God, now I know that I'll never get home again."

He began weeping like a child. We lay there side by side all night, both of us freezing. I went on racking my brains, but I could not remember the rest of the prayer.

The next day was bright and sunny again. The gong sounded, and at seven o'clock Huong went over to the fence around the American compound and turned on his blaring radio. I sat beside Georg all day. He kept saying things I could not understand: "I was always very good at digging excavations; why are people complaining so now?" Another time he said, "If my father could see me working in a hole like this, he would fight on the barricades for me. Even my mother would fight!"

He was delirious. Unaware of the brilliant sunshine outside, he spent the day lost in shadows. In the afternoon he asked to go to the latrine. Rika and I tried to lift him out of bed, but he shook his head. "It's too late now," he said.

We washed him and dressed him in a fresh pair of trousers.

103

Dr. Kushner came with Gus, the American who spoke a little German. Gus said *Lederhosen* and *Riesengaudi* and *Oktoberfest,* trying to make us laugh. After that, he just sat there looking helpless. Dr. Kushner's face looked even graver than usual.

Georg seemed unaware of his surroundings. He lay perfectly still and did not answer our questions. His eyes were closed, his breathing was slow and regular. For the first time, he seemed completely at peace. After listening to Georg's heart and lungs, the *y si* said, "There's nothing wrong. He's just a bit weak. He'll recover." But he was lying, and we knew that he was lying. This time at least, he was probably trying to spare our feelings.

That night it turned bitter cold. Georg's condition had not changed: he was still lying there without moving. Suddenly Rika said, "Couldn't I come to sleep between the two of you? I'm so cold. These so-called blankets don't keep me warm. Can't I lie between the two of you?" She lay down between us. Around ten o'clock I felt myself being pushed farther and farther into my corner of the bed. I asked Rika to move over a little.

"I can't," she said. "Georg is taking up all the room. I've already asked him to move, but he didn't answer."

"Please, Georg," I said, "move over a little. You have so much room left on your side." But he did not answer. Then Rika said, "You know, I think . . . my God, I can't hear him breathing."

I sat up. "What?"

"He's stopped breathing."

It was black as ink inside the hut. Leaning across Rika, I cried, "Georg! Say something. Say something, Georg. Georg!"

But Georg was dead.

I ran outside, calling the *y si* and Dr. Kushner. The guards came running up, closely followed by Huong and the *y si*. One guard was carrying a small oil lamp.

Georg's eyes were closed. He looked very peaceful, as if he were simply asleep. He had dark hair, and during the eleven weeks of our captivity, he had grown a full dark beard. He had been very proud of it and never allowed Little John to do more than trim the ends. A few days before, Georg had said jokingly, "All my life I've wanted to grow a beard, but I had to come to a prison camp to do it."

Standing there, I thought how little separated the living man from the dead man. Georg still looked as strong as ever. How could such a thing happen? Why did God bring a human being into the world and let him grow up, why did he make him so good and so strong, and then suddenly abandon him, leaving him to die a miserable death?

Rika and I undressed Georg, washed his body, and dressed him in his black prison pajamas. Then we covered his body with the faded gray blanket made of rice sacks—the sacks that said "U.S. AID, Rice for the People" and were printed with two clasped hands.

I looked bitterly at the words. Everyone in this country knew that the rice intended for the South Vietnamese people usually ended up in Communist hands. The Americans had told me that twenty percent of all the goods unloaded in Saigon were immediately stolen, and the percentage was even higher in Da Nang. Moreover, it was common knowledge that more than fifty percent of the money sent by the free world to South Vietnam served to line the pockets of corrupt merchants, bureaucrats, and military personnel serving the Saigon regime. The two sacks had traveled a long way before they were torn up and sewed together to make Georg's shroud. First the rice had been misappropriated, then smuggled abroad, and finally sold to the Communists for hard cash.

Georg had not been thinking about facts like these when he first arrived in this country to offer his help. Now he lay beneath the empty sacks.

Rika and I lay down on the other side of the partition, but we could not get to sleep. Then the two of us recited the Lord's Prayer. This time I knew all the words.

It was a dreadful night. The air was damp and chilly, and it was drizzling outside. Neither of us could sleep. Next morning, the Americans came to see us. "We heard that Georg is dead," they said. "It was really a shock. At first we thought that Monika Schwinn had died." Everyone had expected that Monika would be the next to die.

At five o'clock, we got up. The commandant came to see how we were. Rika and I sat on the edge of the bed and stared into space. "Rika," I said, "another one of us is gone. Do you think he will be the last?"

That morning, the Vietnamese led a group of Americans into the jungle to cut bamboo. Meanwhile, other Americans dug a hole behind the camp. Rika and I could do nothing to help. We did not know how to make a bamboo coffin, and we were far too weak to help dig the grave. All morning, we sat side by side on the tree stump outside our hut. Monika was sleeping or unconscious.

Shortly after noon, the Vietnamese wrapped vines around the coffin. Slipping a long pole under the vines, they carried the coffin to our hut on their shoulders and set it down in front of the bed. Then two Americans laid Georg's body inside, lowered the lid, and slipped the pole under the vines again. The black American named Willis and one of his friends picked up the pole and placed it on their shoulders. Then they carried the coffin to the grave, which had been dug in the jungle some fifty-five yards from the camp. Rika was exhausted and very weak, so Dr. Kushner helped her to walk along behind the coffin. I walked alone, leaning on a stick for support. When we reached the grave, the Americans carefully lowered the coffin. The other prisoners, Rika, and I stood around the grave. I said a few words in broken English: "It is easy to become a prisoner. It is not easy for a prisoner to become a free man again. Some prisoners are fortunate enough to survive. Others are even more fortunate: they die and thus are spared the suffering of captivity."

One by one, we each took a handful of earth and threw it on the coffin. Then Dr. Kushner took Rika's arm and led her back to the hut. He tried to distract her, asking if she was married. As I walked along behind them, I heard the doctor caution

Rika to take care of herself. He could tell just by looking at her that she was very ill.

That evening the Americans brought us our food again. Night fell. Rika and I hardly spoke to each other. There was nothing to say.

The American's Dream

BERNHARD DIEHL

Next morning, July 11, Rika got up and began to walk around. I got up, too, and went outside. Then I walked over to a small tree and held on to it while I urinated; but I lost my balance and fell down. Rika could not help me, and I could not get up by myself. Then two of the Americans came over, picked me up, and helped me back to bed. I slept soundly for a couple of hours.

That afternoon I woke up again and saw Rika go outside and disappear around the corner of the hut. She did not come back for a long time. When she entered the hut, she looked exhausted and held on to the doorpost. Going over to her, I saw human feces outside the hut. Rika had not made it to the latrine.

Three days later, Rika Kortmann lost consciousness. For three days she remained in a coma. Then, without ever regaining consciousness, she died. Rika was twenty-eight, the eldest of our group. Since October of 1968 she had been working in our hospital in Da Nang. She died in a prison camp as had her father who, according to the report of a German POW returning from Russia, had been killed in a 1944 bombing raid on a Russian camp.

Hindrika Kortmann died from the effects of malnutrition, edema, insomnia, and inadequate medical treatment. Trying to ease their troubled consciences, the guerrillas later told us that

108

we must all have been sick before we were captured. But I am convinced that the Vietnamese had a supply of the drugs that could have saved our friends. Years later I read the statement of Sergeant Willis A. Watkins, black, twenty-two years old, made after his release from the camp in September of 1969. Willis stated that Rika Kortmann had a stronger will to survive than any prisoner in the camp, and that all the other prisoners were "inspired by her example." Everyone considered her death "very sudden and unexpected."

After Georg died, Rika seemed to know that she was doomed. She had been nursing for over six years and had more medical experience than the rest of us. She had known all along that she was gravely ill; but, not wanting to upset us, she had not talked about it. The day after Georg's death, for the first time she said, "If we don't get out of here soon, we're all going to die." Then she added, "Who knows, it may be for the best. We may be spared a lot of suffering."

She no longer wanted the *y si* to treat her, for she had come to detest him. After Georg's death, one of the Americans had suffered a cardiac arrest. We heard the usual shouting and the sound of running feet. The *y si* was the last to arrive at the scene. He always took his time in coming and strutted around the camp with a ceremonious gait, majestically bearing his aluminum pots and syringes. On this occasion, his behavior upset Rika so much that she began to tremble whenever he came near her. As a surgical nurse she had spent years assisting at operations and was a stickler for cleanliness. She could hardly bear to watch the unsanitary way the *y si* administered injections, not even bothering to clean the patient's skin with alcohol first.

At around one o'clock on the afternoon of July 14, I saw Rika sitting in the sun on a stretch of sand outside our hut. Dr. Kushner, standing by the fence, called over to her, "Of course, sunshine is good for you; it's the healthiest thing we can get in the jungle. But too much sun can harm you."

"I'll go back inside now," Rika replied. She was sitting on the ground and had placed a towel over her head to protect it

109

from the sun. Now she removed the towel and turned her body, trying to rise to her knees and push herself up with her hands. Too weak to get up, she fell on her face, tried again, collapsed, and lay still.

Not waiting for the guard to give them permission to leave their compound, the Americans ran over, picked Rika up, and carried her to bed. Dr. Kushner was with them. Rika's breathing was labored and she could no longer speak. She was completely exhausted. Then the Americans brought a bowl of cold water. I sat beside Rika and used a towel to bathe her face and wipe away the cold sweat. She was obviously in shock. We propped up her legs.

The *y si* condescended to listen to Rika's heart, but he would not let Dr. Kushner examine her. Huong had come with him. After the examination, the two of them began to talk. The *y si* appeared to be asking Huong's permission to administer a morphine injection.

Dr. Kushner knew enough Vietnamese to follow their conversation. Finally he interrupted them. "Either do something now, or just let her die!" He sounded helpless and furious. The Vietnamese stopped talking, and the *y si* gave Rika a morphine injection in the upper arm. It was too little and far too late.

Rika never regained consciousness. She went on sleeping, lying on her back. She never had a chance to wash her lovely hair with real shampoo. It hung in disheveled strands around her face. She was still beautiful. People with beriberi do not look emaciated. On the contrary, their figures are fuller. To me she looked as beautiful as ever. She was wearing her nurse's uniform.

On the following day, July 15, the *y si* paid us a call. He had allowed Dr. Kushner to accompany him so that the doctor could listen to Rika's heart. Then Huong and the *y si* began another whispered conversation. They came back on the 16th and the 17th. I could tell by the look on Dr. Kushner's face that Rika was dying. Still I refused to give up hope. I did what little I could for her, wiping the sweat from her forehead and wiping her lips so that she could breathe more easily. Bob had carved a bamboo gourd which I used to fetch water, and I had a small scrap of cloth to bathe her face.

Then I saw Rika's peaceful face grow twisted; her hands clutched wildly in the air. I ran outside, calling for help. It was the American doctor I wanted, not the Vietnamese. "Kush, Kush, come quickly!" He ran to our hut. The guards could not hold him back. At the same time I saw the *y si* coming out of his hut and walking toward us at a leisurely pace, as if he were saying, "She'll die in any case. There's no need for me to hurry."

Rika was scarcely able to breathe. Dr. Kushner said, "She's going to die. A morphine injection might buy her more time, but she's going to die."

The *y si* walked back to his hut. He *walked* back at a leisurely pace, then *walked* back to us. How I hated him! I hated his sunken chest, his protruding belly, his drooping shoulders. For the first time I *hated*. My mind turned red with hatred. I hated them all, I hated this whole race, and I especially hated this one man walking toward us wearing Ho Chi Minh sandals and black pajamas, carrying a hypodermic. I could have murdered him on the spot. With the air of a high priest, he entered the hut; and then, not even bothering to clean Rika's arm with alcohol, he plunged in the needle, stretching the skin a little with his hand to see if he had hit a blood vessel. I screamed, "Don't touch her! No one has given you the right to touch her!" But he did not understand me. Bending over Rika, he raised her eyelids and then lowered them again. I saw him spread the rice sack over her body.

Rika! I turned toward Monika, who was lying on the bed completely unaware of what had happened. I told her that Rika was dead; but she did not hear me. Shoving the *y si* out of the way, I went outside. The guards, leaning on their rifles, were standing around the hut. They looked at me, apparently surprised that I did not hurl myself to the ground, screaming, weeping, and tearing my hair. I had seen Vietnamese in An

Hoa mourn their dead that way. Suddenly I wished that I could mourn as they did. . . .

Rika Kortmann died at 1:30 P.M. on July 17. She was buried two hours later. The Americans dug another hole, placed her body in the coffin, and carried it to the grave. Then all of us said the Lord's Prayer. I prayed in German, the others in English, some in the Protestant version, some in the Catholic.

After one of the Americans had said a few words, we each threw a handful of earth into the grave. The soil here was pale yellow and had the consistency of clay.

One of the Vietnamese prisoners, a soldier in the army of South Vietnam, approached the grave, made the sign of the cross, and walked away. Then, Willis, John Young, Frank Anton, another American named Ike, and I returned to my hut. Frank always did his best to help us, even though he himself was very ill and suffering from severe edema. They were all allowed to stay with me for a little while.

Earlier that day, some of the Americans had brought two buckets of water and washed the side of the bed where Monika and Rika had been sleeping. Then they dried the area with grass and rags. I was too weak to help.

When the bed had dried, Ike and Willis came to the hut. Monika was just sitting there staring into space. I do not know whether she was aware of what was going on around her. When the Americans lifted her back onto the bed, she fell asleep again at once. Then everyone left me alone.

I saw a bundle of clothing lying in a corner of the hut. Rika had been buried in her white camp pajamas. On the floor I found her nurse's uniform, along with Georg's white hospital shirt. The shirt was covered with bloodstains, for Georg had bled from the nose. Glad to have something to do, I took the clothes down to the stream to wash them.

Kneeling on a little footbridge over the water, I scrubbed the shirt and the dress; but I could not get them clean. Then I thought, "You'll never be able to wear the shirt anyhow. It will always remind you of Georg's death." I decided to throw the things away. Then I felt someone place a hand on my arm. It was Dr. Kushner, who apparently had been watching me for some time. He shook his head and said, "You shouldn't throw the clothes away!"

He seemed to have read my thoughts. Then he said, "I had a dream last night. If you like, I'll tell you about it."

We sat beside the river as he told me his dream. "A helicopter came and circled over our camp. It was flying very low. The pilot must have realized that this was a prison camp. In the dream, I thought to myself, 'Hey man, you're taking a big risk flying that low,' and then I heard the guards shooting at him. The helicopter was so close that I could see the pilot in the cockpit. I saw his face quite clearly. He was smiling at me, as if he were saying, 'Wait a minute, I'll be right down.' But then the smile disappeared. The guards had hit him. The helicopter crashed right in front of the indoctrination hut. The fuselage exploded. Then a bunch of bulky packages fell out—packages of American C-rations. Suddenly hundreds of packages were lying all over the ground."

I looked at the doctor in bewilderment. I did not see the moral of his story. Dr. Kushner smiled sadly.

"Some of the boxes had burst open, and I could see the wonderful things inside—the canned goods, the chocolate bars, the cigarettes. I sprang at them like a savage. Gathering up an armful of packages, I carried them into my hut and then ran out to get more. The helicopter pilot was lying somewhere in the wreckage. He may not have been dead yet; perhaps there was still time for me to save him. I'm a doctor. It was my duty to try to help him. But all I could think about was getting the packages to a safe place, and getting as many as I could before the others noticed them too. . . ."

I still did not understand what he was trying to tell me. He asked, "How long has it been since you were captured?"

It had been eleven weeks.

"After two years of captivity, you will understand the dream," he said. "Perhaps after only one year." Pointing to my friends' clothing, he went on, "I know that these things belonged to

113

people who are dead. But keep them anyhow. Nowhere else in the jungle could you find such a good shirt. One day you'll be happy to have it. You'll wear it without the slightest qualm. It's sad, but one day you'll think only about yourself. No one else, only yourself. While a helicopter pilot is bleeding to death, you will run to pick up a chocolate bar. That's what captivity is all about. In the end, the only thing that matters is staying alive."

I often remembered Dr. Kushner's dream. It told an ugly truth—but a truth all the same.

Coming back from the stream just two hours after burying Rika, I thought, "You want to live. They are dead. There's nothing you can do about that now. It is reality. You must accept it and think no more about it. Try to forget it. *The only thing that matters is staying alive.*"

I did want to live. Now that I saw how alone I was, I wanted to live more than ever. I hung the clothes in front of our hut to dry in the sunshine. For the rest of my captivity, I wore Georg's shirt. Almost four years later, the dark stains had not yet disappeared.

I sat outside on the tree stump. I had sat here after hearing the news of Marie-Luise's death, and after the death of Georg. I was afraid to go into the hut and look at the three empty places. There was no telling how long Monika would survive. Everyone had expected her to die before the others. Now she and I were the only ones left.

Soon it was time for supper. Willis brought me a tin plate containing two portions of manioc and rice and set it down on the tree stump. In addition, there were two tablespoons of bouillon in a small plastic bowl. It was 4:30. At least in the kitchen, everything was business as usual.

I choked down my food and part of Monika's, too. After all, she never ate anything any more. Then I took the rest into the hut, where Monika lay huddled in the corner with her face turned to the wall. She had been lying there for seven weeks.

Then I noticed that my black camp pajamas were not lying

114

in their usual place. I had been alternating wearing the pajamas and my hospital uniform; thus I could wash one outfit while wearing the other. I always used the clean clothing as a pillow. But now my pillow was missing. Then I saw that Monika was wearing the black pajamas. Some time in the last few hours, she must have got up and changed into my clothes.

I do not know exactly what came over me. I lost control of myself and grabbed Monika, screaming insanely over and over, "Who gave you permission to wear my clothes? Who told you you could do that? Those are *my* clothes!"

Grabbing her hand, I pulled her to a sitting position. She sat there staring at me, deep circles under the eyes in her swollen face. Then she murmured something. It was the first time in weeks that she had made any sense: "They laid out the clothes for me. Someone told me to put them on. . . . They told me to put on fresh clothes, otherwise they wouldn't take me in the VW. . . . The VW has clean seat covers." She began to cry.

I could think of only one thing: She was wearing *my* clothes. She must have put them on while we were burying Rika. She had put on *my* clothes, rolling up her own filthy rags and leaving them in place of my pajamas. "If you think you can just dump your dirty clothes here, you're sadly mistaken." Then I went on yelling, "Those are *my* clothes!"

She burst into tears again. She wanted to lie down, but I held her arm and shouted, "I've had enough! Now listen! There were five of us when we were captured. Three of us are already done for. You'll be next if you go on this way. You can go ahead and die for all I care, but not me, I want to live! Even if I have to walk on corpses to do it." I was beside myself with rage. "I want to get out of here! I want to stay alive. I want to get out of here, and you're coming with me! You're coming with me, do you understand? You're coming home with me. No matter how long it takes, we're going home together. Do you understand?"

"Yes."

Had she actually said yes? "Did you really understand what I said? Starting tomorrow morning, I'm going to get you out of bed every day. Then we'll walk. You'll do exercises, and every hour you'll exercise some more until you're on your feet again! Starting tomorrow morning, that's what we're going to do. And you'll do exactly what I tell you. Right now, you're going to eat!"

I fed her the cold rice, one spoonful, then two, then three. For the first time, she did not vomit it up. This was the evening of July 17, the day of Rika's death. On the following morning, I got Monika out of bed as I had promised. Dr. Kushner, who was standing by watching, shook his head and said, "Careful, Bernhard. Are you trying to kill her?"

But I was obsessed with the idea of getting Monika to walk.

Left Foot, Right Foot

MONIKA SCHWINN

"Why is he yelling at me that way?" I wondered. "What does he want from me? Why does he make me keep on walking? I want to sleep, but he won't let me. Why does he keep nagging me that way? Why does he tell me to get up and move around, to go and sit in the sun? I'm so tired. I want to sleep. . . .

"Why does Rika keep calling Georg? Bernhard is calling him, too. Why is Rika taking the cross down from the wall? She hardly has the strength, she has to prop herself up with one hand to keep from falling down. Where did she get the cross from, what's she doing with it?

"They're calling someone again. Why don't they let me sleep? Why are they all yelling so? Why are they running around? I can hear hundreds of feet outside. What are they doing with Georg, why are they carrying him out; are they going to give him another bath?

"I'd like to have a bath and then go to sleep.

"Rika is lying beside me. She can't breathe. There's a rattling sound in her throat. I must help her. . . . Who is this, whose is this strange face bending over me? . . . The Vietnamese nurse . . . She'll never finish unpacking!

"Quiet at last. How beautifully quiet it is. I can sleep at last."

"Why are you wearing my clothes?"

117

"I can hear him perfectly well, why is Bernhard shouting so? His voice echoes as if we were in a huge hall."

"Left foot. Left foot forward. The left one, I said! And now the right, the right one, yes, that's it, hold on to me."

"I can't take another step. I'm tired. My feet hurt."

"Now the left again! The left one, I said! My God, what a fuss you're making!"

"Everything's going black. Everything keeps going black. I can't go on."

"Yes, you can. Wait! Here, take this stick! Now keep going!"

"I'd like to lie down again."

"Now try to stand up by yourself. I'm letting go of you."

"I can't stand up by myself. What's he saying? Who is that?"

"That's Little John."

"Who is Little John?"

"He's an American. He'll cut your hair, he'll give you a splendid haircut if you do what I tell you."

"What's he saying? I can't understand what he's saying."

"He says that you'll never get better! He says that they've already asked the commandant whether I can move in with them when I'm left all alone. Do you want me to be left all alone? Do you want to desert me? Or will you do what I tell you? Keep going now."

"Let me rest, just a little while."

"Once more. Left foot, right foot. You're doing just beautifully. Now you can rest. Sit down here. You'll get some sunshine here. This is where I usually sit."

"Where am I? What's that over there?"

"That's our hut. This is a tree stump. And I built the bench you're sitting on; I did it all myself."

"Everything looks black. The tree is all black."

"It's green!"

"It's black, and it's getting blacker. . . . Everything's getting black. . . ."

Practice Runs

BERNHARD DIEHL

The Americans watched us exercise every day. Now they all came running up, Dr. Kushner in the lead. This morning, Monika had stood alone for the first time and taken her first halting steps. Then she collapsed onto the bench. Dr. Kushner helped me carry her into the hut. Later he took me aside and warned me again not to push her too hard. "This is pretty drastic treatment for someone who's ill, you know. Don't be so impatient. You must go slowly. Keep in mind that if the strain is too much for her, you'll be responsible for her death."

This last remark brought me to my senses. I began to examine my motives. Was I trying to help Monika or myself? Was I really concerned with saving her life, or was I simply afraid to be left alone? I could not be sure.

After allowing Monika two days of rest, I cautiously resumed our exercise program. She was not strong enough to lift her legs from the ground. Thus at first she took tiny steps no more than two inches long. She had to learn to walk all over again.

Walking with these tiny steps, Monika managed to travel more than three yards; but then she was exhausted and moaned that she could not go on. She begged to be allowed to lie down. I rescheduled our sessions so that we exercised more frequently, but for shorter intervals—three times in the morning, twice in the afternoon. By the end of July, two weeks after

119

Rika's death, Monika was able, with my support, to walk more than ten yards forward and ten back.

Then we began to do simple gymnastics, moving our arms in circles and rolling our necks on our shoulders. Around the beginning of August, I told Monika that we were now ready to try our first deep knee bends. I stood directly behind her, holding her under the arms. Then I said, "All right, bend your knees."

I kept my hands under her shoulders but let her support her own weight. When she tried to bend slowly, she started to fall. I caught her, but I barely had the strength to raise her to her feet again. Standing there in her white pajamas, she said, "Oh God, oh God, I'll never get any better."

That afternoon we tried again. This time I gave her a stick, holding on to it myself so that it would support her weight. She managed to do two deep knee bends. I felt very proud and happy.

After a few more days of practice, she managed three deep knee bends. Moreover, she walked more than twenty yards holding on to the stick with her left hand while I supported her on the right. Gradually Monika was beginning to understand what was going on. For moments at a time, she would look at me, know who I was, and understand what we were doing. Then she would sink back into her twilight world.

Sometimes she would make progress and then suffer a relapse. "We're not really getting anywhere," she said. "I can't walk by myself, and I cheat doing the knee bends: you always have to lift me up again." I answered, "No, you do them by yourself. I just hold you so that you don't lose your balance." My words must have cheered her up, for the next day, when I was sitting on the tree stump, she came out of the hut all by herself. I could hardly believe my eyes. She stood in the doorway holding the stick, then climbed down the stairs and walked three or four yards. She was taking steps eight inches in length! Then she fell down and promptly burst into tears because she had fallen again.

After that she got better every day. We added exercises to

120

our repertoire. To stretch her lower back and strengthen her spine, Monika practiced hanging from one of the crossbeams in the ceiling. I sometimes massaged her calves and thighs, for her muscles, unaccustomed to exercise, were stiff and painful.

One day in the middle of August, I went into the jungle to fetch wood for the kitchen. After returning and delivering the wood, I headed back toward our hut. There I found Monika holding on to the doorjamb and weeping like a child. Tears were streaming down her face. I ran over to help her. When I reached her, she said, "It's happened at last! I went alone to the latrine. Just imagine that, all the way there and back." The latrine was about twenty-five yards away. I realized that once she had reached it, she must have crouched down and stood up again without any help. She had a right to weep.

After her magnificent achievement, Monika was completely worn out. I asked no more of her that day.

By the end of August, she could walk all by herself. We had practiced walking up a gentle slope. One day she left the hut alone, climbed over the little hill, and walked down to the stream. Since her arrival in the camp on May 26, this was the first time that she had been able to wash herself.

One thing struck me as strange. Monika had never asked about Rika and Georg; and I, in turn, had never dared to mention them. We both feared the inevitable moment when I would have to tell her what had happened. I resolved to tell her only the bare essentials. One beautiful autumn evening, we were sitting outside watching the sun go down. Suddenly Monika said, "Tell me about it now. What happened to the others?" I answered, "The others are dead."

A Jungle Flower

MONIKA SCHWINN

We sat outside until quite late. One of the guards came over with his rifle and told us to get into the hut and go to sleep; but we went on sitting there long after sunset.

I felt very weak, but the guards and their rifles could no longer frighten me. My illness had affected my vision. I could see clearly only out of the corner of my eye. For weeks Bernhard's voice had sounded very loud. Now all sounds were muffled, as if I had cotton wadding in my ears. When I choked down my rice at mealtime, nothing had any taste. And, strangest of all, I could not clearly distinguish between reality and dream. I was not even certain whether Bernhard and I were really sitting outside on the bench.

Seeing a blue coat draped around my shoulders, I felt confused. Where had the coat come from? I asked Bernhard about it.

"It belongs to Lin Quy."

"Who is Lin Quy?" I was sure that I had never heard the name before.

Bernhard pointed to one of the huts. "Captain Lin Quy, a captive South Vietnamese officer. We spent our first few days in the camp in his hut. When the nights began to get cold, he gave you his coat."

122

"What about these bandages on my arms?"

The bandages looked very old; they were dirty and stiff with dried pus. Bernhard had already told me that we could not get fresh ones.

"The *y si* gave you injections, vitamin B_1 and glucose, I think. He doesn't set much store by cleanliness. He uses the same needle for all his injections."

I looked around. "Is there really a Vietnamese nurse here?"

He gave me a strange look. "Oh, you and your Vietnamese nurse! You went on and on about her. And the VW business, what was that all about?" He looked at me again. "Say, how much do you really remember?"

How much *did* I really remember? I remembered quite clearly the way my friends had stared down at my shoes—Marie-Luise's red linen shoes—as if they were trying to blame me for her death. After that, only fragments, a scrap here and there . . . Rika calling to Georg . . . the cross woven from straw that she took down from the wall . . . all the voices and the sound of running feet . . . I made a mental note to ask Bernhard about all these things.

It had got dark. A few stars had come out. I found the Big and Little Dippers and other familiar constellations. "Well," I thought, "at least the sky is still the same."

Suddenly I heard a sound nearby. I could not believe my ears: it sounded like a hiss. Then I heard it again, the hissing of a giant cat. I was terrified, for I thought that I was still confusing reality and dream.

Everyone in the camp began to wake up. Guards came running out of their huts. I heard cries and saw the beams of flashlights. Then the men began running along from tree to tree, shining their flashlights into the foliage and beating the branches with sticks. A single shot rang out. Then it grew still. I looked at Bernhard. He saw what was frightening me.

"No, no," he said, "you really heard it. It must have been some kind of wildcat. I've heard that there are tigers and black panthers in this area. It must have been something like that."

"You heard the hissing too?"

"Of course I heard it too. In fact I heard it yesterday. The animal must have come here last night and been prowling around the camp ever since. We'd better go into the hut."

"No, wait." I remembered a sentence I had read somewhere: "The tiger comes three times before he strikes." It was the sort of line that sticks in your mind even when you are not certain whether it is true. Then I remembered something else I had read: wild animals dig up dead bodies when they are hungry. For weeks I had huddled inside my little snail's shell, afraid to ask Bernhard the truth. Now the time had come. I asked him, "What happened to the others? Where are they buried?"

Bernhard pointed into the jungle. "The graves aren't far from the camp. I'll take you there tomorrow."

I gathered all my courage. "Who buried them? The Vietnamese?"

"No, the Americans."

He spoke curtly. Trying to reassure him, I said, "Don't be afraid to tell me. Did they have a coffin?" I was still thinking about the wildcat, wondering whether the bodies were protected.

Bernhard told me that right after Georg and Rika died, Dr. Kushner and the other American prisoners went into the jungle to cut bamboo. The Vietnamese split the bamboo with their machetes, forming boards a foot across, and used the boards to build a coffin. Then, perhaps to console me, perhaps merely to fill up the silence, Bernhard said: "You know, it was terrible for them to die that way. And yet, it seems to me that our whole lives are just a sort of imprisonment. We're always surrounded by fences, we're always shut in, we can't get out. Or perhaps there is *one* way to get out. Barbed wire cannot reach as high as Heaven. . . ."

The next day I went to visit the graves. I still walked with a cane, but every day it was growing easier. I went alone. I had asked Bernhard to show me the way.

It was easy to find the graves, for the grass had not yet

grown over them. There was no cross and no flowers, nothing but the two small bare patches in the middle of the jungle. After the next rainfall, they, too, would disappear.

After that, I often returned to visit the graves, always staying for a long time. The night after Bernhard and I had heard the wildcat, I heard the hissing sound again; and again the guards went from tree to tree, hunting with flashlights and sticks. I was afraid that the cat might return. The first thing each morning, I went to the graves to make sure that they had not been disturbed. I checked them again before going to sleep. From time to time I picked a bit of greenery and put it in an empty fish can between the graves.

I could not find any flowers for the graves. It seemed strange that there was not a single flower anywhere. One day, hoping to find flowers or some especially beautiful plant, I began to walk deeper and deeper into the jungle. No one bothered to follow me to see where I was going. Weak as I was, they must have thought that I would be unable to walk very far.

Suddenly I came to a road. It was a real road, wide enough for a jeep and covered with ruts dug by countless tires. Walking along the road, I came to the curve where I had seen the Volkswagen in my dream! "How can that be?" I thought. "I've never been here before." And then it occurred to me that I could run away.

I was already a long distance from the camp. I could hear no sound but the monkeys leaping around in the trees. The guards knew that I always spent a long time at the graves. It would be hours before anyone came to look for me. But how long could I keep walking? Where did the road lead, and which direction should I go? "If they catch you," I thought, "they'll shoot you for attempting to escape."

I remembered what Bernhard had said about everything's being a prison. "No," I thought, "you can't run away, at least not physically. But they can't lock up your thoughts; they can't keep you from being free inside." I decided to go back to the camp.

• • •

When I was able to walk again, I was told that during the noon hour, I might go down to the stream to wash up. At that hour, the Vietnamese usually took a siesta and the Americans were not allowed out of their huts. I followed this suggestion.

The Americans were always decent and treated us kindly. When my friends and I were ill, they even washed our clothing for us, swept our hut, and brought us food. Once I was washing up at the stream, feeling too weak to hurry, when some of the Americans came to fetch water. To avoid disturbing me or making me feel embarrassed, they all stayed at the top of the hill until I was finished. Even under prison conditions, they remained thoughtful and considerate.

However, at no time did the Vietnamese show any consideration for my feelings. They never made sexual advances to me, but neither did they respect my privacy. If they saw that I was partially undressed, they used to stand there and watch me or even come closer.

One day I was given a flower for the two graves. I was to receive two flowers during my captivity. The first was an orchid, signifying death. The second, a rose, meant freedom.

I remember exactly what day it was: September 16, my birthday, my first birthday as a prisoner. Bernhard and I had learned that in two days we were going to be transferred to another camp. We hoped that conditions in the next camp would be better, but we feared they might be worse. In Camp I, the interpreter Tat had raved about the American camp, where prisoners were allowed to drink whiskey and watch films; yet we had found it a place of horror. What reason was there to hope that conditions in the new camp would be any better? Moreover, Dr. Kushner and the others told us that several prisoners had actually been released from the American camp; they advised us to do everything we could to stay there. Unfortunately, our jailers did not consult our wishes.

The guerrillas had a good reason for wishing to transfer all the prisoners. Early in September, American helicopters had begun to fly over the camp. Moreover, day and night we heard bombs detonating all around us; we could even hear guns being fired from low-flying planes. The American prisoners used to take cover in a dugout inside their compound. Bernhard and I had no dugout. When planes flew overhead, we had to sit inside our hut, hoping for the best.

The Americans believed that the entire camp was going to be evacuated. Dr. Kushner brought me some torn clothing which he and the others wanted me to mend before we left.

Planes continued to bomb the area. The shooting raged day and night. Bernhard could tell the difference between the swift, rattling fire of the American machine guns and the slower fire of the Chinese guns. The fighting was so close to the camp that the guards had grown very anxious. On the 17th, the day after my birthday, Huong came to tell us to get ready. We would be leaving tomorrow.

Huong had not told the Americans when they were to be transferred. That evening Dr. Kushner came to fetch the clothes I had been mending. He even took the ones I had not finished. The doctor told us that sometimes prisoners were moved in the middle of the night. He wanted to make sure that he got back his things before we left; for if we simply left the clothing in our hut, the guards would immediately steal it. Then Dr. Kushner said good-by. "Good luck. I'm sure I'll see you again." He was right: this was not our last meeting.

Bernhard and I had been given a straw basket in which to carry our things. As we packed, I saw how much we had accumulated and began to feel quite wealthy. There were the rice-sack blankets, a tin plate, a towel, Georg's hospital shirt and trousers, and Rika's uniform. I did not take Captain Lin Quy's blue coat, which was worn to shreds. We also threw away Marie-Luise's red shoes, which had fallen apart on my journey through the wet jungle. I was now wearing Georg's gym shoes, and Bernhard wore his formerly white tennis shoes, which were almost worn out. In addition to our other treasures, we had Marie-Luise's green pocketbook and her straw hat.

We had not been told where we were going or how long it

would take us to get there. I feared what lay ahead. And I knew that I would never be able to visit the graves again.

Two days before we left, as I have said, my birthday arrived. I had expected Bernhard to remember the day, but he forgot. Feeling sad, I did not bother to remind him. I thought about all the lovely birthdays I had spent in the past. In Lebach, we celebrate "Green Week" in September—a whole week of holidays. My birthday always fell sometime in this week. The holidays began with a horse race on Sunday; on Monday there were other sports events; on Tuesday came the great fair, which has been held in our area for centuries. Wednesday was the soldiers' day, with lots of parachute jumping. Thursday was fashion day; Friday was for politicians; and on Saturday there was a variety show. On Sunday the holiday concluded with riding tournaments and a huge fireworks display. Sometimes my birthday would fall on the second Sunday, so that I could pretend that the fireworks were being set off in my honor. My birthday had always seemed very special. Now for the first time there was no celebration.

Suddenly Captain Lin Quy appeared, holding a flower. He had been in the jungle gathering wood and was now returning with a load on his back. In his hand was a brilliant orange orchid, and he gave it to me. I had received a birthday present after all.

When the captain passed our hut on his way into the jungle, he used to say, "Good morning." Aside from that, he and I had never spoken. He did not know that it was my birthday. It was sheer chance that he happened to find the orange orchid on that day.

Taking the flower, I went for the last time to visit the two graves. I filled the empty can with fresh water and put the flower inside.

Later, someone told me that this species of orchid stays fresh for a long time. . . .

Christmas Presents

MONIKA SCHWINN

The camp lay high in the mountains. To reach it, we had to climb eighty-seven stairs that had been hewn out of the rock. The stairs were reinforced with wooden beams, the halves of tree trunks. I know that there were exactly eighty-seven stairs, for each one seemed an almost insurmountable hurdle.

When we arrived at the camp, it was nearly evening. We were assigned one of two huts that were surrounded by a bamboo fence. The fence was a solid wall of sharp stakes about twelve feet high which had been driven deep into the earth. I had counted the stairs; I counted the stakes as well. There were 1,569. I used to walk along inside the fence, running my fingers over the stakes and making a special mark on every tenth one. I had different marks for every hundredth stake and for every five hundredth. A special sign marked the single stake numbered one thousand. During the six months we were in this camp, I counted the stakes dozens of times. Running my fingers over the rounded wood, I walked around the same circle for hours on end. In Greece I had seen donkeys, their eyes covered, being driven around in a circle to pump water. Now I felt like one of those donkeys. Anyone who had watched me counting the stakes would have thought me mad. In a sense, perhaps I was a little mad. There was not much else to do in the camp but walk in circles.

It took us two and a half days to travel from the American camp to the mountain camp. We traveled uphill all the way. When we reached our destination, we were well over three thousand feet above sea level. Bernhard said that this was the best altitude for rest and relaxation. Sometimes he had a strange sense of humor.

The mountain camp was, in fact, a sort of rest camp for North Vietnamese soldiers—especially wounded soldiers—returning from the front. Bernhard and I were the only prisoners, and no one paid much attention to us. There were no camp regulations. We could do whatever we liked inside our hut behind the bamboo fence—a damp, dark, cold, and cellarlike place, half of it underground. There were two bunks, with a hearth between them where we could build a fire.

The open hearth on the bare earth was the most important thing in our lives. It was the end of September, and winter was coming on. In Vietnam, winter is the rainy season. After our arrival in the camp, the first thing we did was to cut and gather wood and stack it up inside our hut. Some days it was bitter cold. Apart from the rice-sack blankets, we had nothing to keep us warm but our thin camp pajamas and our hospital uniforms. From December on, we kept the fire burning all night. Every two hours, one of us got up to put more wood on the fire. We would gladly have spent all our time sitting beside the fire; but the food here was much worse than in the American camp, and we were too weak to sit up for more than two hours.

During the day, the hut was even colder than at night, for we were not permitted to keep the fire burning in the daytime. The smoke coming from the roof would have been visible to American planes. Twice when it was especially cold, we kept the fire burning after sunrise. Soon the Vietnamese came dashing in. Not saying a word, they beat out the fire with sticks and scattered the coals. Even this high in the mountains, the guerrillas feared the American planes. Bernhard and I had to dig our own bomb shelter. Its entrance lay inside our hut.

When we had done something wrong, the guards here did not shout, threaten, or punish us. The cold, rain, and solitude of the

130

mountain camp affected us all, creating a common bond between prisoners and guards. The guerrillas did not give us
enough to eat, but they themselves often went hungry. They
did not treat us with hatred and indifference, as had our jailers
in the other camps. Later Bernhard and I worked in the kitchen,
helping the guards pound the rice and separate it from the husks.
We also swept the yard between the huts and cleared away
foliage and branches torn down by the wind and rain.

It continued to grow colder. Sometimes it rained for two
weeks without pause. Then there would be a couple of clear
days, followed by more rain. We hardly dared to step outside
the hut. No one told us what they planned to do with us.
We had been forgotten by the world.

Christmas arrived. On Christmas Eve it was icy cold, but
at least it had stopped raining. For days now the camp had
been almost deserted. One after another, the Vietnamese had
disappeared. Only the commandant and the cook stayed behind
with us.

On the morning of December 24, Bernhard went into the
jungle and dragged heaps of palm branches and ferns to the
camp. He decorated the gate in the bamboo fence and stuck
palm branches in the ground before our hut. In the middle of
the hut was a post supporting the roof. Bernhard covered it
with greenery so that it looked like a Christmas tree. I said
to myself, "Perhaps you can find a real tree, a small one."

I did not find a tree, but I found something else. At the
edge of the camp was a hollow tree trunk filled with water.
The water came from a distant mountain spring. Bamboo pipes
conducted it to the camp and into the tree trunk. At the edge
of the trunk I saw a comb and a piece of mirror. I was certain
that their owner did not intend to come back for them, for they
were not worth keeping. There was only a small piece of the
mirror left, and some of the teeth were missing from the comb.
But to me they seemed like the most wonderful Christmas gift
in the world.

Only Marie-Luise had brought a comb along on our Sunday
outing. Hers was the comb that had frightened the Vietnamese

131

who first examined our belongings. She had lost it somewhere on our eleven-day trek through the jungle. During our captivity, we always had to wear the same clothing, and we were never able to wash properly, comb our hair, or look into a mirror. The feeling of being dirty and unkempt was one of the worst things about our life in the camps. Now, seeing the shard of mirror, I understood why Marie-Luise had been so concerned about her appearance. Suddenly I felt afraid. What would I see if I looked into the mirror?

Since our arrival at the mountain camp three months before, we had not changed our clothing. Because of the cold we had to wear everything we owned. Our clothes grew damp and clammy in the humid mountain air, and they got wet when we ran through the rain to the kitchen to fetch our food. The bandages on my arms were now four months old. No, I would not be a pretty sight.

Personal hygiene was out of the question. To trim our fingernails, we simply bit them off. We let our toenails grow until they were long enough to tear off. We cleaned our teeth with "toothpicks"—tiny splinters of bamboo—and rinsed them with tea. Worst of all, I was a woman and suffered from the recurrent problem of menstruation, a nightmare under these curcumstances. I was grateful whenever I managed to find a few scraps of paper to keep myself clean or when I sometimes ceased to menstruate for months on end.

Something else made me afraid to look in the mirror—my hair. It is humiliating for a woman to lose her hair. Almost all of mine had fallen out. A narrow fringe of hair still grew around the bald spot in the middle. I could feel a thin fluff growing in on top. The loss of my hair made me very unhappy. I kept thinking how repellent I must be to the others—a young woman who was almost bald. I always felt ashamed when Bernhard or the guerrillas looked at me; I even felt ashamed when I was alone. At night I used to lie awake thinking, "Oh, what will happen if you're suddenly released and have to go home all bald?" The sense of shame tormented me day and night. Just that morning Bernhard had said, "What do you think, shall we fix ourselves up a bit for this evening?" I wondered whether I could manage to make curlers out of little bamboo sticks, so that I could roll up my hair. Now that I had a comb, I might be able to fluff out the thin wisps of hair to make them look fuller.

Finally I gathered all my courage and looked at myself in the mirror. At once I wished that I had not. I saw an inhuman-looking swollen face with two slits of eyes. The corners of my mouth were cut and sore, my eyebrows pale and sparse. Even my hair looked worse than I had imagined: shiny skin showed through the thin fluff on top. I had found the mirror I had longed for. But what I saw depressed me so much that I threw away the shard of mirror as if it were burning my hand. Standing there, I started to cry.

Then I returned to the hut and crept into my bed. "That thing in the mirror is you," I thought. I could have killed myself that day. . . .

That evening Bernhard and I sat beside the fire as we always did. Violating our former camp regulations, we talked about home. That depressed us more than ever. We also talked about Marie-Luise, Georg, and Rika.

Bernhard was in possession of a small missal in English. Its American owner had died in the other camp. The Americans had given it to Bernhard when he returned Willis's Bible. Bernhard translated the Christmas Gospel for me. We prayed for our three dead friends and sang Christmas carols. It was our first Christmas in the camps, and we felt very close.

We went to bed early. When we felt cold, we got up to re-build the fire. I had washed the comb I had found and given it to Bernhard as a Christmas present. Surprised and pleased, he said that now all he needed was a mirror. I did not tell him that, somewhere outside, a piece of mirror was lying on the ground.

The next day was the 25th, Christmas Day. The cook ordered me to kill a chicken, but I could not bring myself to do it. Finally he killed it himself, leaving me to pluck and draw it.

133

I was looking forward to the fine Christmas dinner we would have. But at noon, Bernhard and I were given our usual portion of manioc with a bit of rice and bouillon. So they had wanted me to kill the chicken for them, not for us!

Bernhard consoled me with the thought that we might be given a better meal that evening. The afternoon passed slowly. Finally we went to fetch our supper. This time we received a large portion of rice with a few scraps of leftover chicken. It was already dark when we finished. Bernhard went to the kitchen, holding our empty dishes in one hand and a burning bamboo torch in the other. Half an hour passed, and still he did not return. I went outside and began counting the stakes in the bamboo fence. Finally Bernhard approached with an oil lamp, carrying a package under his arm.

He had brought powdered coffee for two, fresh water to boil over the fire, a box of cigarettes, and a small paper bag containing candy and four pieces of sugar. These were royal Christmas gifts indeed!

We boiled the water for our coffee and sweetened it with sugar. Each of us smoked a cigarette. Then we went to bed, shivering with cold. We had to keep getting up to lay more wood on the fire. From time to time we heard Clothilde, our house rat, scurrying around. Bernhard had built a small wooden box and hung it from the roof, high above the floor of the hut. We kept our "valuables" here: the towel, a small piece of soap, Bernhard's missal. We put the candy and the two pieces of sugar in the box, but in the morning we saw that Clothilde had managed to gnaw through the bars. The sugar was gone. Well, after all, it was Christmas. She deserved a present, too. . . .

Concerning Diverse Beasts

MONIKA SCHWINN

I have always been afraid of rats and snakes. A stream used to flow behind my house in Lebach. As a child, I often saw rats swimming by with their heads held just above the water. The sight filled me with horror. But in the mountain camp I slept for months eye to eye with a rat: the head of my bed was her favorite place to sleep.

The rat had been living in our hut for some time before we arrived, and she refused to be driven away. We might have been able to capture and kill her, but it never occurred to us to try. She was a living creature like us and shared our captivity. I named her Clothilde, after a teacher who had the same kind of bright button eyes.

After a while, the rat seemed to be quite comfortable living with us. She spent most of the day in the bomb shelter we had dug on one side of the hut. As soon as we lit the fire at night, she came out into our room and behaved as if she owned it. Scurrying around, she would dash up the center pole uttering high, piercing squeaks. While we were sleeping, she stole whatever she could get, sugar or bananas. She never touched our rice, and perhaps it was this that sealed our friendship! I never completely overcame my fear of rats. It disturbed me a little that Clothilde chose to sleep right next to my head. In the morning I always knew when she had been there, for she left

135

telltale traces at the head of the bed. On the other hand, it was fortunate that I met Clothilde and got used to having rats around, for there were rats in all the camps in North Vietnam.

During our four years in the camps, animals played an important role in our lives. Some tormented us and drove us to distraction; others helped us endure our captivity.

Everywhere we went, we encountered insects. The mosquitoes never took a holiday from biting us. Every day in Camp Bao Cao, I watched a parade of large red ants enter beneath the cell door and climb up the bedpost. For some time I could not rid myself of the feeling that a thousand ants were crawling over my body. Camp K77 was infested with bedbugs. One morning I counted them as I shook them out of my mosquito netting: there were sixty-five. In other camps there were spiders with bodies the size of half dollars. The only tree in the yard adjoining my cell in Camp K77 housed hundreds of stinkbugs. The whole yard was filled with their stench. Moreover, they always chose to drop from the tree at the precise moment that I was sitting down in the shade.

The worst of all the vermin were the leeches. We encountered them only where it was especially damp. On our way from the American camp to the mountain camp, we passed through a very damp region. In no time, ten or fifteen leeches were clinging to our hands and legs. They climbed into our shoes and squeezed between our toes. Not knowing the proper method of removing them, we simply pulled them off, leaving large wounds that went on bleeding for a long time. But this was nothing compared to what we suffered on our trek to North Vietnam.

Before leaving for the North, we were warned about the leeches and given a small bag of salt; but no one told us how to use it. The bag was not much larger than a ping-pong ball, and the salt inside was wrapped in several layers of cloth. On our journey, Bernhard and I continued to pull off the leeches, dabbing the wounds with salt. It hurt so much that I almost jumped out of my skin. Our legs were covered with scratches and leech bites that had become badly infected. It was agony to put salt on the open wounds. The pain used to sting me to tears. One day I swore that I would never again put salt on my legs.

We kept walking, blood streaming from our bleeding feet. Bernhard wore close-fitting shoes, and from time to time he had to take them off and pour out the blood. At that time, we were traveling through a region teeming with leeches. I was losing so much blood that I felt very dizzy.

Irony of ironies, Bernhard one day came to me and said that he now knew what we should have been doing with the salt. We were supposed to dampen the bag and nudge the leech with it. Soon the creature would stop sucking and drop off without leaving a bleeding wound. Unfortunately, by the time we learned this technique, our journey was almost over. . . .

In the American camp, I had been afraid of the wildcats. Later, I learned to fear elephants and crocodiles. I never actually saw the elephants but only heard them trumpeting in the distance, sounding like deep-toned horns. The sound reminded me of a story an American officer had told me in An Hoa. After making a parachute landing in the jungle, a squad of twelve Special Forces troops began sending radio messages back to their base. They said that they were under attack and requested that a helicopter be sent to evacuate them. They had been attacked not by the Viet Cong, but by a herd of elephants, which succeeded in wounding two of them!

On our trek to North Vietnam, we encountered crocodiles. An eleven-year-old boy was traveling with us. He had lost his parents in the South and was going north to join a relative, whose name and address were written on a card he wore around his neck. The boy always seemed a little frightened and never strayed far from our group. One day, on a path high in the mountains, we passed a troop of Montagnards, or hill tribesmen, coming from the opposite direction. They were returning from a hunt with their bows and arrows. Their game pouches were slung around their shoulders. One of them was carrying a gray package tightly bound with cords. As soon as the boy caught sight of it, he screamed and started running back the

137

way we had come. All the men laughed: the "package" was a young crocodile whose head and tail had been tied together. To carry it, the hunter had only to slip his fingers under the cords.

Young crocodiles were among the favorite game of the Montagnards. In the evening we used to watch them roast and eat the crocodiles. They also ate roasted snakes, birds, and monkeys.

Full-grown crocodiles often measured more than six feet in length. The young crocodiles were considerably smaller. Hunters did not shoot them with arrows, but captured them alive. In the mountains where we met the hunters, there was a large crocodile population. One day we were passing a shallow pond. It was a very hot day. "How nice," I thought. "You can wade along in the water." At the edge of the pond I saw two cone-shaped baskets. Curious to know what they were, I came closer and almost prodded one of them with my foot; but for some reason I thought better of it. When we camped for the night, I asked the guards about the curious baskets. One guard looked at me quizzically and explained that the baskets were traps used to snare crocodiles. And I had almost gone wading in the pond with nothing on my feet but a pair of flimsy Ho Chi Minh sandals!

Some animals helped us to while away the dreary hours. I sometimes watched the monkeys for hours on end. We also saw many birds and snakes. One snake had made a home of the mountain camp. In September it had a bright red head. As the weather grew colder, its head became brown and then gray. By the time we left the camp, it was beginning to turn red again.

In Camp K77 I often saw lizards hopping among the flag-stones in the yard outside my cell. A gray-and-black-spotted snake lived in the same yard. It spent its days rolled up in a tranquil coil. Sometimes the American prisoner in the cell next to mine used to whistle a tune from *My Fair Lady*. When he began to whistle, the snake often raised its head a little, almost as if it could hear the song.

The soldiers in Camp K77 knew that I liked animals. They

138

used to bring me dogs to wash and sometimes let a chicken and a hare run around in my yard. I was fondest of the birds and managed to get many of them to trust me. Sometimes as many as fifteen birds would be in my yard at once. They were so tame that they used to come and perch on my hand. When the guards noticed what was going on, they would shoot in the air to frighten the birds and upset me; but the birds always came back later.

My closest animal friend was Méo, my cat; but he deserves a chapter all his own. Besides Clothilde and Méo, we named only one of our "pets": Amanda. We met Amanda in the mountain camp. For a long time I was not certain whether the animal was a pig or a dog. Bernhard suggested that she might be some sort of hybrid—a cross between a pig and a dog.

In appearance, Amanda resembled a thin, starving pig. But she behaved like a dog, jumping up on her hind legs. Unlike a pig, she never gained any weight and was constantly in motion. She also fetched sticks for us and came when she was called. I have never seen an animal as good-tempered as she was.

There were two "ordinary" pigs in the mountain camp. They had their own hut and a pen to run in and were fed twice a day with leavings from the kitchen. Amanda was allowed to run around free. During the day she wandered into the jungle, but she always came back. At night she used to sleep in front of our hut like a watchdog. She followed me around wherever I went, frisking at my feet, kicking her hind legs in the air, and begging to fetch a stick.

I grew very attached to Amanda. When we learned that we were going to leave the mountain camp, I told Bernhard that I wanted to take her with us. But one morning she was not waiting for me outside the hut. I whistled and called, but she did not come. When Bernhard and I went to get our breakfast, we heard an animal squealing and grunting. Bernhard looked at me and said, "That *was* Amanda." I could not believe it. Hurrying into the kitchen, I saw a thin pig hanging from a beam. They had slaughtered Amanda. I was so upset that I could not tell Bernhard what I had seen.

The cook prepared the meat with salt and spices and packed it in cans. When we left the camp, each of us was given a can to eat on the journey. Bernhard said, "You see, you're taking Amanda along after all." We had arrived at the mountain camp in September; Amanda died six months later, at the end of March.

In March it appeared that we were going to be released. All along, Bernhard had believed that we would be set free. At first he had thought that we might be home by Christmas. I was less optimistic. My skepticism sometimes made Bernhard very angry. He could not bear to hear me talk about my fears. "You and your miserable doubts!" he said. "Don't be so pessimistic! Stop going around with a long face. What must the Vietnamese think of us?"

From the very beginning, Bernhard was convinced that we would soon be released. Hope kept him alive. I wondered what would happen to him if his faith was not rewarded. . . .

How Do You Like Your Vegetables?

BERNHARD DIEHL

In March the weather finally grew warmer, and we no longer had to keep our fire burning all night. In the past, we had stayed busy gathering wood. Now there was little to occupy our time. We had already swept the yard clean and cleared away all the fallen branches, even though this stripped the camp of camouflage and increased the danger that American planes might spot it from the air. In any case, we now had to find another occupation. To keep busy, I started to help out in the kitchen.

Monika and I may well have been the first prisoners ever quartered in the mountain camp, which served as a temporary rest stop for guerrillas returning from the combat zone, a place where they could recover from their wounds before returning to their northern homeland. Almost every day we saw new faces in the camp. Only the cook had been there since the day we arrived. He was an unfortunate man. The thumb and forefinger of his left hand had been shot off, and he had a large scar on his lower thigh. Moreover, he was still suffering the aftereffects of a gunshot wound in the abdomen that had never completely healed. Remaining infected, it opened periodically and began to drain. Worst of all, the poor man hated being a cook. He tried hard, but the food he prepared showed that his heart was not in his work. After spending so many years at the

141

front, he clearly regarded his new profession as demeaning. On holidays like Tet or New Year's,* he was forced to cede his pots and pans to the camp *y si*. The *y si* was not cut out for nursing the sick. Originally he had been a rice farmer, and he was a good cook. But even for him, taking on the post of cook involved a loss of status.

One morning I was sitting in front of the kitchen in the sunshine, peeling calla leaves. Calla is a vegetable eaten by the Vietnamese. Great quantities of calla grew in the mountains, but Monika and I were never allowed to eat it. When the guerrillas had eaten what they wanted, they gave the scraps to the pigs.

Sitting there peeling calla, I suddenly heard a whistle, the signal that someone was climbing the stairs to our camp. Accustomed to seeing new men arrive, I paid no attention to the two who had just reached the top of the stairs. Moreover, my eyesight had deteriorated recently; I could no longer see clearly at a distance. Thus I failed to recognize one of the new arrivals until he was standing right in front of me. The man was wearing a black uniform with sewn-on pockets. His hair was sheared in a straight line two inches above the ears. It was Huong, the interpreter from the American camp.

I was used to the cordial atmosphere of the mountain camp, where Monika and I shook hands with the itinerant soldiers. Startled at seeing Huong, I involuntarily rose to my feet and offered him my hand. His mouth grew slightly more twisted, and he ignored the outstretched hand.

Then he said in English, "Hello! How are you?"

I did not reply, but merely sat down and continued my work.

"I am glad to see you!" said Huong. "Are they treating you well here? You haven't been thinking too much about home? That's very good for you! You look much better than you did before. I see that the lenient and generous policy of the Vietnamese people is having a good effect on you."

Huong had not changed a bit.

* New Year's according to the Christian calendar, as opposed to Tet, the lunar New Year.—TRANS.

"I see you're keeping busy," he said. "That's very good for you. How do you like your vegetables?"

"I really can't say."

"You can't say that you like them? That's very bad for you!"

"We are not allowed to eat calla," I said. "Calla is not for prisoners: it is only for Vietnamese and pigs."

Huong's eyes grew cold and malicious. "I see that you have not yet learned that you are a prisoner. That is a pity. I came here to bring you some good news. It appears that I may have made the trip for nothing. We'll see. What you need is a couple of days of education. We'll begin our discussion this afternoon. I hope that you will pay careful attention. A great deal will depend on our little talk."

I spent the next few hours wondering whether I had made a mistake in insulting Huong. What had he meant by saying that he had come here to bring me good news?

In the camp that day was a man whom Monika and I had nicknamed "the Artist." The Artist wore his hair longer than the other men and was very skilled at weaving baskets and making various objects from bamboo. Immediately after Huong left me, I saw him go over to talk with the Artist. The man who had accompanied Huong to the camp was also there, holding two rice sacks and a piece of rope. Huong handed the rope and the sacks to the Artist, who clearly had been ordered to make something with the supplies.

What did it all mean? Surely Huong had not made the arduous two-day journey to our camp simply to give us "education"? For a long time I had been hoping that we would soon be released. My hopes were not entirely unfounded. Early in December, a guard we had known in the American camp arrived for a stay in our mountain aerie. He told me that shortly after our departure in September, three American prisoners had been released from the camp. One of them was Willis, who with his friend Ike had carried the coffins of our friends to their graves. After five days of political indoctrination, the three Americans had signed a document testifying that they had been

143

well treated, received excellent medical care and good food, and had never been physically abused. Then they were released. Had Huong come here to offer us the same opportunity?

Returning to our hut, I told Monika about my interview with Huong. I knew beforehand how she would react. She tried to curb my enthusiasm, reminding me of what Dr. Kushner had said shortly before we left the American camp. Three of our group had died in captivity, and Dr. Kushner believed that the Vietnamese would do anything to keep this information from becoming public—including keeping Monika and me prisoner.

"But if they were so concerned about public opinion, they wouldn't have released the three Americans either," I protested. "After all, Willis and the others know all about us; they'll be sure to report what happened." I also reminded Monika that in mid-November she and I had been allowed to write home. Of course, back at the American camp, Dr. Kushner and other prisoners had also been given permission to write home. Weeks later they had accidentally found their letters in the garbage pit beside the kitchen. The Vietnamese had never intended to mail them.

Monika and I spent our days seesawing back and forth between hope and fear. . . .

I could hardly wait until the afternoon. Finally Monika and I were summoned by Huong. The interpreter and his companion had turned one of the huts into an interrogation room. The two of them sat at a table in the center of the hut. Huong's companion acted as recording secretary.

Throughout the interview, I saw the secretary busily scribbling away. He seemed confused, kept dropping his papers, and filled pages with crisscrossing lines of writing. I began to suspect that he was only pretending to record what we said, and that in reality his presence was intended merely to impress or intimidate us.

Apart from the presence of a secretary, our "discussion" with Huong was exactly like discussions in the American camp. First the interpreter admonished us to pay close attention.

144

Then he repeated the same tired old phrases about the cruelty and injustice of the American war of aggression and the justice of the North Vietnamese cause. He spoke of the noble armed alliance of the North Vietnamese soldiers and the depravity of the American-supported Bonn regime. . . . Huong lectured us twice a day for five days, from 6:00 A.M. to 11:00 A.M., and again from 2:00 P.M. to 5:00 P.M. Soon I stopped listening to the words and clung to the thought that after five days of indoctrination, three Americans had been released from the American camp.

On the fifth day, Huong suddenly asked, "Have you been to North Vietnam?"

I looked at Monika, warning her to let me answer the question. "No."

Huong smiled his insincere smile. "Would you like to go to North Vietnam?"

His voice sounded casual, as if he were asking about a little excursion to the Canary Islands. I kept my face impassive. "I would like to go home," I answered, "no matter how long it takes or what route I must take to get there."

"So you believe we will release you?"

Stony-faced, I gave him the answer he was waiting for: "I trust in the leniency and generosity of the Vietnamese people, who have treated us so kindly in the past." He and I looked into each other's eyes. Each of us knew what the other was really thinking. But I had said what he wanted me to say, and he seemed to think that this was victory enough.

"You have finally learned," he said. There was a long pause. "You understand that we cannot turn you over to the Americans or the Saigon army?"

I said that I understood.

"We could take you to North Vietnam and release you there."

He had actually used the word "release." "When will that be?" I asked.

Huong had stood up. "I will consider whether or not to recommend your release. In any case, you should prepare for

145

the journey. North Vietnam is a long way from here. You must get yourselves into good physical condition."

That afternoon, Huong and his companion left the camp. I watched him until the tufts of hair sticking out above his ears disappeared behind the crest of the hill. I hoped that he would soon return with good news. At the same time, I hoped that I would never lay eyes on him again.

Someone touched my shoulder. It was the Artist, holding something in his hand. He had cut up the rice sacks, then sewed them back together forming two elongated pouches, each over a yard in length. Finally, he had laced the bags with rope so that they could be carried like back packs.

I gave the Artist a questioning look. Signaling me to accompany him, he led me to the kitchen, where I saw a pile of stones. The Artist began to pick up the stones and put them in the bags. Still I did not understand what the bags were for. Then the guerrilla told me: "The two of you are going into training. You're going to need it. It's a long journey to the North. . . ."

"Monsieur"

BERNHARD DIEHL

Every day for the next two weeks, I worked out with the back pack full of stones. Wearing the pack, I walked back and forth, descended the eighty-seven stairs, and climbed back up again. Monika was too weak to keep up with me. I behaved like a man possessed, running around as if I felt my efforts might somehow help to hasten our release. But now and then I paused long enough to think, "What if the guerrillas are simply performing an elaborate charade to torment us? Perhaps they are all laughing behind their backs."

Nevertheless, there was good reason to believe that we were about to make a long journey. For the first time since our capture, Monika and I were given meat in addition to our usual rations. In our first week of training, we each received three tiny pieces, in the second week four. Clearly we were being prepared for some crucial event. Then, late on the afternoon of March 31, "Monsieur" arrived in our camp.

Monika and I had just completed our afternoon round of exercise when we saw four men ascending the stairs. Clearly one of them was an important official. We never learned his name, so we dubbed him "Monsieur" because he spoke French. Later his interpreter introduced him as an *officier majeur,* a high-ranking officer, and as the *chef du département;* but we never learned what department he was head of. Monsieur was accompanied by his interpreter and two personal bodyguards. The latter carried his belongings, cooked his food, and lit his cigarettes for him.

Monika and I had observed Monsieur's grand entrance into the camp. None of his party bothered to inquire about us. Thus at first we were not certain that he knew anything about our case. After eating a leisurely supper and drinking the coffee his men prepared for him, Monsieur officiated at a brief decoration ceremony.

Three of the camp personnel lined up at attention. One of them was the cook, with his worn trousers and disheveled hair. Even at this solemn moment, he looked more like Robinson Crusoe than a soldier. His left hand, missing two fingers, rested casually on his trousers. Standing beside the cook was a Vietnamese whom Monika and I called "Mr. Precision." He was an older man with stringy black hair, thin as a rake and suffering from a severe case of tuberculosis. He did not seem to do anything right. He could never get the fire started, and when he went fishing with the others, he never caught any fish. Everyone pushed him around. He was always assigned the filthiest work in the camp, like cleaning out the animal sheds. He was happiest when he had nothing to do and was allowed to sit peacefully in a corner. A third man was standing beside the cook and Mr. Precision. Monika and I simply called him "the Tall One."

At first Monika and I did not understand what was going on. After the three soldiers had listened to Monsieur deliver a brief address, one of the bodyguards walked up holding the decorations, and Monsieur personally pinned them on. It was a brief ceremony. Clearly they were inventing it as they went along. No one seemed particularly impressed by it all. At least the three soldiers appeared to like the decorations, but Monsieur merely looked bored. It was already getting dark. "Perhaps his coming here has nothing to do with us," I thought. Then the interpreter walked over and directed us to follow him.

• • •

We were taken to the hut where we had listened to Huong's five-day lecture series. Now Monsieur was sitting at the table. His two bodyguards stood behind him, ready to spring into action when he needed someone to light his cigarettes. He smoked a great deal. I saw the cigarette box lying in front of him; the brand name was "Rubis." The commandant was there, too. He seemed to be smiling. My hopes soared.

We sat at the table across from Monsieur. To my right I noticed our two back packs lying on another table. After each training session, Monika and I had been ordered to return them to the guards. Beside the packs lay two neat stacks of provisions. Each stack contained a pound of sugar, a small canister of powdered milk with French lettering, and a can of pickled meat, what was left of Monika's beloved pig. I looked at the commandant again. Now I was certain that he was smiling.

The interpreter explained that Monsieur was an *officier majeur* and *chef du département*. Suddenly Monsieur interrupted him. The official had just discovered the two ancient, filthy bandages covering the still-unhealed abscesses on Monika's arms. Monsieur gave an order, and we waited until the camp *y si* came running into the room. His brow furrowed with rage, Monsieur shouted at the *y si*, who turned scarlet and scurried away. Soon the *y si* returned with a clean strip of muslin and a penicillin tablet. Crushing the penicillin, he sprinkled it on the sores and applied the two clean bandages. Silence reigned until he had finished. During this interval, Monsieur went on smoking; the interpreter slumped down in his chair; the commandant smiled a cordial smile that promised us that everything was going to turn out all right.

As Monsieur began to speak, the interpreter translated his words into English. I remember every word. The first two were, "I regret."

"I regret," said Monsieur, "that you have been kept prisoner for so long. You were foreigners, and many foreigners are our enemies. Therefore we had to investigate the possibility that you were spies. We have examined your statements. We were forced to conclude that your statements are true: you are in fact members of a medical organization, and you were engaged in caring for the sick. Thus we have decided to release you and allow you to return to Germany."

"What more need he say?" I thought. "Let's get going. Let's walk night and day, without a pause. Let's walk without eating, without resting." I glanced at Monika in triumph; but there was no joy on her face. She looked as taciturn as ever. I wanted to grab her and dance around the room in front of them all.

"We regret that three of your friends will be unable to return home with you," Monsieur continued. "Even while we are waging our war of liberation, we the Vietnamese people wish to extend lenient and generous treatment to prisoners of war. We regret the death of your friends. We did all we could to help them get well; but you know that in the jungle, our resources are limited. Last winter, as you know, a Vietnamese died in this camp because, unlike the Americans, we could not afford to dispatch a special helicopter to take him to a hospital." I remembered the death. "Moreover, you know that the three men I decorated today are not in very good health either."

"Just hurry up and finish," I thought. "Let's leave the camp right now. Home! Home to Germany!" I had known all along that we would be released. Why was Monika looking so grim?

"I assume that you are prepared to acknowledge the good will of the Vietnamese people toward their enemies and to attest that you have received fair treatment during your captivity." Monsieur leaned forward. "Besides, obviously your friends were ill at the time of their capture. I have here a report from the *y si* confirming this fact." Taking out a cigarette, he waited for someone to light it. The interpreter shoved a piece of paper and a pen across the table.

I thought that I recognized Huong's writing, but I could not be certain: the document was written in Vietnamese. Clearly no one was going to translate it for us. I looked at Monika, fearing that she might be stubborn and ruin everything at the last minute. Long ago I had resolved to sign anything they put in front of me if in return they promised to let me go. Handing Monika the pen, I said in as casual a tone as I could muster, "Don't make any fuss!" I was sure that none of the Vietnamese understood German. Monika signed her copy and I signed mine.

Monsieur stamped out his cigarette and leaned far back in his chair. He began to speak again, in a somewhat more official tone. *"De maintenant vous êtes lebérés,"* he said.

It was not the best French in the world, but it was the most beautiful sentence I had ever heard: "As of this moment, you are free!" The interpreter translated for us, "The Vietnamese people restore your freedom to you. You will return to your country and your families."

Monsieur pointed to the back packs on the table. "You will leave here and travel to North Vietnam. The first ten days will be difficult. Then you will come to a road. From there you will be driven the rest of the way by car. You will be taken to Hanoi, where you will board an airplane. The airplane will fly you home. Have you any questions?"

I had only one. "When do we leave?"

"Tomorrow morning. Three men will accompany you to North Vietnam. I emphasize that these men are your escorts, not your guards. If you want something, go to Mr. Bô, who will guide your group." Once again he adopted an official tone. "Please convey our greetings to your relatives in Germany. I hope that when the war is over, the people of Germany and Vietnam can work together in friendship, to the benefit of both nations."

Monsieur stood up. Monika and I were about to get up, too, but he signaled us to remain seated. Guards brought us tea, and Monsieur offered us some of his Rubis cigarettes. We all sat there smoking and drinking tea. The Vietnamese behaved as if they had never been anything but our friends. . . .

Then Monika and I returned to our hut, carrying our back packs and the provisions for our trip—the sugar, powdered milk, and cans of meat. The pack felt feather-light on my back. I was so happy that I started to sing. Monika was subdued. "He really said we're free?" she asked.

"Stop it now! You see, I was right and you were wrong."

"What did he say exactly?"

" '*Dès maintenant vous êtes libérés*' . . . 'As of now, you are free. The Vietnamese people give you back your freedom.' "

"Do you know what tomorrow is?" she asked.

"No, what do you mean?"

"Tomorrow is April 1. Haven't you ever heard of April Fool's?"

I was furious. I simply could not understand Monika. Her eternal pessimism was getting on my nerves. But say what she liked, that day she could not really make me feel depressed.

The next morning I got up before everyone else. It was a misty day; but no matter what the weather, I would have thought that it was beautiful. I packed the rest of my gear and did my morning gymnastics, inhaling the mountain air. I was in a fever to get going.

Seeing the cook light his fire, I went over to the kitchen. Monsieur, his interpreter, and his bodyguards had already left the camp. Mr. Bô and his two companions had not yet arrived.

The others began waking up. I saw the Vietnamese we called the Tall One coming out of his hut with a machete, looking as if he were about to cut some kindling. The Tall One was a sergeant who had been wounded at the front and had arrived here only a few weeks before. He spoke some English. He had showed me pictures of his wife and children in North Vietnam, and of the rice paddies tilled by his wife and his old father. Laughing with joy at my release, I walked over to the Tall One, shook his hand, and said, "Good luck! We're leaving now. I hope that you will soon be free to return to your family in the North."

His reaction surprised me. His face clouded over, growing grim and hard. I felt that I could read his thoughts. For the first and only time during my captivity, I saw a Vietnamese reveal his true feelings about the war. In his face I read the tale of his long separation from his family, the tale of the war that would not end. . . .

He looked down at the machete in his hand; then, raising his arm, he threw the knife at a tree. The blade pierced deep into the trunk, and the knife stuck there, its handle quivering. The Tall One walked away without a word, leaving the machete in the tree.

This was the only time that a Vietnamese—and a sergeant in the North Vietnamese army at that—bared his soul in my presence. For a moment I understood the suffering of this man who only the evening before had received a military decoration. But that morning there was probably nothing in the world that I would not have understood. . . .

Mister Bô and the Long March

BERNHARD DIEHL

We left the camp at around seven o'clock. It had rained during the night and the air was damp and misty, but we were indifferent to the weather. I was wearing my black pajama trousers and Georg's hospital shirt. Monika wore her white pajama trousers and her nurse's blouse. These outfits represented our "Sunday best."

We all carried our own gear—a change of clothing, a few personal things, the special provisions. Each of us also received a two-week supply of rice, which we kept inside a long stocking wrapped around our necks. We had a heavy load to carry, and Monika and I were glad that we had worked hard to get ourselves in shape. But I was so happy that I could have carried a bag of stones on top of my other gear. After all, we were walking to freedom.

I had assumed that we would climb higher into the mountains, and I was right. The jungle was damp; the plants had thick, fleshy leaves. Then the leeches began to torment us. Soon our hands and feet were covered with them. At around ten o'clock the sun finally came out. As it grew hot, we became weary from climbing the steep mountains. At noon we paused very briefly. Storm clouds were gathering overhead, and it thundered and lightened in the distance. Trying to outrun the storm, we moved on at once. On our first afternoon, we climbed so high into the

154

mountains that our figures were swallowed up by mist. We traveled without pause until evening. When we reached the Montagnard settlement where we were to spend the night, I leaned against a tree and vomited from sheer weakness.

Along the way, it had started to rain. Soaked to the skin, we all took off our wet clothing and hung it up near the fire to dry. Anh Simh, one of our three escorts, took a milk can full of uncooked rice from each stocking and cooked our supper. We had rice with a little salted meat, then finished our meal with tea. Spreading pieces of canvas on the ground, we lay down, covered ourselves with our rice-sack blankets, and huddled together for warmth. Our first day's journey was over.

Three men were traveling with Monika and me. The leader of our group was Ong Bô, or "Mr. Bô." Soon we learned that he was a first lieutenant in the North Vietnamese army, yet he preferred to be addressed as "Mr." Since 1959, Ong Bô had been fighting in South Vietnam. Fortunately—or unfortunately—he had never been severely wounded. In eleven years, this was the first time that he had been permitted to return to his northern homeland. When he joined the army, he was only nineteen; now he was thirty-one. On his upper thigh was a long scar left by a gunshot wound that had barely healed.

Bô wore a black uniform. His belt was fastened with a broad, square metal buckle decorated with the star of North Vietnam. Strapped around his body he carried an East German pistol, and he owned the same kind of water-lily hat that Bob had worn. Every evening when we camped for the night, Ong Bô washed his hat and fluffed it into shape so that when it dried, all the "petals" would stick out at just the right angle. When he finished washing the hat, he would spread a piece of waterproof canvas on the ground, then take apart and clean his pistol and put it back together. Bô was a solitary man who left the rest of us in peace. In return, he wanted to be left in peace himself. During the day, he led the way, walking all alone. In the evening, he sat by himself, chain-smoking and cleaning his pistol.

Our second companion was "the Doctor," who never told us

his real name. We rarely knew the names of the Vietnamese; thus, between ourselves, we often referred to them by nicknames. There was "Sonny Boy," "the Steel-helmed Baron," "Shorty," and "Crisco." This last man was named after a brand of American shortening. The Americans gave him the name because he seemed such a slippery character.

The Doctor came from a region of South Vietnam controlled by the Saigon regime. His parents still lived there. As a boy, the Doctor had traveled to Hanoi to study. After two years' training, he became an *y si* and returned to the South. For the past eight years, he had been serving the Viet Cong as a paramedic. Now he was returning to Hanoi to complete his studies and become a doctor. The Doctor was a real chatterbox and prankster. Climbing up mountains or down, in scorching heat or pouring rain, while the rest of us were gasping for breath, he would race back and forth, his face flushed, chattering away at everyone and telling jokes. He was a tall, thin man with a tough and muscular frame. Like Bô, he prided himself on his possessions—a portable radio and a large pocket flashlight. Long after the batteries were worn out, he used to carry the flashlight around the jungle camps at night, simply to show everyone that he owned it.

Our third escort was a sergeant in the North Vietnamese army who had fought in the South for six years and whose gunshot wounds—in the upper thigh and upper arm—had won him the right to return to the North. He was a small fellow named Simh, so scrawny that the other Vietnamese called him Anh Simh, or "young Simh." He was forty years old. Simh had a wife and two children in North Vietnam and never tired of telling everyone that once he reached home, he planned to grow rice again and raise pigs. Simh, the smallest and weakest of the three men, had the most to carry. Besides his own things and all the cooking utensils, he was carrying Monika's stocking full of rice. Anh Simh was also entrusted with the cameras, watches, and passports that had been confiscated on the day of our capture. . . .

. . .

At first the days all seemed much alike. At night we slept in the huts of the hill tribesmen. These dwellings were solidly built, with roofs that could withstand the most violent downpour. The huts of the *kim,* the true Vietnamese, have roofs of bamboo; the huts of people in the lowlands are covered with rushes. The roofs of Montagnard huts, on the other hand, consist of two overlapping layers of rice thatch.

As a rule, two fires burned in our hut at night. Monika and I spread our sheets of waterproof canvas on the ground and lay down. The nights were cold, but we managed to keep warm, covering ourselves with the rice-sack blankets and hammocks we carried in our packs. The huts were raised on stilts. The pigs and chickens slept under the floor. Lying on the ground, I used to watch the Montagnards sitting around the fire and getting their arrows ready for the next day's hunt. Occasionally one of them would glance over at Monika and me. To them we seemed like visitors from another planet.

We got up very early in the morning. For breakfast we ate our usual fare: rice, canned salted meat, and tea or boiled water with sugar. After breakfast, Ong Bô would bargain with the Montagnards, trying to hire a guide for the day. The guide was paid in bowls of salt. He could earn two or more, depending on how long he was willing to bargain. To the Montagnards, salt was an essential commodity, so they used it as currency. In exchange for salt, they showed us short cuts and led us along mountain paths known only to them. Even with their help, it took us ten days to reach the legendary Ho Chi Minh Trail, which hardly any white man had seen except from an airplane.

I had never quite believed all the tales the Americans in An Hoa had told me about this famous road. They used to talk about it with mingled rage and respect. When the French were fighting in Indochina, the Ho Chi Minh Trail was the main supply route for the armies in the South. Along the Trail flowed troops, weapons and munitions, food supplies, and drugs. The road was some six hundred miles long. Beginning near the training and supply camps north of the seventeenth parallel, it

157

ran south through the mountains and rain forests of Laos until it reached the border between Cambodia and South Vietnam. The main artery pumping fresh blood into the war, it was bombed day and night by American planes. The Americans in An Hoa used to show me aerial photographs of the damage their planes had inflicted—the ruined stretches of road, the burned forests, the deep craters left by the bombs. But in some mysterious way, an unbroken stream of troops and supplies continued to flow along the Trail.

When we arrived at the road, we found the whole area in ruins. We had been walking along a narrow path through dense forest. Suddenly, to the right of the path we saw a steep incline. Looking down, we discovered a road no more than four yards across at its widest point.

The road ran along the foot of the cliff, then twisted and turned until it reached the valley below. The valley had been bombed the night before, and the road lay in ruins, almost hidden by fallen trees. Worst of all, the bombs had hit a dam in the river, and the water had overflowed the banks, flooding the valley. More than one hundred yards of road were covered with water.

However, men were already at work repairing the damage. Wherever had all these people come from? We saw them working away with primitive tools—picks and shovels, wheelbarrows, and little baskets to cart away debris. They also had several bulldozers. Later, traveling along the Ho Chi Minh Trail, we often encountered work detachments busy repairing the road. We passed Montagnards and farmers, mostly women and elderly men, laboring on steep precipices like so many hordes of ants. Soon we realized that the Ho Chi Minh Trail was not really a single road running all the way from North to South Vietnam, but rather a main artery with countless branches.

As we traveled along the road, we began to encounter units of North Vietnamese troops in uniforms and carrying packs and rifles, their trousers pockets full of hand grenades. We also saw transport units laden with heavy boxes. Some of the men carried munitions crates suspended from poles resting on their shoulders. On the side roads we met columns of bicycle units, pushing their loaded bicycles along beside them. We also passed munitions camps camouflaged with branches. At last we were traveling the Ho Chi Minh Trail; but clearly no car was going to take us the rest of our journey. . . .

Once we had reached the road, we stopped spending our nights in the huts of the hill tribesmen. Instead, we paused each evening at one of the countless camps along the edge of the Ho Chi Minh Trail. The camps sheltered the never-ending stream of people traveling between North and South Vietnam. Every night, after a long day's march, we saw a camp miraculously materialize in the middle of the jungle.

Suddenly we would be standing in a large open courtyard ringed with huts. The huts were nothing but long roofs mounted on poles. In the middle of the yard, there was always a sort of ramp about sixty feet long, where new arrivals set down their packs, got their bearings, looked for people they knew, exchanged news about the day's journey, and discussed their plans for the following day. Later, everyone looked for a place to spend the night, stringing his hammock from the poles supporting the roof of the hut. The distance between two poles equaled the length of a hammock. Thus at night fifty people could sleep in long rows under the same roof. Once we had found a place for the night, we took some rice from our stockings and brought it to the kitchen. As a rule, one or two Vietnamese cooked rice for the whole camp. When the rice was ready, the cook called out and beat a gong. After getting his rice and boiled water, everyone went back to his hammock.

Day after day we followed the same routine. Soon we learned to know people in other groups who were also traveling north. Sometimes we would leave the camp with our new acquaintances. During the day, we often lost track of them and might not see them again until two nights later, when we all met at another camp.

Soon after we began traveling the Ho Chi Minh Trail, we encountered a group of ten children wearing bright-colored

159

clothing like that worn by children in the lowlands around Da Nang. Each child had his own pack. The children were orphans fleeing American-occupied territory. They were escorted by an old man, who was leading them six hundred miles to North Vietnam, where they could be educated and trained in some profession. The children were *kim,* the true Vietnamese.

On the following day we met another group of orphans, twelve Montagnard boys and girls, who were also traveling north. They, too, were led by an old man. As the days passed, we saw a spirit of rivalry develop between the Montagnard children and the youngsters from the lowlands. The children of the *kim* were taller for their age and wore better clothing; they showed a certain disdain for the mountain-bred brood. But the Montagnard youngsters, dressed in rags and uncivilized as they were, knew the surrounding country well, could walk long and tirelessly, and knew their way around the overnight camps. In the camps, the *kim* children just played or sat quietly, while the Montagnard children made themselves useful gathering wood and washing the dishes.

We were never alone on our journey. Often fifty to a hundred people slept in the same camp, and many of them left with us in the morning. All day we struggled up and down mountains. During the first stage of our travels, it rained a great deal, especially in the daytime. The ground was slippery, and we often fell down. One bottle of water had to last the whole day. Finally, we had eaten all our salted meat and were running out of sugar and powdered milk.

Crossing the border into Laos, we found ourselves high in the mountains. Soon we saw peaks six thousand feet high. It was bitter cold. Even when Monika and I were walking, our thin clothing did not keep us warm. Our three companions wore sweaters, windbreakers, gloves, and heavy socks. When my tennis shoes went to pieces, I was given Chinese rubber sandals, and Monika received a pair of Ho Chi Minh sandals.

We often had to stop and rest, and sometimes we stayed in one place for days at a time. I had lost a toenail and my foot

160

had become infected. Monika was very weak. She was running a fever and vomited constantly. Once she said, "I'm not sure; do you think I'm dying?" Sick as she was, she had to carry her own pack. She was carrying as much weight as the rest of us, except for the stocking full of rice, which Anh Simh carried for her. Hardest of all was the walking itself: we had to walk long distances to bypass obstacles, and often we had to stoop to avoid trailing vines. Our packs kept shifting position on our backs, upsetting our balance. Moreover, we lost a great deal of blood to the leeches and felt very weak. In the evenings we collapsed into our hammocks, too exhausted to move. Yet, exhausted as we were, we were often unable to sleep.

Monika's fever continued to rise. It was always gone by morning, but when the Doctor took her temperature in the evening, it was over 102° F. He gave her quinine, and Anh Simh administered a "wonder drug" of his own. The wonder drug was mentholated oil, which Anh Simh always carried with him and used to treat every ailment under the sun. Unfortunately, it did not help Monika.

We had been traveling for almost a month. During the day the sky was filled with bombers that came roaring over our heads, dropping their bombs along the road. We had not yet seen the car that Monsieur had mentioned, the car that was supposed to take us north. . . .

The truck looked as if it dated back to World War II. One evening at around six o'clock, we stopped to rest beside the main road of the Ho Chi Minh Trail. Mr. Bô walked to the road and disappeared. Suddenly we heard the sound of a motor and saw a truck emerge from an underground dugout.

The truck was camouflaged. A wide board covered the top of the compartment where the driver sat. The same board extended forward to cover the hood and the radiator, where it was held up by two poles attached to the bumper. Thus the driver could see the road beneath the "canopy," but the front of the truck was invisible from the air. We saw the driver camouflaging the board with branches. As we made our way down to the road, I saw other vehicles in the dugout that had been carved into the side of the cliff.

A soldier holding a field telephone disappeared into the dugout. The place seemed to be a communications center. Finally the soldier came out and called Ong Bô, who informed us that the road was clear. The truck was going to take us to a jungle hospital where we would rest for several days.

We left as soon as it grew dark. All five of us sat side by side in the rear of the truck. Anh Simh showed us how to hold on to one another, firmly grasping our neighbors on both sides around the upper thigh. This technique was necessary to protect us from the terrible bouncing of the truck. The road seemed to be a solid carpet of potholes. Each time the vehicle hit one of the holes, we were hurled into the air, then painfully bounced down again. Whenever we rounded a curve, we heaved from one side of the truck to the other.

We were not allowed to smoke. The driver drove with his headlights on, despite the danger that we might be visible from the air. Men posted along the side of the road signaled with flashlights whenever planes approached the area.

We were driving at breakneck speed. I was amazed that the driver managed to negotiate the narrow curves. I was equally amazed that the truck did not simply fall apart. Judging by the smell, the vehicle must have been losing quantities of gasoline and oil. Moreover, the motor was rattling in a very unhealthy way. But after twelve months' captivity, it felt marvelous to be riding in a car again. Since our capture, this was the first motor we had heard that was not in an airplane. And we were getting closer to Hanoi!

Around midnight we made our first stop, to fill up the truck with gasoline and oil, add water to the radiator, and change drivers. We stopped at a reloading station, a hub of activity in the middle of the forest. For the first time I understood the importance of this highway through the jungle. A column of ten or fifteen trucks lined up in single file. Hastily reloaded with supplies, they sped off into the night. They had scarcely disappeared before more trucks arrived. Half an hour later, the second column departed, loaded with crates of munitions. For an hour we sat there listening to the din of the motors, the screeching of brakes, the grating of tires on the rubble-strewn road, and the men barking orders to keep the traffic moving. Our ears had begun to hurt by the time the road cleared, leaving us free to drive on.

For several hours we had been traveling through an area devastated by bombs. All the bushes and trees on both sides of the road had been razed to the ground. After midnight, we drove through dense forest undamaged by bombs. There was a full moon. The second driver was even more skillful than the first. We were traveling faster than ever along the road to the North.

Our journey ended around 4:00 A.M. Getting out of the truck, we saw several soldiers standing beside the road. Clearly they had been waiting for us. We all started walking through the jungle, the soldiers carrying flashlights covered with cloth to dim the light. The Doctor was ecstatic as he scurried around to all the soldiers and requested new batteries for his flashlight.

The sun was rising. Soon we came to a path and a low wooden fence surrounding a group of bamboo huts. As protection from bombs, the huts had been built a yard deep in the ground. Small embankments outside the doors of each hut helped to shield occupants from fragmentation bombs. So this was our jungle hospital.

It was very clean inside. There were real wooden bedsteads! Two young Vietnamese women wearing green smocks and surgical masks brought us food more sumptuous than anything else we tasted throughout our captivity. There was chicken soup, scrambled eggs, the vegetable called calla, bamboo-shoot salad, green beans, and snowy white rice. For once we could wash and get really clean. We slept in fresh pajamas under real blankets and mosquito nets without any holes in them. For the first time in a year, I slept soundly. I slept through the rest of the day and all night, and did not wake up until late the next morning. . . .

• • •

We stayed in the hospital for several days while fully trained physicians gave us thorough examinations. The Vietnamese were proud of their jungle hospital, which was primarily designed to treat military units on their way south.

The staff took our blood pressure, pulse, and temperature. They also took samples of our blood and applied medicinal herbs to our many sores. Although weak and run-down, I was in fairly good condition. Monika's condition was more serious. She had never fully recovered from her bout of malaria and continued to run a fever. Moreover, she was now showing symptoms of beriberi.

Slowly Monika's blood pressure and temperature began to improve, but we could not wait for her to get well. The time had come to continue our journey to North Vietnam.

At the end of April or the beginning of May, we left the hospital. Once again we had to travel by foot. Monika and I did not know that we still had another month's journey before us.

Our daily routine was much the same as before. We encountered more and more refugees heading north. The overnight camps, stocked with supplies from North Vietnam, furnished our rice and other provisions, so we no longer had to carry the heavy stockings full of rice around our necks. As summer approached, the weather grew warmer and it stopped raining altogether. Monika continued to feel very ill. She could barely drag herself along. Now we were no longer cold all day, but sweating from the heat. From experience we knew that it was better to sweat than to freeze.

And, after all, every day we were getting closer to freedom!

Someone Blows Me a Kiss

MONIKA SCHWINN

I do not know how the woman knew that we had crossed the seventeenth parallel, but suddenly she threw herself to the ground and kissed the earth.

I cannot remember what day it was, nor do I recall anything special about the landscape. I did not see any markers like those we passed when we crossed the border into Laos. I had pictured the seventeenth parallel as a wide strip of no man's land where not a single tree had been left standing; but trees extended on both sides of the border.

The woman had been traveling with us through the jungle. She was a middle-aged, taciturn woman who was taking her children to North Vietnam. During our journey she never spoke to anyone. Then I saw her hurl herself to the ground, gleefully digging her hands into the sand and running it through her fingers, as if she had come to a promised land. What must she have suffered in South Vietnam to rejoice so at leaving it behind? And what did she expect to find on the other side of the border?

"We made it!" Bernhard said. "In just a few days, we'll be free!"

Torn between hope and suspicion, I looked at him, unable to share his elation. My knees were trembling.

For the past few weeks, the hope of our release had kept me

165

going. No matter what the journey cost me, I was determined to get to North Vietnam. Along the way I kept telling myself, "Even if you have to crawl home on all fours, don't let anyone see how sick you feel. Every minute you use up in walking, every hour you take to rest, every day that you make them wait for you to get stronger, is a minute or an hour or a day less of freedom." I repeated this over and over; but no matter what I told myself, I still doubted that we were going to be released. When I saw the woman rejoicing and heard Bernhard say that we had finally made it, all I could think was, "My God, I hope you're right. I hope you won't be disappointed."

When we crossed the border, it was almost evening. A short time later, we arrived at a camp. My fever made me vomit. When we lay down in our hammocks, I was unable to sleep. A couple of hours later, the Doctor came over with his flashlight and told us to get up at once. He said that a truck was waiting for us. When I asked him whether we were going to Hanoi, he did not reply. Probably he did not know what to answer.

As we rode along, Bernhard was very elated. I thought about the many promises the Vietnamese had made us and failed to keep. Sometimes I tried to picture our journey home. "You are free. An airplane will fly you home." Was I going back to Germany in this condition, wearing these old rags? I imagined the faces of the stewardess and the other passengers.

Then I turned to Bernhard. "Did you ask where they're taking us?" He just laughed and said, "Well, where do you think they'll take us? To Hanoi, naturally."

It occurred to me that our three companions were behaving rather strangely. The usually boisterous Doctor seemed ominously still. Somehow, crossing the seventeenth parallel had changed them. They hardly spoke to us and sat some distance away. In the past, they had always behaved as if the five of us were comrades, all part of a single group swept up in the stream of refugees going north. But then, perhaps they had treated Bernhard and me as equals merely to show everyone we met that these white people were not enemies or prisoners and must

166

not be harmed. In the dark truck, I wondered why Lieutenant Bô kept his hand on his gun belt. Or was the night breeding phantoms in my mind?

We traveled all night while American planes flew overhead. We saw the fire of anti-aircraft guns and heard bombs exploding in the distance. The faces of our companions seemed to grow even more somber.

It must have been around 3:00 A.M. when the truck came to a halt. It was still dark out, but we could see that we had stopped near a small town. Many of the houses lay in ruins. The Doctor warned us to keep still and not to speak English: the Americans incessantly bombed the area just north of the seventeenth parallel, and the people passionately hated the *my*'s.

As the truck drove on, our companions led us away on foot. We walked a short distance until we came to a small stone building, a sort of medical aid station. An old woman received us at the door. Inside were two rooms. We passed through the front room to the rear.

Our companions told us that we would spend the rest of the night and the following day here. The next evening, a truck would come to pick us up. Because the people hated all whites, it was not safe for us to travel in the daytime.

But Bernhard and I were not *my*'s, we were Germans! And we had been released. I was still thinking this when I fell asleep. . . .

I drowsed until I heard a deafening noise. Recognizing the voices of children, I thought, "I've been dreaming; I'm still in the children's ward of the hospital in Da Nang." When they started to get well, we used to let the children play in the yard and could hear them outside the hospital windows.

The old Vietnamese woman was standing by my bed. She placed her finger on her mouth, indicating that I was not to move or say a word. Now I recognized that the noise I heard was not the happy sound of children at play. Going to the window, the old woman cautiously peered out.

She must have been at least sixty years old. She was bent

167

with age, and her face was full of wrinkles. Her gray and white hair was partly concealed by a black kerchief tied around her head. In Vietnam, a black kerchief is a sign of mourning. From the way she looked at me and held her finger to her lips, I could tell that she was trying to help us. Prisoners learn what to expect from people just by looking at their faces.

I still did not understand what was going on outside. What were the children shouting about? Looking around, I became fully awake. I was in a sort of storeroom filled with drugs. Boxes of varying sizes lined the shelves along the walls. The room was furnished with a table and three beds. I recalled having seen a row of seven beds in the front room.

The shouting grew louder. It sounded threatening. Getting up, I went over to the old woman. The window was barred, and the bars had enraged the children. Outside stood a group of about twenty boys clad in filthy rags. I did not have much time to observe them, for they had seen my face. Shouting with fury, they bent down to pick up dirt and stones. I drew back as stones bombarded the walls and flew in through the open window.

Looking upset, Ong Bô appeared in the doorway and shouted at me to get away from the window. His face was white. Seeing how frightened he was, I became frightened, too.

Finally the old woman picked up a cudgel and went outside. Cautiously peering out the window, I saw her hitting the boys; but there were too many for her. When she came close, they simply ran a yard or two and then began pelting her with stones and dirt. While the old woman was keeping the children busy, our three companions went outside and nailed wooden shutters on the window. All day the attack continued. With the window sealed up, I was more frightened than ever. The stones striking the wood made an ominous hollow sound. I wondered why the children hated us so. During my year of captivity, I had never seen a Vietnamese look at us with such hatred as had these young boys. I knew that they would not hesitate to kill us. What disturbed me most was that they were children, for I had come to this country to help Vietnamese children. I had taken care of so many, sitting up at night beside their beds. Helping children was the only meaningful thing I could think of to do in this senseless war. . . .

The Vietnamese had planned to leave that evening, but now we were trapped inside the aid station. The men were unable to drive the children away. As the day wore on, more boys came to join the attack. Clearly Bernhard and I were not the only ones in danger. Our companions were no longer concerned only about our safety; they were also afraid for themselves.

Night fell. We did not bother to undress. The door was locked and the windows had been barricaded from inside. It was June, midsummer, and boiling hot inside the tightly sealed building. Outside, the children went on screaming.

I lay down under my mosquito netting, but sleep was out of the question. Cowering under the net, I felt like a caged bird. Finally it grew quiet outside. I could not help wondering what the boys were doing. Were they creeping softly up to the building? Were they fetching weapons, hand grenades? We had left the door between the two rooms ajar, and I could see Ong Bô sitting on the corner of his bed, holding his pistol in his lap.

None of us got much sleep that night. As the hours crept by, I was rigid with terror. Soon I was drenched in sweat— not so much from the boiling heat as from fever and fear.

Next morning, nothing had changed. The children flocked around the building. Our three companions talked in whispers. Early that morning, they had sent the old woman to fetch a truck and soldiers to cover our retreat.

Finally twelve soldiers arrived. As soon as I saw them, I sensed that they hated us just as much as the children did. Lining up in two rows beside the door, the soldiers allowed us to leave the hut. Their faces made me afraid. I could not tell what they planned to do. Ong Bô began to bargain with one of them while the horde of children screamed with rage.

Clearly the negotiations were not progressing quite as Ong

Bô had expected. Suddenly the two men started shouting at each other. I began to think that we were doomed. It would take only one spark to make the powder keg explode.

Only one of us kept a cool head, the one from whom I would least have expected it—the Doctor. This man who had always seemed a clown at heart suddenly wrenched Bô's gun from his hand and started bellowing orders. Standing beside him, I could see the sweat running down his face. He looked white as chalk, but his words and his gun brought everyone else to their senses. The soldiers drew back, permitting us to board the waiting truck. As we sat down in the rear, the truck pulled away. For a moment the children pursued us, screaming and hurling rocks and dirt; but the driver stepped on the gas and we sped off down the road. The Doctor still looked very pale.

We saw no more of the children who hated all white-skinned foreigners. But shortly after we left the aid station, we met another child who, although he could not make me forget that terrible night, did give me something to remember besides hatred.

During our years in the camps, we were always torn by conflicting emotions. For a little while we would feel uncomplicated hatred for the Vietnamese and their callous, cruel behavior. Then something would happen to make us forget our hatred. Often I wished that I could feel nothing but hate. It might have been easier that way.

As the truck sped along, we sat in the rear, looking over the tailboard at the clouds of dust in our wake and watching the groups of refugees we passed by the side of the road. Then I caught sight of the boy.

It was the boy who had been frightened by the crocodile carried by the hill tribesman, the boy who had lost his parents and was traveling north all alone. At night we had often seen him in the jungle camps. For a time he traveled with our group; but after our stay in the jungle hospital, we had lost track of him. Now I glimpsed the boy among the people retreating to the side of the road to get out of the way of our truck.

The youngster recognized us, too. His face had always looked very grave, but now for the first time I actually saw him laugh. He ran along behind the truck until he caught up with us. Then he waved and shouted two words.

"*Duc!*" he yelled—the word means "German"—and "*tôt,*" which means "good." "*Duc tôt!*" he cried once more, completely out of breath. Unable to keep up with the truck, he raised his hand to his mouth and blew me a kiss.

I do not know where he could have learned the gesture, unless perhaps from some Frenchman. I waved back, but he had already been swallowed up in clouds of dust. The driver was speeding along the dusty roads like a madman. It was a hot day, and it had not rained for a long time.

The Storm

MONIKA SCHWINN

For the next few days we traveled only at night, setting out as soon as it got dark and leaving the truck before dawn. We never picked up other refugees. The five of us sat alone in the rear of the truck. When Bernhard and I asked our three companions where we were going, they did not answer. Perhaps they did not know. We were certain of only one thing: we were heading north. Bernhard thought that he recognized the name Hanoi on signs along the road.

We had been told that our journey to North Vietnam would take little more than ten days. The ten days had stretched into almost two months. Yet Bernhard continued to look as serene and confident as he had the day we left the mountain camp. During the day, when we were resting, Bernhard always managed to sleep. He could even sleep at night in the jolting truck. He told me to wake him if anything happened; but nothing did, except that sometimes the planes flew in so low that their noise drowned out the sound of our motor.

I do not know exactly how many days we traveled in the truck. All I clearly remember is the endless hours of waiting, when I was torn between hope and doubt.

Where were they taking us? What was going to happen next? I asked the same questions over and over. But in the end, my doubts always outweighed my hope. I was exhausted and run-

172

ning a fever. Perhaps it was my illness that made me feel so depressed.

One day we had hardly slept for three hours before we had to get up and move on. This time we traveled in a closed ambulance. It was a hot, sultry day. We drove on and on, never stopping to rest. Bernhard and I could not see much through the draped windows, but the traffic was getting heavier; thus we knew that we were approaching a large city. Both of us wondered if it could be Hanoi.

It was still daylight when we drove into the city. We could hear the rumbling of distant thunder. I peered through the windows, trying to see what the houses looked like. We passed a tall clock standing in a square. Staring at its huge hands, I read the time of day. The clock seemed like a miraculous creation.

I thought about all the stores and people in the city. Then I pictured the display windows and imagined myself walking from window to window, looking at all the wonderful things to buy. I wanted only to look at them, not to buy them. I was thinking not about jewelry or elegant clothes, but about much simpler things—a toothbrush, a good comb, underwear, a pair of nice solid shoes. If only I could be one of the people walking around outside; if only I could slip inside someone's skin for just one minute. It would be even better if I had a cloak of invisibility and could move around among them without being seen. And meanwhile, were the people outside wondering who might be riding in this ambulance through the streets of their city? Did they bother to look up as we passed them? Perhaps there had been so many ambulances that no one paid much attention to them any more. . . .

The rumbling noise I had heard was a thunderstorm, not the roar of airplanes. The storm broke just overhead. Lightning flashed through the sky and rain beat down on the ambulance roof. Twice the driver stopped the vehicle. I wondered if he had got lost. Was he asking someone for directions? Directions to where? Asking myself the same old questions, I felt that the

173

dreary weather, the rain beating down on the roof and splashing against the windows, exactly suited my mood.

Where were they taking us, and would they set us free as soon as we got there? Would they say, "You understand, we cannot send you home in this condition; we want to fatten you up a bit first"? Would they delay our release again, leading us on with new lies? I looked at Bernhard, but he was lying on the floor asleep. It had got dark outside.

We left the city behind. When the lightning lit up the landscape, I saw level plains and trees bending in the wind. There were no houses, nothing but wide, empty fields. Would the planes dare to fly in this weather? Was Bernhard right to be sleeping so trustfully? Would we soon arrive at an airport? If there was an airport, it must be outside the city. I thought that the suspense would never end.

Suddenly the driver stepped down hard on the brakes, as if he had just noticed that he had driven past his destination. Or had he simply run out of gas? The ambulance started moving again. The driver backed it up slowly, as if he were trying not to run off a narrow road. The motor died. I saw and heard nothing but the rain. If we were at an airport, we would be able to hear planes. Then I heard voices.

Someone outside opened the double doors at the rear of the ambulance. Lightning shot across the sky and flashlight beams danced before my eyes. A man said something in Vietnamese. Somehow it shocked me to hear him speak. What had I been expecting—someone speaking German, like the formal blond gentleman in my delirious dreams?

I saw that Ong Bô and Anh Simh had already got out. The Doctor nudged me, then pointed to my back pack and the fiber mat, a sleeping roll that had replaced my hammock. Not saying a word, he smiled a strange, embarrassed, apologetic smile and pointed at my things as if he were reminding me not to leave them behind. What use could I have for the worn pack and the fiber mat? What good would they do me in an airplane? People would think I was silly to have brought them.

174

It was still pouring rain. More flashlights had appeared out-side. I saw our three companions walking away through the rain. The Doctor turned around, but then another figure inter-vened, cutting off my view. A voice hidden in the darkness commanded us, "Get out!" For a long time, no one had spoken to us in this tone or pointed rifles at us. It had not been so long that we had forgotten what it meant, but we failed to obey at once, and the man shouted again, "Get out!"

Picking up my pack, I rolled up the fiber mat and tucked it under my arm. Then I climbed out, avoiding looking at Bernhard. I saw a long building with tiny holes along the side. The holes must be windows. It was a prison. Then I turned to look at Bernhard. He stood there dumbfounded, holding his pack and fiber mat, looking as if he could not or would not believe what he was seeing. He seemed about to open his mouth and protest in a very polite but determined voice, "I beg your pardon, but how dare you address us in that tone?"

Our three escorts had vanished. We were surrounded by strangers wearing raincoats and helmets and holding guns. When the beam of a flashlight lit up my face, I closed my eyes to shut out the blinding glare. "You go first!" someone said, push-ing me from behind. I tried to turn toward Bernhard, but the men were pushing me away. Then I noticed that in those few seconds, the rain had already soaked me to the skin.

Soldiers walked along in front of me; others followed behind. After we passed the huge, elongated prison building, I saw a series of small square stone buildings with spaces between them. One of the men in front of me opened a door. I saw a pale reddish light emanating from a bare light bulb. Someone pushed me from the rear, and I staggered into the room, hearing the door shut behind me. Then I heard a sound I had never heard before, a terrible sound—the noise of iron grating on iron as two bars slid into place outside my door. . . .

I was in a tiny square room. One step from the door was the cot, a couple of boards raised just above the ground. A bucket stood on the floor, and a small black box, a loudspeaker, hung

on the wall. Then there was the bare light bulb. That was all.
The floor was gray concrete, the walls were covered with rough
gray plaster. There were no windows.

I heard people whispering and walking around outside. Then
somewhere nearby I heard again the sound of iron bars being
slipped into place.

Suddenly I heard Bernhard cry out. I did not understand what
he said. Perhaps he was not even saying words. As he yelled,
I heard him kicking the door and beating it with his fists. "So," I
thought, "it was all for nothing. They were deceiving you. . . ."

For some time now, Bernhard and I had not been getting
along very well. During our march to the North, things had
grown even worse. He and I were very different, and we reacted
differently to prison life. In the American camp, Bernhard had
in effect saved my life with his rigorous program of physical
exercise. But after that he told me that from then on, he was
concerned with only one thing: survival, getting free any way
he could.

When Monsieur told us in the mountain camp that we had
been released, Bernhard could not bear to hear me voice my
skepticism. Often he was very angry at me, for he believed
that my behavior might influence our captors not to release us.
Our most recent quarrel had occurred in the jungle hospital.
On the first day I was able to get out of bed, Ong Bô decided
that it would be a fine idea to have me sweep up the yard.
Treating me with the contempt Vietnamese men always show
toward women, he threw a broom at my feet. Instead of obeying, I picked up the broom and threw it back at him, loudly
scolding him in German for his bad manners. It was a dangerous
thing to do: one night on the way to the hospital, when I was
too weak to go on, Ong Bô had hit me to make me keep
going. But this time, I had really managed to make him furious.
For a moment he was so angry that he did not know what to
do. Then he pulled out his pistol and held it to my temple.
Strangely enough, as we stood there face to face, I did not
feel afraid. He was more afraid than I, for he was basically a

calm, cool-headed man who knew quite well what would happen to him if he were to pull the trigger. I believe that knowing that he did not dare to kill me made him angrier than ever. Lowering the pistol, he put on the safety catch and slipped the weapon back into its holster.

When the scene was over, Bernhard, looking ashen-faced, started yelling at me in front of the Vietnamese, asking me what I thought I was doing, and telling me that I knew very well how long the Vietnamese could bear a grudge if they were insulted.

"It wouldn't hurt Your Majesty to stoop to sweeping up the yard," he said. He told me that my behavior might ruin everything and keep us from being released. "Just don't get the Vietnamese in a bad mood!"

This was not the first time that he had warned me to be more pleasant. He believed that the only way to earn his release was to do everything the Vietnamese asked of him.

For a few days after this incident, we hardly spoke to each other. For the most part, he walked at the head of our group with Ong Bô, and I brought up the rear. Often my companions and I did not reach the camp at night until an hour after Bernhard had arrived. He and I strung our hammocks far apart.

The Vietnamese had managed to drive us apart. I could not stand these people. I hated having to listen to their language.

Bernhard did not understand my attitude. The two of us continued to quarrel. Often he would scold me for going around with such a hangdog expression on my face. He told me that Anh Simh and the Doctor had both asked him what was the matter with me, and he ordered me to be friendlier to them.

To be friendly! How could he dream of such a thing? "Do you want me to walk through the jungle grinning from ear to ear?"

Yes, that was exactly what he wanted. "The only thing that matters is that we survive. Surely your life is worth a smile or two?" He told me to be careful how I behaved in future. If I didn't do what he said, then I would just have to get along on my own. He, at least, wanted to go home. And after all, we had been officially released and were now on the road to freedom.

"Don't you understand, we're free!" he said.

"Are you quite sure?"

Then he exploded again, railing about my eternal doubts and pessimism. He was convinced that freedom lay at the end of our journey. . . .

Now I could hear him hammering against the door and screaming at the top of his lungs. I knew how much worse it was for him than for me, for he had believed that our captors would keep their word. At that moment, I was almost grateful that I had never really believed that we were free. Hearing Bernhard's cries, I forgot all the bitterness there had been between us. No, I would not let them drive us apart.

Then it grew very still. I had not moved and was still standing beside the door. Outside I heard footsteps approaching. Someone raised a panel in the door. I saw a face. "You sleep!" said a voice. "You sleep!"

Under the circumstances, how did they think we could possibly sleep? As I sat down on the edge of the cot, the light went out. The storm had moved on, but I could still hear distant thunder. I began to cry. Now I was allowed to cry. No one could see me, no one could get angry with me. I did not even lie down. I just sat there crying for the rest of the night.

Bao Cao

BERNHARD DIEHL

Never before had I lost all sense of time. I knew that it was June 4, the four hundred and fourth day of my captivity, but I did not know whether the sun had risen yet. It was dark in my cell. A dark cell. The very words sounded dark and terrifying..

I could think only one thing: "Today you were supposed to be free, but they have locked you in a dark cell." I did not even want to think about anything else. I wanted to remember this moment so that I would never again be foolish enough to hope.

I heard footsteps outside my door. Instinctively I shut my eyes. It was too late to cover my ears; I could already hear them drawing back the iron bars. In the future, I resolved, I would always cover my ears when someone came to the door. I did not want to hear the grating sound of the bars.

Two soldiers with rifles were standing outside. They ordered me out of the cell. Even with my eyes closed, I was blinded by the light. When I could see again, I followed the soldiers, and for the first time I saw the little stone buildings from the outside. They were all the same, square concrete blocks without windows, half buried in the ground. I did not see Monika anywhere.

The soldiers led me along a narrow path until we came to a

179

wall. Behind a narrow gate in the wall lay another prison yard and the large, elongated building I had seen the night before. We entered the gate, climbed the stairs, walked along a passage, and stopped in front of a door. One of the soldiers went inside. I could hear voices. Then the soldier returned and motioned me into the room with his rifle.

Several Vietnamese were sitting behind a long table at the head of the room. I counted the men; there were eight. Two stools stood in front of the table. The Vietnamese sitting at the middle of the table pointed to a stool, saying, "Sit down!" I moved the stool a foot or so forward and started to sit down. Then the same man began to bellow at me. I could not understand what he was saying. One of the soldiers restored the stool to its former position. "Sit down!"

"How are you?" The Vietnamese was quite calm again.

As always, the conversation was conducted in English. I understood the question, but was unable to answer.

"Did you sleep well?"

Did he really expect me to respond?

"Your name is Bernhard Diehl, and you were captured on April 27 of last year."

What was the point of reminding me?

"You are German?"

"Yes, I am German."

"You fought for the Americans."

Were they really starting that all over again? "No, I did not fight for the Americans. I am a medic."

The door opened behind me. A soldier entered and reported something to the commanding officer. Then Monika was brought in. She sat down beside me on the other stool. I could not look at her. I could not forget that I had refused to listen to her when she tried to tell me how she felt. Now I wished that I had listened.

"How are you?"

They were addressing Monika. Turning to look at her, I could see that she was smiling. I thought, "Why are you bothering to smile? You don't need to smile any more."

"You are German?"

"Yes."

"You fought with the Americans?"

"Tell me why you are not releasing us."

I could not stand it any longer; I stood up. Behind me I heard the guards releasing the safety catch on their guns. But I said what was on my mind. "We were released! We were told that we were being taken to North Vietnam and that a plane would fly us home from Hanoi. What right have you to take us prisoner again?" I did not really think that they would pay any attention to what I said.

Or were they trying to provoke us? Were they simply trying to prove how generous, kindly, and humane they were by letting us go all over again? Were they teaching us one final lesson before sending us home?

I was already beginning to hope again. I had to stop doing that. "They promised us . . ."

The official waved his hand, dismissing my question. "We will investigate the matter. You will wait until our superiors have reached some decision."

I tried again. "But we were told quite clearly and unequivocally that we had been released, that we were free."

The Vietnamese gazed impassively across the table. The others were silent, sitting there like extras in a movie. "I am certain that there has been some misunderstanding. You must have misinterpreted something that was said to you. Or perhaps you are lying."

"I am not lying."

"You are not implying that someone lied to *you*, surely you do not mean that? That would be a pity. Let us assume that there has been a misunderstanding. We will clear it up. It may take some time," he said with a studied smile, "and you will be spending this time here with us."

So that was why he had summoned us, that was why he had put on his show with the soldiers and the seven extras. He wanted to introduce himself, to show us that he was the commandant, and to tell us the camp regulations. It almost seemed as if he had too many guards and not enough prisoners in his camp and was happy to add us to his entourage. Some time later I learned that the Americans had dubbed this camp "Farmsworth," because the commandant behaved like an American show host by that name. Monika and I called it "Camp Bao Cao." On that first morning, we were taught the meaning of the phrase *"bao cao."*

"You will obey the camp regulations," the commandant continued, "and the first and most important rule is politeness! Whenever you speak with anyone, whenever you wish to make some request, you must say *'Bao cao.'* "

I asked him what the phrase meant.

He explained that I had already been guilty of impoliteness. I ought to have asked, *"Bao cao,* what is the meaning of this phrase?" *Please, I should like* to know what this word means. *Please, I should like* to wash up. *Please, I should like* to have my food now. That was what *"bao cao"* meant, and every prisoner had to get used to saying it.

I was still standing, but now I sat down. The commandant shouted that I should have asked his permission to sit down. I stood up again. He began shouting that I should have asked his permission to stand.

He called the guards. "Take them away!" As I turned to go, he shrieked that I should have asked the guards to lead me away. . . .

They led Monika and me away separately, taking both of us back to our lightless cells. There was a slight delay before they locked me up again. A Vietnamese arrived carrying a stool and a razor. He looked at me expectantly. Perhaps he was waiting for me politely to *request* that he shave my head bald. Finally he went ahead and shaved me anyhow.

The razor was old and left tufts of hair sticking out here and there. I thought, "Perhaps you ought politely to request that he take off every last hair." I was filled with bitterness. Instead of sitting in an airplane, I was sitting in front of a cell

182

having my head shaved like a war criminal. Was the same thing happening to Monika?

Then once more I was sitting on the cot inside the dark cell. The hours passed, but I had no way of knowing what time it was. *"Bao cao."* Now I had to humble myself, to be submissive to everyone I met. It was stifling hot inside the cell. The air did not circulate. I was sweating and unable to sleep. After doing my exercises, I perspired even more. My body was covered with boils. They bled when I scratched them, but what difference did that make?

How many hours had passed? At some point, the iron bars were drawn back and the door opened. I was blinded by the sunlight. The guards had brought my food. Once again, I did something wrong. When the door opened, I should have stood up at once, bowed deeply, and politely requested that I be given my food.

So we were supposed to bow, too. Well, it was not hard for me to bow. Let them have their bow if they wanted it.

I learned that lesson quickly: whenever the door or the small panel opened, I had to bow. Also, prisoners were not permitted to speak first. They had to wait until they were spoken to. Moreover, when they spoke, they could not talk out loud, but had to whisper. Camp Regulation Number Two in Camp Bao Cao was, "Prisoners must speak in a whisper to guards and camp officials."

Suddenly there was a terrible racket in my cell. For the first time I became aware of the small loudspeaker on the wall, which broadcast news and propaganda in English. The acoustics in the bare cell were very poor. There was so much static that I could barely make out a word. Lying on my cot, I thought, "At least now you are closer to Monika, for she is hearing the same sounds in her cell."

Footsteps; the panel in the door was raised. I stood up and bowed. But the Vietnamese was not satisfied with that. Pointing to the loudspeaker, he said, "When the news is on, you are not permitted to lie down! You must *sit* on your bed and listen! That's an order!"

After that, I sat on my bed and listened three times a day to radio broadcasts of "The Voice of Vietnam." I had learned another lesson.

Darkness. More hours that I could not count. The door opened. I bowed. I asked to be given my food, the tin plate with cooked squash and a piece of bread, and the two small cups of water. That was my ration for half a day. We were served two meals a day and were allowed fifteen minutes to empty our plates. The time was ample. When the guard returned, I asked his permission to hand back the plate. How quickly I had got used to it all.

Shortly after my meal was over, the panel was raised again. The guard handed me a cigarette. Holding the cigarette in my left hand, I reached for the matches with my right. Horrified, the guard shook his head and hurried away. I must have committed so great an offense that he could not explain it to me himself and had gone to report the matter. I stood there with my cigarette and no match.

After a few minutes, the guard returned with an official. They discussed the situation in front of my cell. Then the door opened and the official explained my error. "You have no discipline!" he shouted. "You have no breeding! Are you trying to cause trouble?" When someone offered me a match or anything else, he explained, I was supposed to hold out both my hands! Moreover, I must give back the matchbox with both hands. "We are going to teach you to be polite!"

This rule was not a security measure designed to keep a prisoner from hitting a guard with his free hand; it was simply a form of humiliation. Holding something with both hands is a token of submission.

For the next few days, I kept on learning. One evening I recited a poem out loud in my cell. I do not know exactly why I did this, except that it was very dark and terribly still. I wanted at least to hear the sound of my own voice. I recited a poem I had learned in school, the first poem that came into my head.

184

The little trap door opened again, and the grim-faced official asked what I was saying.

"I am reciting a poem."

"What kind of poem?"

"A German poem that I learned in school."

"A West German poem?"

Was Goethe a West German? He had lived long enough in Weimar to qualify as an East German. Deciding to risk it, I said, "An East German poem."

For a moment he hesitated. Then, clearly annoyed, he said, "You know that you are not permitted to talk out loud! Keep that in mind."

Well, at least I knew it now. He went on to explain other rules. Prisoners do not knock on the walls. Prisoners do not talk to themselves. Prisoners do not sing in their cells—I wondered whether very many prisoners felt like singing in their dark cells.

Then I was alone again, sitting in the dark. I did not know what was happening to Monika. "What a fool you've been," I thought.

Then I discovered the lines on the walls. Someone sitting in my cell had scratched the lines with a nail on the gray plaster walls. There were many lines, in groups of five, representing the days of the month. Then came a single thick line: that was a year! There was more. I kept on counting. There were more groups of five. The lines became crooked and much thinner, as if the prisoner had given up after a year had gone by. I counted 397 lines in all. Could it be true? Could a man survive 397 days alone in a dark cell?

I tried to imagine what it would be like. Three hundred and ninety-seven lines. I stared at the gray wall. Who was the prisoner? What was his name? Where was he now? Was he reciting poems? Was he singing songs?

Three hundred and ninety-seven lines. "You'll go out of your mind," I thought. "Unless you do something, you're going to go crazy in this cell. . . ."

The Fever King

BERNHARD DIEHL

I kept hearing voices, and many strange faces were bending over me. It was summer, it had to be summer; and yet if I stretched my hand out from under the covers, I felt freezing cold. My forehead was bathed in cold sweat. I was parched with thirst. Where was I? Who were these people? Why were they wearing white smocks? What did they keep murmuring about? I had to move around and speak; otherwise they would think I was dead. I had read stories about people who were buried alive by mistake. Were the stories true?

Buried alive! I tried to sit up. The voices grew louder. Then for a long time I heard nothing at all. When I regained consciousness, they were all standing around in my cell, just as before. I still did not have the strength to sit up, but I managed to keep my eyes open and I could move my lips. I asked, "What's wrong with me?"

One of the men said in English, "You were very ill. But now you're on the road to recovery."

I looked at the man. It was the one wearing the white smock. There was only one man there with a smock. A stethoscope dangled from his breast pocket, and he was holding a hypodermic syringe. His hands looked as if he worked very hard. Again I tried to raise my head. "What's the matter with me?"

"Probably malaria," the doctor said. Probably? These bun-

186

glers! Couldn't they ever do anything right? Why didn't they take a blood sample? Then I saw all the puncture marks around my wrist, which was covered with blue and yellow bruises. These accursed bunglers, they could not even manage to draw blood correctly! Doctors have always said that I have prominent veins, very easy to locate. I watched the doctor dab a spot on my arm with a cotton swab and then stick in the needle. The needle was very dull. God knows how many times it had been used. He injected some liquid and, when the syringe was empty, drew blood from the vein. My hair almost stood on end. What kind of results could anyone get from a blood sample like that?

I felt too weak to protest. The men left my cell. I heard a key being turned in a lock and then fell into a deep sleep.

As soon as I awoke, I remembered the sound of the key. No, I had not been mistaken, there really was a lock on the cell door, not an iron bolt. Light entered my cell through a narrow barred window. Light! They had taken me out of my dark cell. I looked around. I was in a strange cell. For an instant I thought that I had never seen it before. But then I began to remember, pieces of the puzzle began to fit together. . . . I am in another camp. . . . It is night when they take us from the dark cells. . . . I scarcely have time to grab my things. . . . They take me to a jeep. . . . Monika is there, too. Four men are guarding us. . . . We drive through the night, through a large city. Hanoi? An asphalt road, streetcar rails, people riding bicycles, a single flickering neon sign above a barred storefront . . . We are outside the city again, traveling for half an hour over bumpy, uneven roads. . . . A long wall, a gate with a pagoda-shaped roof. Watchtowers . . . Long cellblocks . . . Monika and I are separated again. We are led off in different directions.

And then?

My memory is growing clearer. Interrogation sessions! They interrogated me for six days, asking the same old questions they had asked a hundred times before. No hint that we might be released. The disappointment and, after that, nothing more . . . I want to sleep, I want to forget, I do not want to realize that

CAMP K77

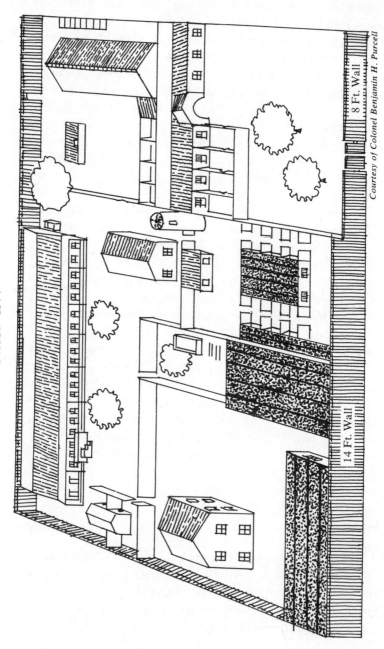

14 Ft. Wall

8 Ft. Wall

Courtesy of Colonel Benjamin H. Purcell

nothing has changed, that it is all going to continue, that it will never end. . . .

I sat up slowly. I was surprised that I felt strong enough to sit up. So this was my new prison—a bare-walled cell about seven feet square, with a wooden door containing a small trap door that at the moment was closed. Above the door was a window covered with iron bars but open so that light and air could enter. Then there was the wooden cot on which I was lying, and a bucket that served as a toilet. On the wall opposite me hung a placard.

Lowering my feet to the concrete floor, I stood up and wobbled over to the wall. The placard listed the camp regulations, in English. The letters were faded, as if the notice had been hanging there for many, many years:

CAMP REGULATIONS
American servicemen participating in the war of aggression by U.S. administration in Vietnam and caught in the act while perpetrating barbarous crimes against the Vietnamese land and people should have been duly punished according to their criminal acts. . . .

The regulations went on to state that despite the "crimes" committed by the prisoners, the lenient and generous policy of the Vietnamese people guaranteed them a "normal life." There followed ten rules which prisoners were supposed to obey. The rules were similar to those in the other camps, particularly Camp Bao Cao, but there was one difference. Here we were called not prisoners but "detainees," and we were in not a prison camp but a "detention camp." My cell was a "detention room." From the placard it was clear that Monika and I were being accorded the same treatment as the American prisoners.

Outside, footsteps approached; then the door opened. The men stared at me as if I had risen from the dead. Did I really look as bad as all that?

At the door was one of the men who had always accompanied the doctor. I remembered him because on his narrow hand he wore a large gold signet ring engraved with the image of a horse. He was one of the interpreters in this camp, which was called Camp K77. Later I nicknamed him "Sonny Boy." I decided on the name while I was reading the third volume of the selected writings of Lenin. Having completed the chapter on "The State and Revolution," I asked Sonny Boy what was the difference between socialism and communism. He hemmed and hawed for a while and then gave up, announcing with a beaming smile that he was "an easygoing person," and suggesting that, instead of talking about politics, I should ask him for tips on becoming a good table-tennis player. He told me that he had won the last regional table-tennis championship and thus was the "champion of the entire region."

Sonny Boy smiled as he stood in the doorway. "You really seem to have recovered," he said. "Do you know that they'd given up on you?"

"What's the date today?"

"August 4," he said.

I knew that we had arrived at Camp Bao Cao on June 4, 1970. "How long have I been here?"

"Since June 11." Again he grinned broadly. "Do you know that you are now the Fever King?"

"I'm what?"

"You really made it! You are the Fever King. You beat them all! All the Americans and all the Vietnamese. You had a temperature of over 107°, and that's the record in this camp. You are the Fever King, and I think you'll hold your record for a long time." He twisted the ring on his finger. "Now you and I are both champions."

I asked him about Monika, wanting to know why we had been separated and whether I would be permitted to see her.

The smile left his face, and he answered curtly, "She is here." Camp regulations did not permit prisoners to visit one another.

Thinking about the interrogation sessions and about our promised release, I asked Sonny Boy whether I would be permitted to write home. He answered only, "Do you know that people talk when they are sick with fever? Do you know all the things you said? You said very bad things! If you said things like that when you were conscious, you wouldn't be treated nearly so well."

Was he bluffing? If I had raved when I was delirious, then I must have spoken German. Did he or some other Vietnamese know enough German to have understood me? It was possible that I had talked about how much I hated them. One thing was certain: I was still their prisoner, and there was no reason to hope that they would ever let me go. . . .

For the next few days, I continued to get better. My temperature dropped to normal. Every two weeks or so I suffered a minor recurrence, complete with chills, which lasted a day or two. Then I was given injections, and for two whole weeks I received a lemon every day. In other respects, the food was very bad. In the morning I was given a piece of bread, a spoonful of sugar, and boiled water. At noon and in the evening, there was thin, watery squash. I was allowed to leave my cell only to put the chamber pot in the outside yard, or when the guards took me to the well to wash up.

The yard outside the door was part of my tiny prison. It was no larger than my cell and surrounded by a wall about ten feet high, with barbed wire strung along the top. Sometimes I was locked out of my cell in the yard and allowed to sit for an hour or two in the sun.

Perhaps I was no worse off here than in the jungle camps of South Vietnam, but I could not get used to the change. In the South I had spent all my time with Monika and the other prisoners; I had even been close to some of the guards. Here in the North I was alone, in solitary confinement, inside a cell that measured only three paces and a yard where there was nothing to look at but walls. The walls suffocated me. They reminded me that I was nothing but an animal in a cage.

In the mountain camp and on the long journey northward, I had almost been free. Our guards had always shared our privations. Here, on the other hand, the men who guarded me looked well fed and well rested. They wore rings as Sonny Boy did and talked about their plans to spend the weekend in Hanoi.

I was always aware of the large city and the many people nearby; yet I was more alone than ever before.

In the jungle, my sole concern was, "How are you going to survive? What are you going to eat? How can you keep warm? How can you get through the next day?" Here I began to ask, "How can you keep the loneliness from driving you crazy?" In the South, I had devoted all my energy to physical survival. Here I struggled to keep from being destroyed by my own thoughts and feelings, by my self-pity.

For weeks I lay on my cot staring at the ceiling, indifferent to everything. After all, what was the use of trying to keep busy? Nothing mattered. They were never going to let us go.

At first I did not believe that anyone could sit in a cell reciting poetry and singing songs; but in less than two months, I began talking to myself all day. Monika had had to learn to walk all over again. Now I had to learn again how to think. I knew that unless I did something soon, I was really going to lose my mind.

First I tried to remember everything I had learned in school. After reconstructing the opening monologue from *Faust*, I walked up and down in my cell, three steps forward, two steps back, declaiming the lines. I managed to remember almost all of the 104 chemical elements. Then I arranged the elements in groups according to their physical and chemical properties—valence, melting point, and electrochemical properties—and reconstructed the periodic table. For weeks I worked out new combinations: two elements in group K, eight in group L, eighteen in group M. But I knew that soon I would have to get hold of books, paper, and ink.

My only hope to obtain these materials was Sonny Boy, the table-tennis champion and "easygoing person," who did not know the difference between socialism and communism. I was not certain whether he had the authority to grant such privileges, for the bureaucratic hierarchy in Camp K77 was far more complex than that in the southern camps.

Camp personnel fell into four basic categories. At the top

of the ladder were the commandant and his two deputy assistants. Next came the staff of English-speaking interpreters. Third was the group the Americans called the "turnkeys," the men responsible for opening and closing the cells. At the bottom of the ladder were the guards. In reality, however, the chain of authority was more complex. An interpreter like Sonny Boy held a higher position in the hierarchy than a turnkey, yet the turnkey could order an interpreter out of a cell any time he chose. A turnkey held a higher rank than a guard, but the guards determined when a cell could or could not be opened. Even the commandant made no decisions without consulting his deputies and interpreters. Thus the system was one of mutual checks and balances. It was almost impossible for a prisoner to obtain any privileges, for no one person had the power to grant them.

One day Sonny Boy appeared and asked whether I would be willing to teach him German. This was the opportunity I had been waiting for. I explained that "we" would need paper and ink so that I could write out his exercises. Another camp official also asked for lessons. He had never spoken to me before, but when he learned that our Aid Service had maintained a dispensary for the Vietnamese in Quang Nam, he became very friendly. "Axel," as I called him, was born and raised in a village near An Hoa.

Thus I had suddenly acquired two "pupils." I was given sheets of coarse brown paper, pen and ink, and even some reading material. First I was allowed to read the censored newspaper printed by the VNA, the "Vietnamese News Agency," especially for American prisoners. I also read the *Vietnam Courier,* a propaganda sheet published for foreign distribution. Finally I was given books. First Sonny Boy brought me the third volume of Lenin's collected works. Strangely enough, I was always given the concluding volume of each collection first—the third volume of Mao's works, the fifth volume of the collected works of Ho Chi Minh—and received the first volume last. Besides all these, I read English translations of Sholokhov and Maxim Gorky. . . .

I was really allowed to read! I learned whole chapters by heart and recited them aloud. Then, using my paper and ink, I began to assemble an English-German dictionary that eventually contained two thousand words. I converted Marx, Engels, and Hegel into Alexandrines and composed a three-act play containing six hundred lines of verse, based on a passage from *Das Kapital*. I also wrote my own poems, some six thousand lines in two years. Not long before, we had trained with sacks full of stones to prepare for our journey to freedom. Now I was trying to train my mind.

And most important of all, I was learning Vietnamese.

Do You Speak Vietnamese?

BERNHARD DIEHL

As the months passed, my life changed very little. The food was as bad as ever, the cell as small, and I was not allowed to spend any more time in the yard than I had been before. I had heard no news of Monika and wondered whether she, too, had been given paper and books. I continued to read and memorize long passages, and I went on writing, seated on the cot in my cell and using the stool as a desk. When I was permitted to sit in the yard, I read or wrote outside.

Each cell had its own little yard. There were long blocks of adjoining cells, with wooden doors connecting one yard to the next. I was housed in Section A, Cell 1. One of the two wooden doors in my yard opened into the large prison yard, which was always patrolled by guards. The guards could look into my yard through a crack in the door. Repeatedly the guards came over and asked me the same question, something that sounded like, *"Anh lam chai chi?"* When I asked Sonny Boy about it, he said that it meant, "What are you doing?" Wanting to answer the guards, I asked the interpreter to write down the Vietnamese for, "I cannot tell you what I am doing in Vietnamese." The sentence looked endless. Then Sonny Boy smiled and said that in future I ought simply to reply, *"Toi không thê nói duoc tiêng viêt,"* which meant, "I do not speak Vietnamese."

My attempts to teach German to Sonny Boy and Axel proved

an abysmal failure. I tried to approach the subject systematically, beginning with grammar; this gave me an excuse for using so much paper. Unfortunately, Sonny Boy and I got off to a bad start. The two of us were sitting outside in the yard. I began my lesson with the German sentence, "I am ready to teach you German." When I translated the sentence into English, Sonny Boy jumped up and hurried to the wooden door to make sure that no one had overheard us. Then he returned, visibly outraged. "You cannot say that to me!"

I did not understand what was wrong. What exactly was I not supposed to say? "To teach you German!" I, as a prisoner, could not possibly teach a Vietnamese anything. What if someone should overhear me! It was not polite or respectful to speak to an official in this way. I should have said, "I am ready to help you understand German." It was all right to *help,* but not to *teach.*

From that moment on, Sonny Boy's desire to learn German rapidly dwindled. I *helped* him learn simple phrases like "Good morning," "Good evening," "How are you?," and "I am a high-ranking official." Once he had mastered that, he was quite satisfied. I feared that my paper supply might soon be cut off. When I asked for writing materials for my own use, I was always told that there was no paper, that the storeroom was closed, that there was no money to buy supplies, or that the ink had all dried up. But if I explained that I wanted to write out Sonny Boy's German exercises, I was given whatever I asked for, even though the interpreter never showed up for his lessons. As an additional precaution against losing my supplies, I asked Sonny Boy to teach me Vietnamese. In this case it was quite proper to use the word "teach," for of course a camp official could *teach* a prisoner.

When we were captured, I knew only a couple of words of Vietnamese. In An Hoa, we had always relied on interpreters. I knew that when addressing a man, one said *"Chao ông"* for "Good day"; when addressing a woman, *"Chao ba."* *"Cam ông"* was "Thanks very much." These phrases exhausted my vocabulary. In the American camp and the mountain camp, I began to learn more, mostly by conducting conversations in sign language.

I remember one "conversation" I had with the cook in the mountain camp. Pointing to his left hand, the one missing two fingers, I asked him in German, "What caused it?" He pointed to the sky and said *"Máy bay my."* I knew that *"my"* meant "American," but what was *"máy bay"*? Extending his arms like wings, the man imitated the sound of airplane motors; thus I knew that *"máy bay"* meant "airplane." First he pointed to his left hand, then to the sky, and then at the ground, making the sound of a machine gun. I understood that guns firing from an American plane had shot him in the hand. Then I asked a question I had already learned, *"Bac si lam chi?"* "What did the doctor do?" He answered, *"Bac si kat!"* I interpreted this phrase to mean, "The doctor amputated my fingers!"

This was a rather primitive method of learning a language, but my strange conversations had a certain charm. Sometimes it took me five or ten minutes to figure out a single word, another five to pronounce it correctly, and a whole hour to piece all the words together so that they made sense. The Vietnamese soon grew accustomed to conducting these fragmentary conversations with me.

One day in the mountain camp, I left the hut with my pajamas draped over my arm and approached one of the guards. *"Tôi in di tam?"* (May I go and wash these?) *"Không duoc!"* (No!) Then it occurred to me that, while addressing the guard, perhaps I ought not to hold anything in my hand. Laying my pajamas on the ground, I asked again, "May I go wash?" He answered, "Prisoner not good. Very bad. Too late. No washing today. Back to the hut."

One morning I left the hut and asked, *"Tôi in di tói kia?"* (May I fetch the machete?) *"Di lam chi?"* (What for?) "I'd like to cut wood." "No." "We have no more wood." "Not today. Today it's raining. Clothes would get wet. Not good. Sick. Headache. Fever. *Bac si không có thuôć.* Doctor has no medicine."

"We cannot build a fire. We are freezing."

"Good. Take the machete. Go!"

"Hôm nay tôi di dao Hanôi," one of the guards in Camp K77 suddenly announced. We were standing in the yard outside my cell, where I had just placed the toilet bucket. I had learned that *"hôm nay"* meant "today." *"Tôi"* was the pronoun "I." *"Di"* meant "go." That much was clear: "Today I am going to Hanoi." But what was *"dao"*?

The Vietnamese turned, walked a couple of yards at a leisurely pace, and then walked back. The word meant "to go for a walk." So the sentence was, "Today I am going to walk to Hanoi."

Then I asked him the words for "at two o'clock." When Sonny Boy visited my cell a few days later, I surprised him by announcing in Vietnamese, "This afternoon at two o'clock I am going to walk to Hanoi."

Instead of laughing, Sonny Boy looked very grave and told me that I could not use this expression. He was a man who believed in drawing fine distinctions and explained how unthinkable it was that a prisoner should go walking toward Hanoi. A prisoner could not even ask permission to do such a thing!

Sonny Boy continued to teach me the fine distinctions. He did not condescend to write out exercises for me as I did for him; but sometimes he would take a stick and draw words in the sand outside my cell. He also explained the five accents and the mysteries of Vietnamese word order. Used in different positions, the same word could have radically different meanings. I learned words and fragments of sentences, concentrating on phrases I needed to communicate with the guards and turnkeys. I made notes, but the most important words I wrote on the frame of the little trap door in my cell. *"Giat"*—"to wash," *"uông"*—"to drink," *"lanh"*—"cold," *"dau"*—"pains," *"thuôc"* —"cigarette," *"hút"*—"to smoke," *"giây"*—"paper," *"múc"*— "ink," *"tai sao"*—"why," *"xin lôi"*—"I beg your pardon."

Always remembering to begin my sentence with *"Bao cao,"* I could now say, "Please, I would like a light," "Please, I would like some water," "Please, I would like to speak to an official who understands English." Moreover, now I could understand what the guards said to me: *"Máy bay my không tôt!"* (American planes are not good!) *"Nixon không tôt!"* (Nixon is not good!) *"Dông duc tôt làm."* (West Germans are not good.) East Germans were very good, as were the People's Republic of China and the USSR. Very, very good was Uncle Ho. I also heard, *"Chung tôi dánh my."* (We are destroying the Americans.) Soon I was able to conduct brief conversations with Axel, Sonny Boy, and the slippery Crisco.

"What will you do when you get home?" Crisco asked me in Vietnamese.

"I will study medicine."

"Are you married? Not yet? Why not?"

"I'm not even twenty-four. That's still very young."

"Have you any children?"

"No."

"Why haven't you any children?"

"Because I am not married yet."

"Oh, in Vietnam you can have children even if you're not married."

"Not in Germany."

"West Germany is not good. Vietnam is very good."

Another conversation went like this: "Hey, you. Today I'll cut your hair!"

"Please, I would like to ask that you not cut my hair!"

"Why?"

"Because, Mister Official, you do not know how to cut hair."

"What do I do wrong?"

"You cut it all off."

"Prisoner, be quiet. I know how to cut hair."

"I would like to say that you cut it very badly."

"The prisoner is not speaking politely! The Vietnamese official cuts hair very, very well."

"Please, can't you cut my hair tomorrow?"

"Banat is impolite. Banat bad. West Germans are bad. I will cut your hair, that's enough now. Forward march."

One day Crisco came to me and said, "You have read a lot. Now do you understand Kac Mac?"

"I do not understand the official."

"You, Banat, are German, and yet you don't understand Kac Mac!"

"Please, I would like to ask that you write the word for me." He drew it in the sand in front of my cell: K-a-c M-a-c. I shook my head.

"Kac Mac is a great German! You read Kac Mac all the time."

"You mean Karl Marx?"

"How did you say that? *Anh nói chái chi?*"

"K-a-r-l M-a-r-x!"

This time he shook his head. "Oh, German is very hard. German prisoners are a lot of trouble."

I filled up more and more sheets of the cheap brown paper with notes. In other respects, my life went on as before. I was not permitted to see Monika or anyone besides the camp personnel. My brief encounters with the Vietnamese did little to relieve my loneliness. My cell grew no larger and the wall around my yard no lower. And, as before, I had to suffer through the long nights alone in my cell.

When I asked about Monika, I received curt replies. "She's well. All the prisoners are well." Then I was told that we had committed barbarous crimes against the Vietnamese people; nevertheless, they were treating us with leniency and generosity!

On the morning of September 2, 1970, Sonny Boy took me from my cell and conducted me to a large office building, formerly a villa. He told me that one of the commandant's deputy assistants was granting me an audience. I inquired whether I was allowed to ask questions. Sonny Boy replied that I was only supposed to answer them. "Mister Deputy Director" entered the room, and Sonny Boy began to translate for us.

"Have you recovered from your illness?"

"Yes, I think so."

"Do you get enough to eat?"

"No, I do not get enough to eat. Besides, the food is of poor quality."

"We will do something to improve the food."

I knew that he would say that; I also knew that nothing would be done about the food.

"Do you get enough sleep?"

"Yes, I get enough sleep."

"Do you often think about home?"

"Yes, I often think about home."

"Don't do that. Are your parents still living? How are your parents?"

"I don't know. I have not yet been given permission to write them."

"We will make arrangements for you to write home. Do you know the date today?"

"Yes, today is September 2, and I have been a prisoner for four hundred and seventy-one days."

"Today is Vietnamese Independence Day. Today in Hanoi there will be a giant military parade and fireworks. In honor of our Independence Day, we will permit you to meet with your friend."

Sonny Boy led me away. Guards accompanied us as we walked through the camp. For the first time I realized the size of the camp and got some idea of where the various cellblocks were located. I had not yet seen a trace of the American prisoners.

I was taken to the room in which I had been interrogated. Here I saw a table, two chairs, and two stools. Monika had not arrived yet. She and I had not seen each other for almost three months. I wondered how she would look, what had happened to her in the interim, and how she was coping with solitary confinement.

Sonny started to offer me a cigarette but stopped when Crisco entered, a cigarette dangling from the corner of his mouth, his hands buried in his trousers pockets. Crisco straddled one of the chairs backward, resting his arm along the back of the chair. He began asking me the usual round of questions.

"How are you? Do you know what today is? Did you know that it is a great holiday for the heroic Vietnamese people?"

At that moment, Monika entered the room. I was startled when I saw her. She had grown even thinner. Her face appeared sunken, and she had deep black circles under her eyes. But it was not her appearance that shocked me most. She looked like a person who has been dragged from darkness into light and would like nothing better than to be allowed to return to the darkness.

Crisco proceeded to ask her the same questions he had asked me. Monika looked at me. "Tell them to leave me alone. Or tell them whatever they want to hear."

They did not leave us alone together. I asked Monika whether she had been given any books. She answered no. Did she have paper and ink? No. I told her that she must try to keep busy. For the first time she smiled a little and said that she knew a wonderful way to pass the time; but she did not tell me what it was. After ten minutes, the guards told us that the meeting was over and led us back to our cells.

It was September 2, 1970, Vietnamese Independence Day, the four hundred and seventy-first day of our captivity. That evening I really did see fireworks in the sky. . . .

Dream Houses

MONIKA SCHWINN

It was a dream house: a white façade, lots of windows with white shutters, a staircase, and a projecting roof resting on columns. The house was surrounded by green trees. It resembled Scarlett O'Hara's home in *Gone with the Wind,* but it was smaller and more graceful, which made me like it even more. They had chosen to turn this beautiful old colonial-style home into a prison, an office building for the camp officialdom. Perhaps the former owner of the house had been the first prisoner in the camp.

On the evening we were brought here from Camp Bao Cao, all the windows in the house were lit up, so that it looked especially beautiful. It made a deep impression on me, for it was the first real house I had seen after spending a year in the jungle. Houses have always meant a great deal to me. When I first saw the house at Camp K77, I remember thinking, "That's a place where I'd be happy to live."

I did not see the house again until September 2, when I was permitted to meet with Bernhard. The meeting took place so abruptly that I did not have time to think of anything to say. Afterward, in my cell, I thought of all the things I wished I had asked and told him. For months I had tried to think of some way to find out how Bernhard was, some way to get a message to him. I was not even certain that he was still alive.

I had seen Bernhard just one other time, in the interrogation room. I was being led into the room just as he was being led out. Interrogation sessions were always the same. We were told that we had to stay in the camp "until your case has been settled," and that it would be settled very soon, for "our superiors" were planning to deal with the matter. Until they had done so, of course, we would remain where we were. . . . I knew that I would never, never again believe anything they said, and I was certain that they would never even charge us with any specific crime. Moreover, nothing we did could influence them to release us, for our freedom did not depend on how we behaved. Sometimes I asked permission to write home—not because I believed that they might comply with my request, but simply to prove to myself that I was still alive, that they had not yet crossed me off their list, that they still acknowledged my existence, if only on paper. . . .

My cell was the last in a row of five. To get there, I had had to pass through the yards adjoining the four neighboring cells. The other cells in my block were unoccupied and the yards strewn with rubbish. I saw and heard no signs of life. From time to time the cell next to mine was used for interrogations; then for a little while I would hear voices. Otherwise I was completely alone. I used to scratch lines on my cell wall to represent the days. There was nothing else to do, although I would gladly have done the filthiest work in the camp in order to keep busy. Finally I began to build houses.

The walled yard adjoining my cell had once been inlaid with tiles. Tiles and fragments of tiles still lay around the yard—white, light-gray, and dark-gray ones decorated with a small pattern. I collected them and stacked them in different piles to use in building my houses. The Vietnamese had refused to give me books and writing materials, so the broken tiles were all I had.

At first I built real houses, using the tiles, bits of wood, and the sand in my yard. But soon I saw that I did not really need all those materials. My houses would be much larger and more beautiful if I simply sat down in the yard, smoothed out a patch of sand with my hand, and drew the floor plan with a small bamboo stick. Even using this improved method, I ran into problems. My brother, a structural engineer, kept looking over my shoulder and criticizing my houses. He worried about statics and how much weight the ceilings would support, and he complained because I ignored base lines and all the basic rules of construction. He was always there, correcting me and making me feel self-conscious, the way older brothers often treat their younger sisters. So I started to build purely imaginary houses.

This method was supremely successful. Freed of my inhibitions, I worked away for days and weeks and months. I did not even need to stay in the yard any more, for the cell worked just as well. I always had several building sites in different stages of construction and had to go around tending to each one.

At first, as a sort of warming-up exercise, I rebuilt houses with which I was already familiar, like my brother's home and the homes of various relatives. Then I received contracts to remodel houses, to add a conservatory or make improvements in the attic. Finally I grew bold enough to build houses of my own. I even tackled large buildings like hospitals; but my favorite buildings were hotels.

The main advantage in building a hotel was that there were so many things to think about—especially if, for example, one wanted to build along a wild and lonely coast in Sardinia. It took some time to select the proper location and arrange the financing. After that, there were wells to be dug, and I had to figure out some way of conveying electrical power to the site from a long distance. Then there were all my conversations with the man who had commissioned the building, when I had to convince him that some of his ideas simply were not feasible. Once I built a hotel containing five hundred beds. I myself got to select all the beds, for I only accepted contracts that appointed me to pick all the furnishings.

I enjoyed furnishing my buildings even more than building them. To furnish them properly, I often had to go on long journeys to find some special object—a painting, a certain kind of wood for the paneling, a Gobelin for the entrance hall, preferably one with a blue background. And of course there were the dishes for the various restaurants, the silverware, and the linen, all designed in a special pattern.

I was always working on several buildings and sets of furnishings at once, but sometimes I miscalculated the date on which I would complete them. Suddenly I would find that I had finished both the buildings and their furnishings and had not yet got around to drawing up any new plans. Those were terrible days indeed.

Sometimes reality intruded once more, and I felt as if the ceiling of my cell had fallen down and crushed me. Then I had no recourse but to pray. I prayed as we pray only when we are desperate, and went on praying for almost two years. I never received any answer to my prayers, and this fact made my life doubly bitter.

I doubted the existence of God. Lying in my cell, I told him, "I am praying to you from the depths of my soul, and yet I receive no answer, I see and hear nothing, you do not give me the slightest sign. I am a prisoner; can't you relieve my suffering a little? I am losing my mind. I may end up killing myself. Don't be surprised if I do! It is a terrible thing to lock up a person like an animal, leaving her nothing to do for months on end."

Sometimes I was tempted to pick up the stool and the bed and try to break down the walls. At those times, I prayed until I grew a little calmer. . . .

I had lost my faith in God. I continued to build my dream houses, but now they seemed to topple down before they were completed. I never really slept, just drowsed day and night. The guards brought me food twice a day. Once a day I put my toilet bucket outside to be emptied. One day I was given a piece of cloth, scissors, and needle to sew myself a blouse. Then I asked to be allowed to make clothes for children, but my request was refused. Summer and fall were over, and winter had come. In January I was transferred to another cell.

The yard adjoining my new cell was larger than the old

yard, and inside stood a tree. The place looked like a garbage dump. Broken objects and rubbish of all kinds lay around in heaps, and everything was overgrown with weeds. But now, for a while at least, I had something to do. With no tools but my bare hands, I began to clean up the yard. I spent all day arranging the trash in piles—bits of wood in one pile, broken glass in another, miscellaneous scraps and weeds in a third. A little fence about two feet high encircled the tree, and the space inside the fence was piled high with earth. By placing the stool on the raised ground and then standing on the stool, I could reach up to twist off the barbed wire on top of the wall. I made a cross of wood and mounted it with an image of Christ made of barbed wire.

I also dug a flower bed, where I grew weeds. One of the turnkeys used to spit out melon seeds into my yard. I gathered and sowed the seeds and managed to grow little plants. In mid-January, one of the turnkeys gave me a pepper plant which I raised with loving care. It developed beautiful heart-shaped leaves and buds, but I watered it too much, so it never bore fruit.

I saw Bernhard only once during this time, at Christmas. We met in the same room as before. A small tree stood in the room, hung with paper garlands, and a picture of Santa Claus, painted by an American, was hanging on the wall. Once the Vietnamese had told me to write down information about myself and had given me four sheets of paper to write on. I used one sheet to write a letter to Bernhard. Then, taking my needle and thread, I sewed a false bottom in an empty cigarette pack, concealing the letter inside. But when Bernhard and I met at Christmas, the two guards did not let us out of their sight for a moment; thus I did not have a chance to give him the letter. After ten minutes, we were led back to our cells.

A new year had begun, 1971, our third year of captivity. I kept remembering two dates: April 27, the day of our capture, and March 31, the day when Monsieur had "released" us. Both these events had taken place in the spring. We had spent a year in the southern jungle and a year in North Vietnam. What was going to happen to us this spring?

I began to receive better treatment. The guards and turnkeys occasionally talked to me. The food improved. Now I was given meat once a week, as well as bananas. Against my better judgment, little by little I found myself hoping again.

March 31 had passed. April 27 arrived. All day I sat in my cell, my heart pounding madly, staring at the door. I was certain that someone was about to open it and tell me that I was free. But nothing happened. In fact, on the following day they seemed to have decided to treat me more harshly. I had scarcely taken the food into my cell when they slammed the door and locked it behind me. Surely there was some reason for this sudden change in their behavior. Did they want me to go to pieces, to do something foolish that would warrant further punishment? Or did they want me to throw myself at their feet, whining for mercy?

I racked my brains, trying to understand. Something had to change, or I could not go on. I had spent two years, twenty-four months, seven hundred and thirty-one days of my life in prison, and still there was no end in sight.

I did not want to kill myself. There was no need for me to go that far. All I had to do was lie down in my cell, close my eyes, and stop eating, and then I would be sure to die. The Vietnamese themselves had once told me how easy it was to die if one simply lay down and did not move. Wasn't death the best thing that could happen to me? Death was the only thing I still had to look forward to. Was there any life left for me in a world where I could no longer even believe in my dream houses? . . .

Two Saxon Gentlemen

MONIKA SCHWINN

The wooden door opened, and the turnkey stood there holding his great bunch of keys and calling, *"An com!"* (Food!) I was lying on my cot and did not move. Jingling his keys, he called more loudly, *"An com!"* Recognizing his voice, I answered, *"Toô com an!"* (I won't eat!)

I was sorry that it had to be this particular turnkey who found me, for he was by far the friendliest of them all; it was he who had given me the pepper plant. He had told me that he was fifty, but he looked much older. A small, emaciated fellow, he had lost some of his teeth and was also losing his hair. He was crooked and bent when he walked. I called the man "Ba Cham," Father Hundred, for with his wrinkled, leathery face, he looked as if he were a hundred years old.

Standing in my cell, Ba Cham looked very unhappy. He toyed with his bunch of keys and said once more, *"An com?"* Then he turned around, still bent over, and locked the door behind him.

I heard him talking with the guards outside. I knew what was going to happen, and I did not have long to wait. Almost at once, three men appeared, led by the commandant with his turned-up nose and receding hairline. The commandant smiled, confident of victory. I could endure their shouting, but whenever a Vietnamese smiled at me, I felt afraid.

209

He began to question me. Why did I not want to eat? I had no right to refuse to eat: that was disobedience of the camp regulations. He commanded me to start eating immediately.

I did not answer him. There was no reason to reply. Turning my face to the wall, I remained silent.

Strangely enough, he did not begin to shout or threaten me. He told me that if I would simply explain my grievance, he would give me anything I wanted. I knew perfectly well that they would promise prisoners anything to get them to cooperate. But I decided to try it anyhow. I asked for paper and ink.

Asked what I intended to write, I answered that I wished to write out a complaint. What did I want to complain about—about him, about the camp? He said that no prisoner had ever complained before. I replied that I wished to submit a petition requesting that I be told why I was being held here. I wanted to have a trial where I could defend myself and have my case decided one way or the other.

"You will be given paper and ink and allowed to submit your petition. I will pass it on and make sure that your case is settled. I promise that you will have your trial. Now will you eat?"

"No," I replied. "I do not believe anything you have said." I saw that the commandant was no longer smiling and seemed uncertain what to do. They had lied to me too often for me to believe a word they said. Therefore I decided to continue my hunger strike. That first day I was actually given paper and ink and allowed to write my petition. I requested that Bernhard and I be released or immediately tried in a neutral court of law. I also asked permission to write and receive letters from home and demanded adequate medical care. I did not hope that any of my requests would be granted.

For the next few days I did not eat a thing. One day one of the turnkeys opened my door and told me that I was being allowed a visitor. I had often told them that I wanted someone to talk to. Now a Vietnamese woman entered my cell, smiling and looking very friendly.

Since moving to this new cellblock, I had often heard women's voices; thus I knew that other women prisoners were housed nearby. For a long time I had wanted the chance to talk with another woman. I offered the Vietnamese woman my stool. At first we found it very hard to communicate, for she spoke only a few words of French and English. Using signs and gestures, we managed to carry on a conversation.

I learned that she was a nurse, twenty-eight years old, who five years before had married a *bac si*. She had been a widow for four years. Her husband had died in South Vietnam, fighting on the side of the Viet Cong.

But if her husband had fought with the Viet Cong, why was she a prisoner in this camp?

She said that she had worked in the German-Vietnamese Friendship Hospital in Hanoi.

"Is there really a German hospital in Hanoi?" I asked.

She replied that it was East German. She had tried to steal vitamins and medicine from the hospital for members of her family, but she had been caught and sentenced to two years' imprisonment.

It was now eleven o'clock, and my midday meal was brought in. I never touched my food, but every day the guards continued to bring me my meals. This morning, the guard was a man I had never seen before. I was struck by the intimate way the Vietnamese woman addressed him. Later she explained that he was a friend of hers but cautioned me not to tell anyone.

Beginning to distrust her, I looked at her more closely. She wore new, very white clothing. How could a prisoner have such clean clothing, when the water we were given to wash with was always dirty and full of insects? I saw that her hair was neatly combed. Where would a prisoner get a comb? And she had plucked her eyebrows! Getting my paper and ink, I drew a pair of tweezers. She told me that tweezers were called *"dip"* in Vietnamese. Then I asked her to lend me her tweezers, but she said that she had none. In that case, how could she have plucked her eyebrows?

A little later, I detected another lie. The woman told me that she had married when she was nineteen. "What's this?" I thought. "She said that she got married five years ago, yet she claims that now she's twenty-eight? She certainly hasn't learned her story very well!" Just before the woman left that afternoon, she said that she hoped to be released in a few days and promised that, if I wanted to write a letter, she would smuggle it out and send it to Germany. Now I knew that she was an undercover agent who had been sent to spy on me.

She was such a poor liar that I almost felt sorry for her. Perhaps she really was a prisoner who had lost her husband, stolen a few drugs, and been locked up for two years. But what did she hope to gain by spying on other prisoners? Our captors might have promised to release her. If so, I doubted that they would keep their promise. And what would happen to her if she did not get me to do what they wanted? Soon I began to feel genuinely sorry for her. She was in the same predicament I was.

Every day she came to visit me again. She continued to be very pleasant and kept urging me to write a letter, but I pretended not to understand her. Then she took a piece of paper and indicated that I should write on it. She also brought me candy, and crayons so that I could draw pictures. Roses are my favorite flowers, so I drew a rosebush for her. I felt sad to think how much I had longed for someone to talk to. Now that my wish had been granted, I had to stop and think twice before saying a word. I did not write the letter as she suggested. But after eight days, I finally ended my hunger strike. I no longer had the strength to resist. Moreover, I thought that this way, at least, the Vietnamese woman would have accomplished part of her mission and would be spared the consequences of total failure. . . .

My hunger strike produced another unexpected result. One day, without warning, the commandant personally visited my cell and told me to put on the blue blouse I had made myself.

I was given soap and a towel to wash with, though both were immediately taken away from me again. The commandant did not tell me what was going to happen.

I was taken to the villa and brought to a room divided in half by a curtain. A bed stood behind the curtain. I saw a broad table, a flag on the wall, and a ventilator in the ceiling. But at first I was almost unaware of the furnishings, for I was amazed to see two white men sitting behind the table!

The men had blue eyes, and one of them had light hair, the other dark blond. Both wore short-sleeved shirts that were open at the collar. One of them was very thin, with a sunken face and deep circles under the eyes; his skin had an unhealthy pallor. The younger man was very fat. His chest was covered with thick tufts of hair which poked out through the opening in his shirt. He had clearly developed breasts. One of the men said, "Please sit down," and the other added, "As you can hear, we speak German." Both of them spoke with Saxon accents.

For months I had secretly been hoping for help from the East German embassy in Hanoi. I had learned that the embassy was nearby when I asked the Vietnamese to get some German books for me, and they replied that they were not on the best of terms with the German embassy in Hanoi. At once I began scheming, trying to think of some way to escape from the camp and seek asylum in the embassy. I believed that I could escape, and that Hanoi was not more than twenty miles away. I could travel that distance in one night. But how would I find the embassy, when there was no one I would dare to ask?

Whoever the two men were, they were German. Suddenly I felt a wild hope. . . .

"Now listen carefully," said the lean, older man. "To begin with, from now on there will be no more hunger strikes! And no more protests either. Is that clearly understood? In future you will undertake no further actions of this kind. You do not have the power to disobey us, and you had better not write any more letters of protest. Is that clear? These histrionic gestures won't help you at all. Quite the contrary: you're making your position worse. And now, will you be kind enough to answer a few questions. . . ."

As a child I used to build houses of cards and would burst into tears when my lovely building collapsed just as I was putting on the very last card. Once more, my house of cards had tumbled down. I had allowed myself to hope again.

The two Germans asked me the same questions I was always asked, but they wanted more precise information. "Was your father a member of the Nazi party? Was he a soldier? Where was he stationed? What was his field post number?"

I answered yes or no to two or three questions and then remained silent. My interrogators appeared nervous. One of them would light a cigarette, take a couple of puffs, and put it out. The fat man began to shout at me; but instead of intimidating me, his rage merely stiffened my resistance. The men broke off the "hearing," and I was taken back to my cell. Later that day I was brought back for more questioning. I did not see Bernhard. Eventually he told me that he had been interrogated on the previous day.

I do not remember how I answered their questions at the second session. I had suffered through many interrogations, but this was the worst of all, for it was conducted in German, our native language. At one point I tried to remind the men that we were all Germans. They answered in chorus, "We have nothing at all in common. Not even our language is the same!" They seemed to me more cruel than the Vietnamese.

From that moment on, I could no longer even bear to look at them. I stared at the flag hanging on the wall above the commandant's bed. It was a red flag embroidered in gold, but it was not new like the flags that fly from flagpoles or hang down outside windows. The cloth and the embroidery were old and faded, and the lower end of the flag was in tatters. It looked like a regimental flag that had seen many days of battle.

Did it belong to the commandant? He had a scar on his left temple. Had he fought in a war, and did the flag belong to the troop he had fought with? Did he hate serving here in the prison? At night when he slept beneath this flag, did he think

214

back to the days when he had captured prisoners instead of guarding them?

What did he matter to me, what did I care about any of the Vietnamese? I did not want to understand these people, for they had not bothered to understand me. . . .

I heard the fat man shouting at me, saying that I must answer their questions if I wanted them to be kind enough to continue working on my case. Apparently they were only interested in getting me to state my opposition to the "filthy war of aggression perpetrated by the U.S." "Kind," indeed! They disgusted me. I could not stand any more. My whole body was trembling. I could not bear to listen to them. I was sick to my stomach, and they had to return me to my cell. I collapsed just outside the door.

On the following day, they brought the Vietnamese woman to my cell to visit me. She knew what had happened and tried to comfort me, asking why I was so upset and assuring me that the two Germans were only concerned for my welfare. She said that I would surely be released very soon. Then once again she began to talk about the letter she wanted to smuggle out for me, promising that I could express my true feelings, without fear that the letter might fall into the wrong hands.

It was time to stop playing this cat-and-mouse game. I told the woman that I would never give her any letter and would not speak to her at all, for I believed that she would turn the letter over to our jailers and report every word I said. Her reaction surprised me. She laughed and, looking quite cheerful, said how relieved she was that she did not have to betray me.

What kind of people were they? The longer I lived among them, the less I understood them. A spy who was happy when she did not need to betray her victim; a prison commandant who liked to sleep beneath a tattered battle flag; a turnkey who was sad when his prisoners did not eat. I was lost in a world where nothing made any sense.

A trivial event made me feel better. One day I heard someone whistling and knew that a new occupant had moved into

215

one of the cells in my block. The prisoner was outside in his yard, whistling the same tune over and over—a few bars from *My Fair Lady*.

It had to be an American. The whistling sounded so happy and carefree. "If only I could see him," I thought. I wanted to see a happy and carefree young American.

He was not in the cell adjoining mine, but two cells away. The cell next door was unoccupied. I kept watching for my chance to get a glimpse of the prisoner. Then one day I noticed that the turnkey had forgotten to lock the door leading into the neighboring yard. I waited until I heard the whistling, then picked up my stool and hurried into the next yard, where I placed the stool in front of the wooden door. At the top of the door was a wide crack.

Peering through the crack, I saw the man standing in the yard beside the water trough, shirtless. He was busy shaving. I had pictured a young man; what I saw was a living skeleton. He was so thin that I could see every rib, and his collarbone almost poked out through his skin. His hair was gray and cut so short that he looked nearly bald. He turned around as if he could tell that I was watching him, and I saw that his face looked gray and sunken. There were deep hollows around his eyes. Yet he went on whistling just as cheerfully as ever.

He was the first American prisoner I had seen in North Vietnam. "Just look at him," I thought. "Think how long he must have been a prisoner, think what he must have suffered."

After that, I always felt better when the sound of whistling came sailing over the high walls. Now I was no longer alone!

Cargoes . . .

BERNHARD DIEHL

I was sitting outside in my cell yard. It was evening; the sun had almost disappeared behind the ten-foot wall. Then someone knocked on the wooden door connecting with the neighboring cell, and I saw a note being pushed through the crack high in the door. It was such a tiny scrap of paper that I might easily have overlooked it. Jumping up, I took the note. I barely had time to conceal it in the hem of my pajama trousers before the other door—the one leading into the large prison yard—opened behind me. My time outside was up, and the turnkey had arrived to lock me back in my cell. I stood behind the locked door, my heart pounding madly. This was the first note I had received during my year in Camp K77, and already I had almost been caught. Later I learned that the attempt to communicate with other prisoners was punished with three months' strict solitary confinement, a cut in rations, and the loss of yard privileges.

I waited until I could not hear a sound outside. Then I looked at the note, written in tiny letters on a piece of toilet paper. It was in English: "We are Americans. No names for now. We have heard about you. We'd be happy if you answered. If not, that's O.K., too. Be careful. Use this paper for the purpose it was meant for."

I lay on my bunk, holding the note as if it were a priceless treasure. Just a few days ago, I had been transferred to another cell. I was now in Section C, Cell 1, and I had heard voices coming from the neighboring cells. At least two men must have been sharing Cell 2, for I had heard two voices, a deep, sonorous bass and a high-pitched, almost feminine falsetto. The higher voice seemed to have been reciting numbers. I was never to forget that voice or the man to whom it belonged.

The night I received the note, I did nothing but read it over and over. How could they even dream that I would not want to reply!

In my former cell in Section A, it had been virtually impossible for me to communicate with the American prisoners. The Vietnamese were bent on keeping us all in total isolation. They separated prisoners by leaving an empty cell between each two occupied cells, or by placing a Vietnamese prisoner next to an American. In Section A, I had been in Cell 1; Number 2 was empty; Number 3 housed an American, Number 4 a Vietnamese, and Number 5 another American. When a prisoner left his yard to be interrogated or to wash at the well in the prison yard, he had to pass through the yards belonging to the other cells. Before he was led through, all the other prisoners were locked in their cells with the trap doors closed. I often tried to catch a glimpse of my neighbors, but I was lucky if I saw as much as a hand or a foot or a head.

During my stay in Section A, I succeeded only once in contacting an American. One day I was outside in my yard when suddenly I heard someone call out, "Happy birthday, Tom!" The prisoner in Cell 3 called back, "Thank you, Frank!" Taking advantage of the opportunity, I called softly over the wall, "Happy birthday, Number 3."

Then I asked him his name. He answered, but I could not understand him, for we did not dare to raise our voices above a whisper. I asked Number 3 to spell out his name, using the NATO alphabet. He said, "Tango, October, Mike . . . Tom. Romeo, Uniform, Sierra, Hotel, Tango, October, November . . . Rushton."

And his address?

"Papa, Alpha, Romeo, Kilo, Ecco, Romeo . . . Parker Street."

The town?

"New . . ."

New what?

"November, Ecco, Whiskey, Bravo, Ecco, Delta, Foxtrot, October, Romeo, Delta . . . New Bedford, Massachusetts. Got it?"

I thanked him, gave him my name and address, and said that we must keep in touch. Unfortunately, I never had another opportunity to speak with Number 3.

Inside my new cell, I listened to the voices next door. Was Tom Rushton one of my neighbors? It seemed likely that he was, for the note said that they had heard about me. I could hardly wait to find out.

I was lucky. As a rule, the Vietnamese never let me out into my yard for two days running, but the next afternoon I was allowed to go out again. I had not expected to get back to the yard so soon and thus had not yet written my letter. Outside, I sat there planning what I would write, feeling excited and nervous, and wondering whether anything would go wrong. Then I heard a sound. Glancing at the door, I saw nothing. Then I heard the sound again, a soft "pssst" just above me. Looking up, I saw a face above the wall, behind the barbed wire. The man's head had been shaved bald, his large ears stuck out, and his wide mouth was smiling, showing the teeth.

I jumped up, beads of sweat on my forehead. Still staring at the American, I dragged over my water trough, climbed up on it, and shook his hand. I cannot express how much it meant to me to be able to shake hands with one of my fellow captives. But the joy lasted only a few seconds. Then, fearing that we might be observed, I whispered, "Go back!"

The other door, which led into the prison yard, had a large crack in the middle. The guards had formed the habit of glancing into my yard whenever they passed. I never knew when one of them might be looking in. The door was a problem that

219

I would have to solve if my neighbors and I were to exchange notes in safety.

That evening I learned how important it was to be careful. Entering my cell, Sonny Boy came directly to the point: "You know that you are not allowed to communicate with the prisoners in the cell next door! Do not attempt to do so. It will only cause trouble." I did not think that he could prove anything, so I denied that I had communicated with my neighbors. Dismissing my words with a wave of the hand, Sonny Boy said, "We'll find out about it, I warn you. We'll know by the next day."

I paid no attention, for I was determined not to lose touch with the Americans. But first I had to find some way of solving the problem of the door.

I found the solution with unexpected ease. Whenever I was allowed to go out in my yard. I went to the door and peered through the crack at the prison yard, deliberately attracting the attention of the guards, who came over to scold me, threatened to report me, and immediately locked me up again inside my cell. Unabashed, I continued to peer through the crack. After several days, they took the door off its hinges and locked me in my cell for a whole week, until the new door was ready. It was a brand-new, very solid door—without a crack. The Vietnamese were proud of the clever way they had outwitted me. But I had what I wanted: they could no longer see inside my yard.

The evening of the day the new door was installed, I wrote my letter to the Americans. I wrote not a brief note but a long letter on a large sheet of my brown paper. This was the first letter I had written since my capture over two years before and I wanted to say everything that was on my mind. My first letter! Best of all, I knew that it was going to reach its destination.

I wrote down everything I had been wanting to say for so long; I poured out all my feelings, vomited out my rage against the Vietnamese. I did not know that this letter, or the information in it, would be circulated throughout the camp, earning me

220

my code name among the American prisoners: "Y.G.T.," standing for "Young Guideless Tiger."

Three days later I sent the letter through the crack in the door. Soon I received a reply listing the names of my neighbors. I had been right: Tom Rushton was one of the men sharing the cell. The man with the bass voice was a black named Don Rander. The man I had shaken hands with was Captain Thompson. I was certain that there was a fourth man in their cell, the man with the falsetto voice; but strangely enough, they had not given me his name. I asked about him in my next letter, but they simply ignored the question. I decided that I must have been mistaken. . . .

For the next few weeks, we kept up a lively correspondence. I learned that the Americans called our notes "cargoes," and that there were two kinds of cargoes. Simple communications about what was going on in the camp and friendly greetings between prisoners were torn into shreds and thrown into the toilet pails. A second type of message, called a "hot cargo," was immediately burned over the oil lamp. Hot cargoes contained information received from outside the camp, or names.

The names of other prisoners were always considered "hot." Before writing anything else, prisoners exchanged names and addresses. Hot cargoes also listed the names of new arrivals in the camp and the names of men being transferred elsewhere. It was important that every man know all the others' names, so that if one prisoner was released, he could carry news of the others to the outside world. Whenever I read a name, I immediately memorized it before burning the note. Often I spent whole nights walking up and down in my cell, repeating the names and addresses. Some of the names were those of dead men. . . .

James Dibernardo, lieutenant, Television Station Hué; last seen in April 1968 in a camp in North Vietnam. Andrew Anderson, Television Station Hué; captured 1968, last seen near the nineteenth parallel on July 3, 1968. Don Doin, sergeant, TV Hué; last seen in April 1968 in a North Vietnamese camp.

221

Harry Ettmuller, a sergeant in the same unit, same story. Tom Rexdale, agricultural expert, CORDS Hué; died in March 1968 in a camp in West Quang Tri province near the Laotian border. Sol Godwin, CORDS Hué; died July 25, 1968. Ernie Brace, shot down over Laos in 1965, in North Vietnam since 1968, believed dead . . .

Without ever seeing or talking to one another, we learned one another's stories. Often it took months to piece together the details of a man's life. Soon I learned that Captain Floyd Thompson had been captured in 1964 and imprisoned for seven years, the first three in solitary confinement in the jungle. Just before taking off on an L-19 reconnaissance mission, he had learned that his wife was about to give birth to their third child. The pilot of the plane had been killed, and Thompson himself had been listed as MIA/PD, or "missing in action, presumed dead." It was not until shortly before his release that Thompson learned of his official status and realized that for nine years his family had not known whether he was alive or dead!

Usually we all used pseudonyms when writing our cargoes. One man signed his "T.B.R.," for "The Black Ram." This was Lieutenant Colonel Ben Purcell, who was something of a legend: he was the only prisoner in the camp who had attempted to escape.

"The Black Ram" first attempted to escape from Camp K77 in December of 1969. He hoarded his sugar ration and toasted bits of bread over the oil lamp to eat on his journey. He drilled holes around the edge of the bottom part of the door so that he could remove the wood between the holes. On Pearl Harbor Day, he removed the panel from the bottom of the door, slipped out and replaced the panel, went over the wall, and walked in the direction of Hanoi. On the road, he was offered a ride on a bicycle. The cyclist, however, delivered him into the hands of the police, and the next day he was back in a punishment cell.

I was in the camp when Purcell made his second escape attempt, in the spring of 1972. We had all been transferred to Camp K49, which the Americans called the Mountain Village. This time Purcell planned to go to the coast, "requisition" a boat, and try to make contact with the U.S. Navy. After thirty hours of freedom he was ambushed by a group of soldiers and returned to K49. He paid for the thirty hours with thirty days of confinement to his cell and short rations.

To pass the time, many of the prisoners played chess, read, or learned a language. Ben Purcell, too, had to find some way to keep busy. Later I asked him why he had twice attempted to escape. He just smiled and said, "I think it was worth the trouble. I had to do something, right?"

... and Hot Cargoes

BERNHARD DIEHL

We devoted more time and energy to thinking about cargoes and hot cargoes than to anything else in prison life. We all worked to keep our lines of communication open, to reestablish contact whenever it was broken, and to invent new techniques for passing on the notes. Every prisoner in the camp racked his brains to come up with methods of keeping the messages flowing. We did not dare to send them often, for the guards and turnkeys were always on the alert.

At first the Americans and I passed cargoes back and forth through the door between our yards. But sometimes two weeks would go by before we were out in our yards at the same time; thus there was little opportunity of exchanging notes. We had to find other ways of getting our messages through.

Every morning a large toilet pail was passed along from cell to cell, so that each man could empty his chamber pot into the container. After first testing the system with a blank piece of paper, we began to stick notes under the lid of the pail, to be removed by the next man in line. This method did not always work. It was difficult to remove a note without being seen, for the guards always stood behind us when we were emptying our pails. Moreover, each man was locked in his cell before his neighbor came to drag the pail into the next yard, so that there was no direct contact between the prisoners.

224

One of the Americans noticed that a rat had gnawed a hole at the bottom of my cell door. The hole was large enough for a note to be pushed through. The American told me that, when an opportunity presented itself, he would try to get a message through the hole.

I waited for days, but nothing happened. Then one morning I heard someone shouting outside. My door was unlocked and one of the turnkeys entered, shouting and gesticulating wildly. I caught the word *"giấy,"* meaning "paper." Then Crisco arrived, crying, "Where did you put the note?"

"I don't have any note. What are you talking about?" I guessed that the American must have been caught trying to slip a note under my door. But wouldn't I have heard him if he had tried? In any case, I knew that I was in trouble. I had not received a note; but in preparation for the next exchange, I had just written my own cargo and concealed it in the hem of my trousers.

"You are lying! You are lying to an official. You're going to pay for this!"

Once more I assured Crisco that I did not know what he was talking about. I was lucky. The guards left me and went to the cell next to mine. But I knew that they would soon be coming back. There was only one thing to do: I had to swallow the note! Unfortunately, I had written my cargo on a piece of cardboard taken from an empty cigarette box, and, as always, it was a long message. Gagging, I chewed the cardboard for five minutes until it was soft enough to swallow. I had no sooner choked down the last of it than the guards returned.

This time they asked no questions, but turned my cell upside down. They made me strip naked and proceeded to search my clothing. Naturally they found no note and they left looking puzzled and angry. I was not given my midday meal. At noon I was taken to the interrogation room.

Sonny Boy was my interrogator, but it was useless to hope for any help from him. He was so furious that I hardly recognized him. He went on shouting insults until I finally managed to say, "I didn't receive any note. Therefore I can't possibly have one. Besides, the guards didn't find anything. What do you want me to do?" But he was clever enough to guess the truth: "Of course you don't have a note any more. The guards left you alone for half an hour."

"Unfortunately, they were gone only five minutes," I thought, still feeling the cardboard in my stomach. I asked Sonny Boy for a glass of water.

He said that he would give me ten minutes to think things over. "But I advise you to confess everything. You'll be sorry if you don't."

When Sonny Boy returned, he was somewhat calmer. Placing a full box of cigarettes in front of me, he promised to give them to me if I would tell him the truth. After all, he said, we were old friends.

"I can't tell you anything more than I've already said. I don't have any note."

"All right, so you don't have a note. But you know the names of the others. With whom were you exchanging messages? How many names do you know? Tell me all the names. Be sensible. Think about all the books we've given you. Think about the paper and writing materials. Now, will you talk?"

"I can't say anything but what I've already said."

He began to yell at me again. "You are ungrateful. And you're stupid too! *I* can tell *you* whom you were sending messages to. Do you want to hear the names?" He proceeded to list them all. "I don't need your confession! I already know all I need to know. But I'll still give you another chance."

Saying nothing, I merely shook my head.

The cigarettes disappeared from the table. Sonny Boy summoned Crisco, and they announced my punishment: the confiscation of all my books and writing materials, a cut in rations, and three months' confinement in my cell, without yard privileges.

They kept their word. For three months I stayed in my cell, except for the few times when I was allowed to wash outside. The guards and turnkeys were forbidden to speak to me. I heard no news of Monika or the other prisoners. I could hear strange voices in the cell next door. Apparently the Americans had been moved somewhere else.

I knew that the three months would pass. After two and a half years of captivity, the thought of three months' solitary confinement did not frighten me. What *did* frighten me and make me angry was the thought that someone had betrayed me! Sonny Boy had not been bluffing. He had correctly listed the names of all my contacts. I thought that I knew who the traitor might be: the American with the falsetto voice in the adjoining cell, whose name the others had refused to tell me.

His name was Fred C. He was a captain in the U.S. Army Intelligence Service, and I hated him until I heard his story. I did not see the man face to face until shortly before our release, when we were both in the Hanoi Hilton, and then I was ashamed of the hatred I had felt. But that day was still far off.

Without knowing it, I had already had indirect contact with Fred C. Often I had seen messages and numbers scribbled in the margins of the propaganda newspapers I was given to read. The turnkeys themselves took the papers from cell to cell, so I knew that the scribblings were not secret messages from one of the prisoners. The writing was thin and scrawled and the words made no sense. The scrawled words and numbers always made cold shivers run up and down my spine, for clearly the person who had written them was not in his right mind. They were the work of Fred C. Later I saw the "books" he wrote, which were even more frightening. Sometimes they contained as many as two thousand pages, in which not a single line made any sense.

Once I had actually seen Fred C. without knowing who he was. Coming to wash at the well in the prison yard, I saw a tall man who seemed to stoop. His prison clothes hung loosely around his body. As he talked with one of the guards, he bowed with folded hands. I was surprised at his obsequious manner and the submissive tone in which he addressed the Vietnamese. He did not seem to me quite normal. He looked like a broken man.

Eventually I learned his story. Fred C. had been captured

227

during the 1968 Tet offensive and taken north to Camp Farmsworth—our Camp Bao Cao, where Monika and I had spent seven days in dark, windowless cells. There the Vietnamese began to interrogate him. But this man was more than just one of the hated *my*'s: he was an intelligence agent, and they treated him accordingly.

Lieutenant Colonel Ben Purcell occupied the cell next to Fred C. and knew what was going on. The American would not talk, so they tied a rope around his left wrist and hung him from the ceiling of the cell. They left him there for an hour before taking him down and then repeated the process eighteen times.

Purcell heard him screaming. Night after night he screamed the same thing. He begged the Vietnamese to kill him, to let him die. They did not want to let him die. They wanted him to talk. After a month they managed to break him. Fred C. told them whatever they wanted to hear. But he no longer knew what he was saying. . . .

This was the man I had hated and despised. Later, in the Hanoi Hilton, he and I were quartered in a group cell, where we slept in adjoining beds. Like the other men, I tried to talk with him. But Fred just sat there playing with his hands as children do and talking to himself. He talked to himself all day long, only pausing to fill page after page with writing. When I woke up at night, I used to see him sitting on his bunk, talking to himself again.

He was an emotional wreck, one of the living dead created by the war. No words could describe what he had become. Once an American prisoner named Phil expressed what we all felt. "Back home we have a saying: 'I pitied myself because I had no shoes, until I met a man who had no feet.' "

My three months' confinement seemed to pass quickly. One day Sonny Boy appeared in my cell, smiling and as easygoing as ever. He had decided that he wanted another German lesson. Glancing at the marks I had made on my wall, I saw that three months had in fact gone by. Sonny Boy claimed to have forgotten the whole matter. "Let's talk about something else," he said. The Vietnamese were like that. How could anyone understand them?

I began to receive cargoes again. There were not many, but at least they were getting through. Soon I learned the names of the new American occupants of the cell next to mine. Then, in early December, a year and a half after Monika and I had come to Camp K77, I received a hot cargo reporting a rumor that we were all going to be transferred to another camp.

All the prisoners were eager to hear rumors and took them very seriously. We had no way of obtaining more accurate information. Besides, rumors often turned out to be substantially correct. In the Hanoi Hilton, our obsession with rumors turned into a kind of game. Whenever one prisoner met another, the standard greeting was, "Got a new rumor?" The proper response was, "Sure, I've got a great rumor: we're all going to be released!"

As soon as the rumor of our transfer had circulated through the camp, we all began preparing ourselves for the move. Quantities of cargoes streamed from cell to cell. Apparently the guards had orders to ignore them. Once more, names were exchanged and committed to memory. We all agreed on a signal: the first man led off to the new camp was supposed to whistle the opening bars of the song "Goodbye, My Love."

On December 10 I heard someone crossing the prison yard on the other side of my wall, loudly and cheerfully whistling, "Goodbye, My Love."

So we were really leaving. Once again we were being transferred. In the past, a new camp had not meant a change for the better.

Méo Means Cat

MONIKA SCHWINN

There are two old sayings, that when cats eat grass, or when chickens refuse to enter their coop at night, it means that it is going to rain. In prison one learns to sense things the way an animal does. In some primitive way, I sensed that something unusual was about to happen. Also like an animal, I was attached to my den and did not want to leave it. The cell and the yard outside were a cage, but they were the cage I was used to.

The guards came for me late one afternoon. They were in a great hurry. Having spread a blanket on the floor, they threw in my things and handed me the bundle. The jeep was already waiting. It was December 11, 1971, my thirty-second month of captivity.

The jeep was waiting with its motor running, and Bernhard was sitting in the back seat. On top of the jeep our captors had constructed two cages separated by sheet metal and bars. They transported us like animals being taken from one zoo to another. We were accompanied by four zookeepers to keep us from running away. It was already quite cold, but during the journey it grew even colder. I assumed that we must be climbing higher into the mountains. As we drove along, I told myself that there was no point in hoping for improved conditions in the new camp. But if necessary, I could always try another hunger strike. At least the last strike had accomplished something.

During the journey, I was not allowed to talk to Bernhard. As soon as we arrived at the new camp, he and I were separated. But before we were led away, I whispered to him, "You must back up what I'm going to say. Tell them that unless they want a dead woman on their hands, they have to give me what I want. I want paper and something to write with, and I want them to put you in a cell near mine and to let us see each other."

We had been traveling for almost two hours. The camp was, in fact, higher in the mountains, and the first thing I noticed was the bitter cold. The Americans gave the camp the romantic name "Mountain Village." I did not consider it very romantic. Standing outside my cell, my first thought was, "Well, you'd better get started with your hunger strike right away."

I saw a row of five cells with adjoining yards, just like the cellblocks in Camp K77. The cells looked very new and apparently were not quite completed. My cell was damp inside; the gray walls and floor glistened with moisture. I saw a wooden bunk, a table, a stool, and a bare light bulb. There was a massive double door of wood, fitted with iron hinges and lock. I saw the usual barred trap door and an open, barred window above the door. I could not stand any more. It was just too much. Everything was sopping wet; I could not even sit down. I was freezing cold. As I stood there holding my things, tears began to stream down my face. "Well, you have to do something," I thought. Then I saw bread and a piece of bacon on the table.

I was ravenously hungry and I had been dreading the thought of another hunger strike. I was not sure that I had the inner strength to go hungry for days on end. But once I had seen the cell, I felt so angry and defiant that I picked up the bread and bacon and handed them to the turnkey. He put them back on the table. Picking them up again, I set them down in front of the cell. He brought them back. This time I left them where they were, thinking to myself, "You'll see soon enough that I'm stronger than you are. . . ."

It was a cold night. I had put on all the clothes I owned, but

231

I was still freezing and miserable. This time I was determined not to cooperate with my captors. I lay down on my bunk, turning my face to the wall.

Soon the commandant arrived, accompanied by two interpreters. The cell was crowded with Vietnamese. I did not look at them or answer their questions. I was disobeying all the camp regulations at once. Finally they gave up and left.

I was determined not to touch a morsel of food. Ironically, the food here was better than in any of the other camps. When the guards left my cell, I used to get up and look at it. There was always some meat, and vegetables, and once even a fried egg! I did not know whether this was the usual prison fare, or whether they served me special food to entice me to eat. In any case, every day I found it harder to resist the sight and smell of the food. I recovered from my initial shock at my surroundings, and soon the cell dried out. It was larger than my cell in Camp K77 and even contained a table and a stool. The latrine and the wash tank were separate. And I was so hungry! But I knew that the first few days of a hunger strike are always the worst.

The Vietnamese here had more finesse than those in K77. They did not pay any attention to me at all. Not saying a word, they brought food to my cell every day and left it there all night. They did not remove it until the next day, when they brought fresh food. The quality of the food even seemed to improve somewhat. I saw things that I had not eaten for years. Beginning to weaken, I wondered whether my strike would really accomplish anything.

I made it through the first week, drinking water and occasionally swallowing a spoonful or two of rice. The portions were so large that the Vietnamese would not be able to tell that I had eaten a little. For the first few days, when I knew that I was unobserved, I did a few exercises, for I did not want to grow weak and ill. Still the Vietnamese showed no sign of relenting. Then, after ten days of fasting, I achieved my first victory.

It was already dark out. As a rule, no one came to my cell

that late. Then, hearing sounds, I lay down and turned my face to the wall, as I always did when I heard someone coming. One man unlocked the door; another entered and placed something on the ground. He said nothing. Then I heard a soft purring sound. I could not resist turning around. On the floor was a small bamboo cage which I immediately recognized as the cage in which Ba Cham, Father Hundred, had once brought me a bird he had captured. It had been a beautiful, brightly colored bird. But as I could not bear to watch it almost kill itself trying to escape from the cage, I had given it back at once to Ba Cham.

I glimpsed something gray behind the bars of the cage. Bending down, the guard pressed a wire, opening a small door. My cat walked out of the cage with small hesitant steps. . . .

The kitten, too, had been a present from Father Hundred, the only one of my guards who showed any compassion. For days I had heard a plaintive mewing. Finally I asked Ba Cham to let me keep the animal for a little while. It was so small that he could hold it with two fingers by the scruff of the neck. It was only a few weeks old and appeared to be starving.

I fed the kitten, chewing first the rice myself, for it could not even eat on its own. Then I placed my stool against the bed, so that the back of the stool would prevent the kitten from falling off, and lined the nest with some of my clothing. The animal slept there the first night. And fortunately, Ba Cham never remembered to take her away again.

I spoiled the kitten, feeding her my food and lifting her up and down from the tree in my yard. The Vietnamese used to scold me, for they believed that a cat should climb trees by itself and hunt its own food. But the kitten was so small that I could not help pampering her.

When the guards came to take me to the new camp, the kitten crouched under my bed, watching me get ready to leave. During the ten days she had been with me, she had grown very attached to me. At night she slept with me under my blanket, and she spent her days sitting in my lap. It was

233

December and very cold; thus even when she was in my lap, I kept her wrapped in a blanket. She used to cry when I got up to wash and could not carry her with me in my arms. Now suddenly I was leaving the camp, and I had to leave the kitten . behind. I had prayed and prayed that we would not be separated, but it was no use. . . .

The little cat had come to mean a great deal to me. I was overjoyed to see her again, jumping up on my bed and curling into a ball.

The man who had brought the cat was standing there watching. Then he asked, "Now will you start eating again?" I thought of the lovely large portions of food that they had been bringing. If I continued my fast, only the cat would get to eat them. But I shook my head no.

"We sent someone especially to get the cat for you." The interpreter seemed quite offended. Then he paused, apparently wondering what else he might offer me. "Would you like to have some sand and stones for your yard?" He explained that he had heard what nice flower beds I had dug in Camp K77. "If you agree to eat, we'll give you sand and some fine stones."

"Aha," I thought, "I'm on the right track," and resolved to go on fasting. After all, I no longer needed food: I was happy just to have my cat with me again. Now that she really belonged to me, I decided to give her a name. I called her Méo, which means "cat" in Vietnamese. . . .

I went on fasting for twenty days, until December 31. I could not go any longer without food, for I was so weak that I could do nothing but lie on my bunk. The moment I stood up, I felt very dizzy; everything clouded over and I almost fainted. Besides, I had achieved a second victory. Bernhard had been placed in the cell next to mine, and we had been given permission to see each other twice a week for half an hour.

Méo had profited most from my hunger strike. She had grown big and strong from eating all my food. She was too big now to spend the whole day inside my cell, so I tried to think of some way of letting her out for a run. Then Bernhard and I solved the problem.

234

It was spring now, and it rained a great deal. Often the water stood foot-deep in the cell yards. The Vietnamese had drilled holes in the walls to drain the water, but most of the holes were no larger than a pencil and thus not very effective. However, they had drilled a fine large drain in Bernhard's yard, which was at one end of the cellblock. Whenever I went to visit Bernhard, the cat used to slip out through the hole; but I went to Bernhard's yard only twice a week. In the evenings, when I knew that no guards would come to my cell, I began to let the cat out through the window over the door. A long beam led directly from my door to the door of Bernhard's cell. Méo used to walk along the beam into Bernhard's yard and then slip out through the drain. She returned to my cell the same way.

This gave Bernhard an idea. He had told me about the cargoes, and now he suggested that we might attach messages to the cat. Although we occupied neighboring cells, we were strictly forbidden to exchange a single word. Any attempt to do so was immediately punished, and the Vietnamese had already threatened to separate us again and to take away our visiting privileges.

I sewed a tiny pouch to hold our notes and fastened it to the cat before she began her evening rounds. Bernhard and I established our own postal system, and it functioned flawlessly. I would knock on the wall to let Bernhard know that Méo was coming out. He took hold of her as she passed his cell window, removed the pouch, and released her again. Then he waited until she returned, fastened on the pouch containing his message, and knocked on the wall to tell me that she was about to enter my cell.

Now Bernhard and I could write each other every day. Our notes and letters grew longer. Méo performed beautifully. I even sent Bernhard a small package of sugar and bread. I always fastened things to Méo's left side, so that if the guards happened to be looking her way, they would see nothing but a cat prowling along the beam.

Unfortunately, our lovely postal system broke down at the end of April, after only a few months. Our conspiracy was

235

never detected, but Méo had grown so big that she could no longer slip through the drain hole in Bernhard's yard.

Méo no longer needed the hole. "She" had turned out to be a tomcat who passionately loved his freedom—which was only to be expected from a cat of mine. To get out of the yard, Méo jumped up onto the ten-foot wall. Now he was far too independent a fellow to spend his time running about with little pouches tied around his neck. Every evening he disappeared; but punctually at 5:00 A.M., when the camp was beginning to stir, I would hear a purring sound next to my bed, and he would creep wearily under the covers.

At the end of April or the beginning of May, around the time when Méo stopped carrying our messages, Bernhard and I acquired a new correspondent. One morning I heard the sound of whistling outside. Bernhard was in Cell 5, and I was in 4. The whistling came from the yard of Cell 3, just next door. It sounded cheerful and carefree, and I recognized the melody. It was my old friend whistling his tune from *My Fair Lady*.

The Garden of Wishes

MONIKA SCHWINN

It was my neighbor who later picked the rose for me, and who also gave me a chess set. He molded the chessmen from bread that he could not eat because it was full of vermin. After molding the figures, he dried them in the sun. He made a complete set, using toothpaste to color the white men and ink for the black. He also composed a birthday poem for me:

> On this day I send a bunch of roses,
> Gathered from my garden of best wishes,
> In the center there's a big carnation,
> Chosen by my heart's imagination.
> Never think you are alone.

So my old neighbor was back, in the cell right next to mine. Almost a year had elapsed since I had caught a brief glimpse of him through the crack in the door. I still did not know his name or anything about him. But as soon as I heard him whistling, I wrote a cargo to Bernhard. It took me a long time to learn enough English to write cargoes. For weeks I had been carrying around a note listing my name and the date and location of my capture. I wanted to give the note to my American neighbor, but I did not have the courage to throw it over the wall in broad daylight. Bernhard had warned me to be careful. He had not

237

forgotten that once an American had betrayed him to the Vietnamese.

One morning I washed my clothes and hung them up in the yard to dry. Suddenly I noticed that the note I had been carrying was gone. I always kept it concealed in my clothing, but now I could not find it anywhere. After searching feverishly through my belongings, I finally saw the note lying in plain view on the doorstep of my cell.

I went on sweating even after I found the note. "They'd have taken your head off if they found that," I thought. "You'd better get rid of it right away." Fetching my stool, I placed it against the wall. Then I knocked once and heard the sound of my neighbor's cell door being opened. I had wrapped the note around a stone. Taking a deep breath, I threw it over the wall.

My heart pounding madly, I waited to see what would happen. For a while I heard nothing. Then someone knocked on the other side of the wall, and a note flew over to me. Dashing into my cell, I flattened out the piece of toilet paper and read the tiny letters.

The American had written that his name was Philip Manhard and that he had been captured during the 1968 Tet offensive. He was married and had three children. The note gave his home address. Then he added, "My folks back home don't know that I'm alive. If you get out before I do, please tell them about me. Thanks a lot. Burn this note. So long, Phil."

I memorized the note, and during my next visit to Bernhard's cell, I told him all about it. We began a lively correspondence with Phil. He and I never spoke with each other; yet as the weeks and months went by, we became closer than many people who live together all their lives. We each formed an image of what the other was like, an image which was both true and false. Our image of each other resembled the dream houses I had spent so much time building, or the garden I had planted, full of invisible flowers. Sometimes when Phil was outside in his yard, I would sit there staring at the wall; if I stared long enough, the wall turned into glass and I could see through to the other side. . . .

238

The other Americans called Phil Manhard "the Diplomat." He was not a soldier, but before his capture he had been chief of CORDS in Hué. Before that he had served in American embassies in Korea and Japan. He had also spent a long time in Communist China, working to extradite American citizens trapped there during the 1948 revolution. Thus "the Diplomat" had had considerable experience dealing with Asiatics and with Communists. The best informed of the American prisoners, he sent out most of the hot cargoes that circulated in the camp. Phil was extremely adept at interpreting information; thus he seemed to know more about what was really going on than a lot of the camp personnel.

Every month Phil received two "visits" from a young, inexperienced Vietnamese official who served in the Foreign Office in Hanoi. The young man was supposed to pump Phil for information, but Phil usually learned more than the official did. Most of us were bewildered by the propaganda newspapers we were given to read, but Phil knew how to read between the lines. When we read news of the victorious 1972 Tet offensive, Phil sent around a cargo saying that the North Vietnamese had suffered heavy losses. The rest of us read that Podgorny and Chou En-lai had received an enthusiastic welcome in Hanoi, but Phil immediately guessed that China and the Soviet Union had pressed the North Vietnamese to adopt a conciliatory attitude toward the United States. Once he circulated extracts from the French newspaper *Le Monde,* describing Nixon's visit to Moscow: the young Hanoi official had carelessly brought Phil a can of milk wrapped in a newspaper only a few days old.

"The Diplomat" not only kept us informed about current events, but also gave us tips on how to treat the guards and turnkeys and served as a confidant to whom we could pour out our impotent rage against the Vietnamese. At first Bernhard had opposed the idea of our corresponding with Phil, but soon he began to write the American letters many pages long. The two of them argued about politics and literature, and Phil had a restraining and subduing influence on my friend.

"The Diplomat" was gravely ill, suffering from severe stomach problems and cysts. It was almost a miracle that he had survived several years of captivity. Once he became so ill that the Vietnamese sent him away for a week's stay in a Hanoi military hospital. When he came back, I heard him laughing. In his next letter he explained that the only thing wrong with him was that his stomach was too small. At first the doctors thought that his X rays had got mixed up with those of a child. Phil had the stomach of a Vietnamese child in the body of an American man!

Bananas were almost the only food that Phil could digest, so when I was given bananas, I used to throw them over the wall to him. When Bernhard knew that I had thrown a banana, he would sit in his cell yard, as he said, "sweating blood." He felt that two or three bananas a week were not worth the risk of our being separated and having to give up our flourishing correspondence. Finally he grew so disturbed that he wrote Phil a letter requesting the American to tell me not to give him any more fruit. Knowing that he would have to give the letter to me so that I could forward it to Phil, Bernhard wrote it in French, thinking that I would be unable to read it. Then the Vietnamese stopped giving us bananas, and the problem solved itself.

Once again, Bernhard believed that we would soon be released. This time he expected to be free some time in the summer of 1972. For years he swung himself along from one hope to the next. When I dreamed about Bernhard, I saw him as a trapeze artist swinging from bar to bar in a circus tent. I was always running around by myself in the ring below, trying to spread out the heavy net that would break his fall. . . .

On September 16, Phil sent me the birthday poem. This was the fourth birthday I had spent in a prison camp. From then on, most of Phil's cargoes contained commentary on the political scene.

Had we noticed that, in the *Vietnam Courier,* there were an increasing number of reports about Kissinger's private conferences with Le Duc Tho? Had we read between the lines and realized that General Giap had complained about Moscow's

240

unwillingness to break the American sea blockade? Had we understood that Moscow and Peking had reduced their military aid to North Vietnam, and did we know what this implied? Then came a note saying simply, "Elections will be held in America in four weeks!!" We noticed the two exclamation points. Then the elections were over, and still no peace agreement had been signed. All the prisoners were deeply disappointed. Then Phil's next bulletin arrived: "Nixon reelected by a 63% majority!!!" This time there were three exclamation points.

Soon I saw other, more tangible signs that something unusual was going on. At the end of October, the turnkeys went around from cell to cell, distributing wonderful gifts. I received a piece of toilet soap, a washbowl, a comb and mirror, and a thermos jug, which I used not for hot water but for tea. Six exclamation points!!!!!!

That summer we had eaten the same meal twice a day for four and a half months—a bit of rice and "spinach à la vietnamienne," which was not really spinach but a kind of grass. Suddenly the food became as good as it had been during my hunger strike, and we were given six cigarettes a day. Moreover, at mealtimes we were handed a notebook listing everything we had been given to eat and were asked to sign our names. "Aha," I thought, "they're trying to fatten us up in a hurry, and protect themselves against accusations that we might make later."

We were very frightened when the Americans began to bomb Hanoi. At night we could hear the airplane motors and the exploding bombs. Everyone was very tense, and the cargoes were full of wild rumors. Since mid-November, the American prisoners had been allowed to meet once a week in a large recreation room where they played table tennis and exchanged notes. Bernhard and I remained in our cells, but Phil always told us what went on.

After Christmas came New Year's, 1973. In spirit, all of us were at the Paris peace talks. Phil reported that on January 8, Kissinger had met privately with Le Duc Tho. Ben Purcell went on a hunger strike, trying to get permission to write home.

The suspense increased. We were all holding our breath. On January 25, an interpreter distributed stationery and air-mail envelopes, and we were allowed to write home. During four years of captivity, this was the second time that Bernhard and I were allowed to write letters; but the letters were never mailed.

On January 27, when the Vietnamese came to pick up our mail, I was outside in my yard. Now we were permitted to spend all day outside. Méo was lying in the cell, resting up from the previous night's adventures. The day was passing uneventfully. Another day. It was strange to remember that not long ago we had counted time in months and years; now suddenly we were counting the days again.

Late that afternoon, I heard the Americans being taken from their cells. This was not the day when they were allowed to meet for recreation. Hearing them walking along outside the high wall, I could tell how hard it was for them to walk. Or was I just imagining that? "You and your glass walls!" I thought. "Now you really need a glass wall."

A half hour elapsed. What was that sound? It sounded like something roaring. Was it a roar of happiness? "My God," I thought, "can't you even tell any more when people are happy?" Then I heard the Americans returning. It sounded as if they were running and jumping. Someone was whistling just outside the wall. I did not recognize the melody, but Bernhard did. It was "Goodbye, My Love," and it meant that the Americans were going to leave the camp.

A little later, a piece of paper sailed over the wall. It was our last cargo. But it was not the kind of cargo we were used to seeing—tiny letters on a little scrap of paper. It was a large piece of paper with giant letters on it: "PEACE. Signed in Paris today. They turned over a list with the names of all the prisoners. We're leaving the camp in thirty minutes. Chin up! Lots of luck! I hope we'll see each other when we're free."

Peace. A list containing the names of all the prisoners. Were our names on that list?

242

Remember Us Kindly

MONIKA SCHWINN

They were smiling and sweet as honey. The commandant had put on a jacket over his white shirt. His eyes smiled behind his gold-rimmed glasses. The interpreter smiled. In the background, the guards were smiling, too.

So I wanted to take my cat along? Of course I could! After all, the cat belonged to me. They would give me a special basket to carry him in! The commandant himself would write a letter explaining that the cat was mine and ordering that I be given extra food for him and allowed to exercise him whenever I chose. It was so important for a tomcat to get enough exercise. They all smiled.

Oh, so I wanted to take the cat back to Germany with me? Well, of course I could. What a perfectly splendid idea. A German nurse takes a Vietnamese cat back home with her; we must tell the press all about it right away. So that there would be no problems later on, the commandant promised to give orders that I be allowed to take the cat home with me when I left. We must remember the Vietnamese people kindly; and of course we must remember him, the commandant, too.

Pouring us all glasses of apricot liqueur, he drank to our health. Then he drank to our new friendship, telling us to forget the past few years. He raised his glass.

We did not drink. Nor did we smile. But our coldness did

not disconcert him. Of course, he said, he understood that we could not drink: our health did not permit it. Yes, the winters were harsh in Vietnam. The winters, he said, but not the prisons. He smiled. They all smiled. After all, it was peacetime. Everything was fine now. To friendship!

As they stood there smiling at me, I feared them as much as ever. Suddenly I remembered the way the old rice farmer had smiled as he came out of his paddy, luring us into a trap. Seeing his smile, I had thought, "It's a pity that you can't speak their language and that you know so little about these people and their country."

Now, four years later, did I really know much more? I understood a few things better. I understood how many enemies these people had to combat, beginning with nature, the jungle and the rain, the floods and the drought. The *my*'s were not their first enemies, but simply the most recent. A thousand years ago it had been the Chinese, then the Japanese, and for the last one hundred years, the French. I understood how a people who had known nothing but enemies could learn to be enemies themselves.

I understood this, but it did not help me much to understand. It helped me not to hate them for what they had done to me, but it did not keep me from being afraid when they smiled. . . .

Our interview with the commandant took place in a large meeting hall. When Bernhard and I were led back to our cells to pack up our gear, it was already dark. The Americans had left the camp late that afternoon. We were the last to go. We were going to join the others where, the commandant had assured us, we would be very comfortable. We were to remain in the new camp until our release.

Returning to my yard, I saw Méo sitting on the wall. He looked very impatient, as if he could not understand why I had stayed away for so long. Peace or no peace, he wanted to be off on his usual nightly excursion and was waiting to be fed before he left. He had found a female companion somewhere in the

244

camp and could not understand why I was delaying dinner. And why was I trying to lure him inside this ridiculous basket? Our departure was delayed for over an hour while everyone waited for me to catch the cat.

There were four of us in the jeep—the driver, an interpreter, Bernhard, and I. As we rode along, I held Méo's basket in my lap. It was cold, and I had covered the cat with a blanket. I could tell that he did not like the basket or the motion of the car, and I understood his feelings. He was a camp cat descended from a long line of camp cats, and he must have known that no good ever came of moving to another camp.

We traveled for three or four hours. It was almost midnight when we reached the center of Hanoi and drew up at the camp the Americans called the Hanoi Hilton. The Americans were inveterate optimists.

As usual, we were barely given time to get out of the jeep before being locked in our new cells. Bernhard and I were assigned two adjoining rooms with tiny barred windows. Both rooms were filthy. The commandant was on the scene to greet us. Not bothering to smile, he told us to obey the camp regulations. Then he asked who had told Bernhard and me that we were being released. The commandant at our last camp? Well, he was commandant here! He knew that the Americans were being released, but he knew nothing about us.

Méo wandered restlessly through the dark rooms, jumping against the wooden door and scratching it until his paws were sore. He did not understand why no one let him out. I felt sorry for him. *I* knew that peace had been declared and that we were going home, but the tomcat knew only that he had lost his girl friend back at the other camp. . . .

For the next week, we were not allowed out of our cells. We kept hearing the Paris accords being read over the camp loud-speaker; but we spent all day inside our filthy cells, eating three meals and drinking three cups of water. Méo ran back and forth between the front and back doors. When night fell, he suffered

THE HANOI HILTON

Courtesy of Colonel Benjamin H. Purcell

even more. By the fourth day, I could no longer stand to see how unhappy he was. He had stopped eating. When the guards brought our evening meal, I managed to let him slip outside.

The next morning at exactly 5:00 A.M., Méo came back to my cell as he had always done in the Mountain Village. I heard him scratching and crying at the rear door, but I could not open it. Now that it was five o'clock, all the camp radios began broadcasting propaganda. Running to the front door, I called one of the guards and begged him to open the rear door, explaining that the commandant had promised me that my cat would have his daily run. For the first time in four years, I broke down and pleaded with my captors. "What do you care about a cat?" the guard answered. "There are dozens of cats here; in fact there are too many." He refused to unlock the door.

For the next few days, I kept hearing Méo outside. Every morning at five o'clock I was awakened by the sound of his scratching. People say that cats are very independent creatures and quickly forget their human masters. But Méo kept coming back to my cell, scratching and yowling at the door. I could not get any of the guards to let him in. Then Bernhard and I were transferred to another section of the Hanoi Hilton, and Méo could not find me. Everyone in the camp knew that the cat was mine. The Americans had passed the word that a girl had brought a cat to the camp in a basket and intended to take the cat home with her. Several prisoners came to tell me that they had seen or heard my cat, and I asked them to look for him. I kept on looking myself; but I never saw Méo again. . . .

Four hundred and seventy-six Americans were being held in the Hanoi Hilton. They had been brought here from all the camps in North Vietnam. Now the "hotel" was full up. Most of the prisoners were housed in large group cells, twenty or thirty men to each cell. Ten days after our arrival, Bernhard was moved to one of the group cells. I was given a cell by myself.

Bernhard and I were allowed to move around freely in our

section of the camp. Soon we encountered our old friends from the American camp. Dr. Kushner was still wearing his shatter-proof glasses; Frank, the pilot, still suffered from terrible nightmares; and Gus could still entertain me with his eccentric pronunciation of German. Little John, the contented barber, could have had a field day cutting all the hair in this camp! But John Young was not with his friends: he had died of starvation.

Many old friends had died; and here, for the first time, the prisoners learned what had happened to their comrades. The survivors shook hands and embraced one another warmly. Many had never met face to face and knew one another only through the cargoes that had passed from cell to cell. Now they walked over to greet one another, all moving rather unsteadily, looking gray-faced and emaciated. Some needed canes and crutches. I saw many of them cry when they embraced. They all seemed faintly bewildered, as if freedom were a dazzling light that had blinded them, so that for a moment they had to close their eyes.

Two weeks after we arrived at the Hanoi Hilton, the first group of Americans were released. Two weeks later, at the end of February, a second group left the camp. The peace agreement had stipulated that women were to be released first; yet Bernhard and I had not been freed. The Hanoi Hilton would soon be empty. Had Bernhard and I not been included on the prisoners' list?

We had both been given new clothing. Bernhard received a suit from the Soviet Union, a white shirt, a tie, and a pair of shoes. I was given sandals, a jacket, and a blouse with a pair of trousers, but no skirt. Before being presented to the press, we were warned not to say anything that might delay our release. Then we were permitted to go on several "tours of the city," accompanied by an interpreter. Our guide showed us Bach May Hospital, which had been destroyed by American bombs. The most prized possessions of the Revolutionary Museum were the clothing and sandals worn by Ho Chi Minh when he proclaimed Vietnam a republic. The Museum even contained the microphone Ho had spoken into. Later our Vietnamese guide showed us Independence Park and the zoo; but I had had quite enough of prisoners, including imprisoned animals.

Longing to see a large city, I had imagined how lovely it would be to walk around the streets, look at the stores, and move freely among the people. But in Hanoi, I did not feel free. When people walked toward me along the street, I shied away from them, and I jumped whenever someone behind me talked in a loud voice.

On the evening of March 4, Bernhard and I were told that we would be released the next day along with thirty-four other prisoners. We would be released if the weather was good, if the American plane arrived on schedule, and if the plane was able to take off again. . . . If!

I was given a large bag to hold my things. Cutting open the lining, I concealed whatever I did not want the Vietnamese to see—letters, notes, the addresses of American friends. Then I sewed the lining shut again. I worked slowly, but soon the bag was ready, and I had finished packing my things. Now I had nothing to do but wait. It was the longest, but also the shortest, night of my captivity.

Morning arrived. I ought to remember what the weather was like, but all I can remember now is that when I stepped outside, I prayed, "Dear God, don't let anything go wrong." I am not sure that I even dared to breathe. The Vietnamese arrived to inspect me and my belongings. I told them that only the people from the Liberation Front had the right to search me. We argued until they gave in.

The jeep was already standing outside with the motor running. Bernhard was beside the jeep, quarreling with the commandant. I had simply decided to keep my notes. Bernhard, with his usual boundless optimism and desire to do everything *comme il faut,* had turned over his papers to the commandant, asking official permission to take them with him. The papers had all been confiscated.

Everything was gone, all his notes, notebooks, and poems.

He did not want to leave without them. "Dear God," I thought, "make him be reasonable." But, insisting that he wanted his papers, Bernhard told me to leave in the jeep without him.

The jeep drove away, and soon I heard the driver shifting gears. Ahead of us, at the end of the narrow passage between the cells, I saw the gate just about to open.

"There lies freedom," I thought. "Another hour or two, and you will no longer be walking on Vietnamese soil; you'll be flying high in the sky." I wondered whether the plane was already in sight. But I hated to leave Méo. I would have left everything else behind, I would have left a bag of gold, if only I could have taken my cat. I had told him how pleasant things would be for him in Germany; but now I was leaving without him.

"Why don't you yell?" I thought. "Why don't you shout for joy?" I had always imagined that when this moment came, the coldness would disappear, the armor I had worn for years would fall away, the shell would crack. "What's the matter with you?" I thought. "You're like a stone."

Suddenly I heard someone whistling a tune from *My Fair Lady,* and the tune sounded as cheerful and carefree as ever. Leaning forward, I placed my hand on the driver's shoulder. He actually stopped the jeep.

Turning around, I saw Phil, "the Diplomat," come running up. This was the last time I saw him face to face while in prison. He was wearing a dark suit and tie and black shoes, but his gray hair was cut as short as ever and his face still looked deeply lined. Holding out his hand, he said, "Monika, we've beaten them." That was all.

There was a tiny garden outside one of the cells. Next to the cell door stood a rosebush with two flowers. Phil walked over and bent down by the bush, then returned holding one of the roses.

It was the first rose anyone had ever given me, and it smelled of freedom.

Vietnam, Where's That?

BERNHARD DIEHL

They must all have thought that I was out of my mind. A group of reporters were standing around in the yard watching the jeeps pull away. A few American prisoners watched us enviously, for they were not in the group being released that day. And here I was, refusing to get into the jeep because the Vietnamese had taken away a few poems! One of the Americans shook his head and asked me in a voice loud enough to be heard by everyone in the yard, "Did you know that in the Hanoi Hilton there's a Frenchman who's been locked in an unlit cell since the fall of Dien Bien Phu? And do you know why he's here?" He paused solemnly to make sure that he had our attention. Politely I asked, "No, why?" Laughing so hard that he could hardly talk, he said, "He lost his poems, too!"

Everyone around me started laughing. Even the commandant laughed. "Well, which do you prefer?" he asked. "Do you want to be released, or would you like to join the Frenchman in his dark cell?"

"I want my poems and papers back, as I was promised."

The commandant stopped laughing.

"Take him away!" he said.

Once again I found myself inside a cell, with the door being locked behind me. Why, for the sake of a few notes and poems, had I risked being kept a prisoner here? Was I making one last attempt to force the Vietnamese to keep their word to me? They had made us so many promises and never kept one. Perhaps I had been hoping that just this once they would not lie to me.

Half an hour later, an entire delegation, led by the commandant, came to visit my cell. Smiling again, he expressed his hope that I had calmed down and regained my senses. "So, do you want to stay here, or would you like to be released?"

"You took my papers and poems, and you . . ."

"Please," he said, interrupting me, "don't make any trouble at the last minute. Go! I beg you to go! You are free! Go home. Give your parents my greetings."

It was insane. A Vietnamese was pleading with me, a prisoner, to leave my prison!

"You promised to give me back my poems," I said.

"I don't have them. I can't give them back to you."

"Who has them?"

"Government Security."

"My poems?"

"I had to submit them to the proper authorities."

"Then you were lying to me when you said . . ."

"Go!" he shouted. "For the last time, I ask you to go!"

Seeing that it was no use, I followed them outside. The commandant asked me again to give my parents his most cordial greetings. I climbed into the jeep. . . .

Monika was waiting for me in the office of the NLF, where Liberation Front officials were going to turn us over to a representative of the German embassy in Saigon. Shortly after my arrival, we heard a car drive up, and then a young man entered the room. He had dark hair and was wearing a light suit with a black tie. Walking over to us, he explained that he was from the German embassy in Saigon.

He spoke perfect German, but what did that prove? I could not help distrusting him. "Would you please show us your credentials? You must have documents confirming your right to take us into custody."

He stared at me in amazement. Apparently he did not understand my request. Why did he not understand? Had he only been in this country a short time? "You could be anyone," I said. "Surely you understand that."

Opening his black diplomatic attaché case, he took out a diplomatic passport and a telegram from Bonn, addressed to the German embassy in Saigon. Even now I did not quite trust him, but there was nothing more I could do. . . .

Some official papers were lying on the desk. After glancing through them, we signed them. Then we listened to a talk by a representative of the NLF. Finally we were invited out for a meal in the city. The German diplomat protested that the plane was waiting and that we were already late; but our protests went unheeded. We were told that on such an occasion, we could not refuse to eat one meal with them "to seal our friendship."

We all rode into the city to a French restaurant in a large hotel. The Vietnamese delivered many toasts and ordered a large meal. Our man from Saigon was concerned about our health and kept warning us not to eat too much; but even without his warnings, Monika and I felt too excited to swallow a bite.

Waiting for us at the airport was a remodeled C-142 called a "Starlifter." I was familiar with this type of plane, which had been used to transport jeeps, weaponry, and troops to Vietnam. In addition to the crew, the plane took off with thirty-two Americans, two Filipinos, a German diplomat, and two workers in the Aid Service of Malta. Our destination was Clark Air Base, an American Air Force base in the Philippines.

Our German companion told us that we would be given clothing and medical care in the Philippines. Moreover, at the air base we could buy anything we wanted—cameras, perfume, portable television sets. Our salary had been accumulating for four years; Monika and I were suddenly quite affluent.

Except for the other prisoners, the people around us belonged to a different world. They knew nothing of our world; and after four years what could we know of theirs? We did not even know that men were now wearing their hair much longer and had been quite puzzled by two long-haired French reporters we had seen at the Hanoi Hilton.

We were told that we would be allowed to telephone home from Clark Air Base. Each prisoner was entitled to a fifteen-minute call to his closest relatives. I wondered why they had decided on exactly fifteen minutes. What could two people say to each other in fifteen minutes? It was such a short time—but such a long time, too. Trying to picture what the call would be like, I imagined the crackling sound I would hear as the connection was made. Then I would hear the voices of various operators, and finally someone would say, "All right, go ahead now!"

"Hello, Mother!" Then there would be a long silence, followed by her voice: "Bernhard! My God . . . Son!" "Hello, Mother, can you hear me? Am I coming through clearly?" "Son, is it really you?" "Yes, Mother, it's me." "My God, Son, it's been so long!" "Yes, Mother, it's been a long time." "How are you?" "I'm just fine, Mother." "Really?" "Yes, Mother, really. How are all of you?" "Fine, fine, we're all in good health. You'll see, everything will be all right, Son." "Of course, Mother . . ." Fifteen minutes was such a long time.

No one would ask us what it had been like. At least at first, they would be very careful not to ask. At Clark Air Base, a general order had been issued to all personnel who might come into contact with prisoners: "Do not ask the prisoners about their experiences in Vietnam."

I imagined what it would be like when I got home—the reporters asking questions, the special attention, the receptions. For a few days or a few weeks, we would be treated as celebrities. People would tell us how brave we had been and what shining examples we were to our fellow men. They would cite us as victims of Communist oppression and cruelty and boast of the superiority of their own system: for we of the free world, of course, had never unjustly deprived anyone of his liberty.

I remembered the friend I had told of my decision to go to Vietnam—the one who had answered, "Vietnam? Where's that?" Now I was asking myself, "Germany? Where's that?"

• • •

Three times during our flight in the C-142, the prisoners began to cheer—when we took off, when the pilot announced that we had left the Democratic Republic of North Vietnam, and when we landed at Clark Air Base. But each time, our cheers sounded different. The first time, we roared with joy. The second time, our cries were more subdued. The third time, the sound was softer and tinged with fear. A profound and oppressive silence was settling over us all.

Huddling down into our seats and lowering our heads, we broke off our eager conversations and stared into space. Our initial feeling of euphoria was beginning to wear off. We were afraid of our new-won freedom.

Turning my head, I looked at Monika sitting beside me. She, too, had slumped down into her seat. She was holding the rose between her clasped hands as if she were afraid to let go. I knew that for once we were feeling the same thing.

Chronology of the Indochina War

1945   On September 2 in Hanoi, Ho Chi Minh proclaims the independence of the "Democratic Republic of Vietnam." French troops reoccupy Vietnam.

1946   The French bomb Haiphong. The Indochina War begins.

1954   The battle of Dien Bien Phu. Vietnam is divided. Ngo Dinh Diem becomes president of South Vietnam.

1955   President Diem proclaims the Republic of Vietnam.

1956   The U.S.A. sends military advisers to Saigon.

1958   The first outbreaks of violence in South Vietnam.

1959   The first battles with the Viet Cong.

1960   The foundation of the National Liberation Front (NLF).

1961   President Diem petitions President Kennedy for a sizable increase of American combat strength in South Vietnam.

1963   Military uprising in Saigon. Diem is assassinated.

1964   Establishment of a new military government under General Nguyen Khan. Escalation of U.S. aid and the first American bombing attacks of North Vietnam.

1965   U.S. troop strength reaches 184,000 men. Air Vice-Marshal Nguyen Cao Ky becomes premier of South Vietnam.

1968   On January 31, the holiday of Tet, the Viet Cong attack all major cities, the U.S. embassy in Saigon, and dozens of other strategic points. U.S. forces now comprise over 500,000 men. In Paris, the Americans and the North Vietnamese begin preliminary peace negotiations.

1969   Nguyen Van Thieu, the President of South Vietnam, states his opposition to the unilateral withdrawal of American troops from South Vietnam. American forces are reduced to less than 500,000 men.

1970   Mrs. Nguyen Thi Binh, "Foreign Minister" of the Provisional Revolutionary Government, submits an eight-point peace plan to the eighty-fourth session of the Paris peace talks. The Americans reject her proposal.

1971   Despite continual bombing attacks on North Vietnam, North Vietnamese units pursue their steady infiltration of South Vietnam.

1972   A major North Vietnamese offensive. In an effort to cut off North Vietnamese supply routes, President Nixon orders the mining of the North Vietnamese coastline and steps up the bombing of North Vietnam.

President Nixon reports that the U.S. government has been conducting secret negotiations with North Vietnam to end the war. On December 18, 1972, the Paris peace talks come to a halt.

1973   On January 27, the "Paris Agreement on Ending the War and Restoring Peace in Vietnam" is signed in Paris. North Vietnam releases the POWs.